Emma Goldman: Still Dangerous

Emma Goldman
Still Dangerous

C. BRÍD NICHOLSON

BLACK
ROSE
BOOKS

Montreal/New York/London

Black Rose Books No. NN369

Library and Archives Canada Cataloguing in Publication

Nicholson, C. Brid
Emma Goldman, 1869–1940 : still dangerous / C. Brid Nicholson

Includes bibliographical references
ISBN 978-1-55164-327-4 (bound) ISBN 978-1-55164-326-7 (pbk.)

1. Goldman, Emma, 1869-1940. 2. Women anarchists—United States—Biography. 3. Anarchists—United States—Biography. I. Title.

HX843.7.G65N43 2009   335'.83092   C2008-905057-6

BLACK ROSE BOOKS

C.P. 1258	2250 Military Road	99 Wallis Road
Succ. Place du Parc	Tonawanda, NY	London, E9 5LN
Montréal, H2X 4A7	14150	England
Canada	USA	UK

To order books:
In Canada: (phone) 1-800-565-9523 (fax) 1-800-221-9985
email: utpbooks@utpress.utoronto.ca
In the United States: (phone) 1-800-283-3572 (fax) 1-800-351-5073
In the UK & Europe: (phone) 44 (0)20 8986-4854 (fax) 44 (0)20 8533-5821
email: order@centralbooks.com

Our Web Site address: http://www.blackrosebooks.net
Printed in Canada

Contents

Acknowledgements / vii

Introduction / 3

1 An Exceedingly Dangerous Woman / 23

2 New Americans and Anarchy / 38

3 Into the Public Eye / 67

4 Words and Deeds / 81

5 Ideas, Life and Deportation / 96

6 Nowhere and No One / 127

7 Writing an American Story / 141

8 Sex and Sexuality: The Silenced Skein / 163

9 Posthumous Reputations – Scholarly Biographies / 178

Conclusion / 189

Bibliography / 201

Notes / 207

Index / 227

In memory of my grandmothers

Bríd Bean Mhic Niocaill and Mary Ward Brennan

two women for whom war and

revolution were all in a day's work!

꒰꒱

Acknowledgements

The simplest truth is that you never write a book alone. So many people help along the way, with a whole lot of encouragement. So thank you to everyone who has encouraged, supported, listened, or even asked the simple question, "So how is the book going?" A special thanks to those of you who had enough confidence in me to pre-order!

Thanks to my colleagues at Kean University, Frank Argote-Freyre, Thomas Banit, Christopher Bellitto, Frank Esposito, Sue Gronewold, Elizabeth Hyde, Dennis Klein, Mark Lender, Robert Mayer, Jonathan Mercantini, Brian Regal, Jay Spaulding, and Lawrence Zimmer, who have all provided me with great understanding, knowledge, and support. To Maria Perez and the staff and the Professional Development Center at Kean – thank you all.

Thanks also to the library staff at Drew University, in particular, to Jody Caldwell and Bruce Lancaster, who always manage to find the impossible.

I would like to thank everyone at Black Rose Books for their help in getting this from my computer into print. A special thanks to Drew Nelles for piloting this project from start to finish and to David LeBlanc for his design and production.

Growing up, my love of history was encouraged by two people in particular: Mary Callan of Scoil Carmel in Limerick, and the late Brid Culloo of the Model School in Limerick. Miss Culloo passed away recently. She was honestly the last of a generation of teachers who saw teaching as education and, who organized as broad a curriculum as possible, in order to show her students the wonders of the world.
Ar dheis Dé ar a h-anam.

Special thanks also goes to my family: Sean, Caitlín, and Shay, who always believed.

Extra special thanks goes to Paula L. Cameron, who helped by editing, making coffee, and most of all by listening during those very long phone calls.

Finally, but most of all, thank you to my husband Mark, who has lived this book in its many forms. It's finally done!

Emma Goldman, (second from left) with Alexander Berkman and others,
St. Tropez. Labadie Collection, University of Michigan

Alexander Berkman
Labadie Collection, University of Michigan

Alexander Berkman standing on boardwalk, Nice
Labadie Collection, University of Michigan

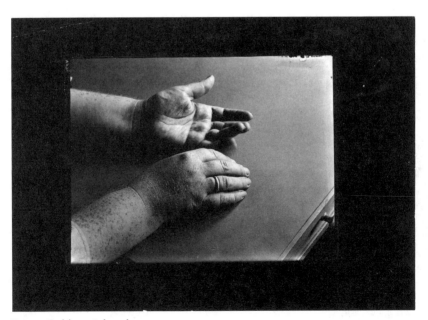

Emma Goldman's hands
Labadie Collection, University of Michigan

Emma Goldman
Labadie Collection, University of Michigan

Memo. for Mr. Creighton, -2- 8/23/19 JEH-GPO
Re Berkman and Goldman.

of the Bureau of Immigration to have a search made of their
files and to submit the same to me for consideration relative
to these two cases.

Emma Goldman and Alexander Berkman are, beyond doubt,
two of the most dangerous anarchists in this country and if
permitted to return to the community will result in undue harm.

Respectfully,

J. Ea. Hoover

Memo written by J. Edgar Hoover recommending the deportation of Emma
Goldman and Alexander Berkman, 1919. August 23, 1919, Unites States
National Archives, Record Group 60

"Emma Goldman, High Priestess
of Anarchy Whose Speeches
Inspired Czolgosz to his Crime,"
Chicago Daily Tribune, September
8, 1901.

Harper's Weekly
May 22, 1886.

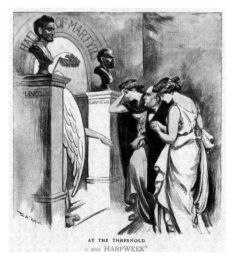

"At the Threshold," *Harper's Weekly* September 14, 1901.

Emma Goldman: Still Dangerous

The anarchists as I knew them, were always right and always ineffective. They never resigned themselves to making compromises, which are necessary in any struggle. Emma Goldman did somewhat better than most, however. She was interested in immediate issues as well as philosophy. She was extraordinarily motherly in her relations with other people, partly because her motherhood had been frustrated by her not being able to have children. She was an extremely literate person, who lived in books as well as history. Her lectures, which I began to attend in 1911 while in St. Louis, opened up all kinds of new literature to me – Ibsen, Schopenhauer, the Russians. She introduced many people to a whole literature of protest.
–(Roger Baldwin, founder of the American Civil Liberties Union)

Introduction

[Emma Goldman] wrote an enormous number of letters all over the world, to friends, relatives, comrades. Sometimes she made notes first, sometimes she dictated right out. Her mind was very keen. She was able to think very quickly.

   That was the greatest period of my life. Just knowing her and being with her is something I'll never forget. I'll cherish it forever. Her ability to do the things she did, her clear mind and strong intellect, her determination to fight the ills of society – I often wish I could have done all that. I wish I had the strength of character, the ability. She was a strong personality. She was also a good housekeeper and an excellent cook.[1]

I found Emma Goldman on a day filled with desperation. I was a graduate student, looking for someone (anyone) about whom I could write a proposed intellectual biography as a final research paper for a class. Bored with my own thoughts, and failed ideas, I eventually wandered into the local bookstore and found Paul Avrich's wonderful book *Anarchist Voices*. What fascinated me was how vivid this collection of memories was. It was not just that assorted people remembered various anarchists, but they recalled how they felt around these anarchists, what the public thought of them, how the government reacted to them, how newspapers described them. In short, the reputations established by individual anarchists were far more enthralling and long-lasting than any political action taken by any individual anarchist.

   In this book was a chapter on Emma Goldman, described by Freda Diamond as someone who "spoke well. She had an odd voice with a peculiar accent. But she was a good speaker and made an impression. Emma was more than a bit vain. She thought she was the Queen of Sheba. She thought she was very attractive, beautiful woman. She held herself that way."[2]

While Ida Gershoy described Goldman more simply as "lots of fun."[3] She soon fascinated me. She seemed to have been annoying, endearing, loving, off-putting, crazed, determined, and yet had softness to her, and seemed to have doubts about so much, and yet a firm belief in education. So when Emma Goldman wrote in her autobiography: "I was not hewn of one piece like Sasha or other heroic figures. I had long realized that I was woven of many skeins, conflicting in shade and texture,"[4] I realized much, much later it was probably the most insightful comment she ever made about herself. For me it describes not only Emma Goldman the person and political activist, but also the Emma Goldman of this project. This phrase gave me my starting point, as I set out on a complicated journey to dig deeper into a world where Goldman was apparently well-known, where she was feared, and then into Goldman's private world of letters. It was in this private world that her high political beliefs clashed with the mundane realities of the private world.

But studying an anarchist was problematic in itself. Anarchy was, and is, a difficult topic to explain. I was soon bombarded by questions about violence and terrorism. I was asked questions about jails, and institutions. But the simple truth is that anarchy is a complicated concept, too often confused with something it is not. It is not necessarily violent, nor does it automatically imply that there will be no personal property. Anarchy at its simplest is instead a system, which (perhaps optimistically) believes that people are fundamentally good and will voluntarily act in an ethically and morally appropriate way for the betterment of all.

Yet by insisting that each individual must be completely free to act, anarchists also believe that neither law nor any form of authority should control or limit personal actions in any way. The result of this is that people may choose to form mutually beneficial societies, but these are set up in such a way so that people are free to withdraw without consequence at any time. These chosen voluntary institutions are, for most anarchists, best suited to the needs of all the people, and are therefore philosophically closer to the more natural order of the world.

The common aspect of all forms of anarchy is a rejection of authority, whether that is a government, or an institution of that government, such as the police or army. No matter how democratic any form of government appears to be, it is simply unacceptable.

In summary, therefore, it is fair to say that anarchy is the most complete anti-state philosophy and system of organization of society.

Where do our views of anarchy come from? What is usually understood in modern and popular culture as anarchy is a nineteenth-century version, one made known through the writings of a group of mainly Russian, German, Italian, and Spanish revolutionaries. The actual term *anarchism* comes from Greek; the word *av* means absence, while the word *apxn* means authority or government. Anarchists usually date the history of anarchy back to the Greek philosopher Zeno (342–267/270 BCE), who believed that any form of regulation, or any means of restraining people's natural tendencies, obstructed the natural impulse in people to seek perfection. He argued the state had no right to interfere in an individual's rights.

Two later individuals who can be seen as predecessors of anarchy are Gerrard Winstanley (1609–c1660), and William Godwin (1756–1836). While it should be noted that neither used the term "anarchist" in their writings, their actions, philosophy, and ideals can be seen as anarchistic in nature.

Winstanley was a linen draper who led the small movement of Diggers during the Commonwealth in England, from 1649 to 1650. The Diggers protested the excesses of the New Model Army by squatting on land in southern England and setting up communities that shared work and goods. The communities failed, but a series of pamphlets written by Winstanley survived. These advocated a rational Christianity, noting the corrupting force of authority. Each person had the right to share in liberty, and Winstanley noted the unjust link between property ownership and lack of freedom. He promoted a society where work would be done in common, with shared products without commerce.

Godwin, whose work was lost for many years, was instead to become known through his relatives: he became the father-in-law of Percy Shelly, and the husband of Mary Wollstonecraft. Nevertheless, in his own book *Enquiry Concerning Political Justice*, published in 1793, he insisted it was fundamentally unfair to bind all generations to a contract made once by hypothetical ancestors. Influenced by the English tradition of dissent and the French Enlightenment, Godwin rejected the notion that one man should have power over another. He preferred the idea that small groups of people seeking out truth and justice could make up a society of free individuals. According to Godwin, justice was based on immutable truths, but laws were merely man-made, and therefore fallible.[5] This meant that it was necessary that people use their own intellect, rather than simple obedience or blind fear.

Everything in this new society would not be achieved through violence, but instead through education. Education would support the natural, rational principles in people to forward change for the betterment of all. Finally, in this new society, everyone would take part in, and benefit from, production, resulting in the breaking down of all class barriers.

Godwin, whose book was published mere weeks after Thomas Paine was forced to leave England following the publication of his book *The Rights of Man,* was also in danger of being branded a traitor. However, the high cost of his book – three guineas – meant few people could afford it and so the government assumed it had nothing to worry about. Nevertheless, copies were made available through a variety of revolutionary clubs that had sprung up throughout England, Ireland, Scotland, and Wales, and Godwin's work became popular overnight. Yet the reality was that by the time of his death, any possible thoughts of revolutionary change in England had died out, and Godwin died in poverty, his work forgotten.

The modern, and better-known, version of anarchy made popular in the nineteenth century results from a combination of Hegel's notion that history can be understood as a march towards reason, and the very basic Marxist notion that the proletariat would inherit the earth.

What Hegel offered anarchy was the notion that the history of man is one of progression toward freedom. Hegel's notion of progressivism states that the mind is free, and it is therefore vital for humankind to continue toward creating a situation in which all people are free. For Hegel, history consisted of three phases: the Oriental, Greek and Roman, and Germanic. In the Oriental world only the rulers were free. In the Greek and Roman world, while there was a greater understanding of freedom, in practical terms freedom was only found in fulfilling those things that were fundamental for the state. One's own needs were never taken into consideration and indeed the slaves in this society could not experience freedom of any kind.

Hegel summed up this view in the phrase, "Man as man should be free."[6] This was particularly true of the Germanic version of

Protestantism, which had grown out of the Reformation and influenced institutions and states in Europe and the United States.

The aspect of Hegelianism that appealed to the anarchists was a possibility of revolution now. History's logic dictated that progress, something one should move towards, demanded that the revolution occur within these times. Further emphasis on the moral need for a revolution was found in Ludwig Feurbach's *Essence of Christianity*.

Feuerbach argues that humanity is the true subject of theology. Truth is found in man's love for man; thus, anarchist philosophers had a moral duty to bring humankind to the spiritual and moral realization that a new form of society needed to be created by the proletariat. These were the people who, in the present system, had little or nothing materially, yet who philosophically had as many rights and needs as anyone else in society. History was a natural progression toward freedom for all people and so the only question became when this would happen. For the anarchist, it soon became a matter, if necessary, of pushing history along.

Another equally important influence on practical anarchy was Max Stirner, who stated, "Nothing is my cause." Stirner was an atheist, and though he never applied the term "anarchist" to himself, he has had the term "individualistic anarchist" applied to his thinking. Stirner rejected notions of society as well as the state, and indeed rejected all forms of organizations as nothing more than a collection of egos.

Though the French anarchist movement of the 1890s was heavily influenced by individualistic anarchy, the anarchist movement with which people are most familiar is the populist anarchist movement that came to existence at the end of the nineteenth century. This movement is a product of the industrialization of society, its social re-organization, and the constant hope and bitter frustration of a better life for most people.[7] The person who is seen as the "father" of modern anarchy is Pierre-Joseph Proudhon (1809–1865). Born into what could be called a petit-bourgeois family in French Comte, his father was a brewer and his mother a cook in a local brewery. His father was not successful in business and poverty was a common experience. At a very young age, Proudhon was sent to look after the herds in the nearby countryside and much of his writing reflects a nostalgia felt for a society and a way of life that no longer exists – a rural simple society, full of natural order, goodness, and beauty.

The importance of Proudhon's work is neither in his theoretical arguments nor in his revolutionary phrases, but instead in his basic notion of humankind and society. According to Proudhon, work was natural to man; therefore, not working was contrary to man's natural instincts and would prevent man from leading a full and fulfilling life. Logically, then, labour was both a social necessity and a moral virtue.[8] The working class was dignified by Proudhon, and thus of vital importance to anarchist thought was the idea of a worker's duty to himself, his class, and society. The revolution must take place to protect workers and to stop once and for all the degradation and exploitation of the capitalist system.

Proudhon was, for the most part, self-educated, teaching himself Hebrew, Latin, and Greek, as well as theology and philosophy. In 1838 he was awarded a Suard scholarship, which enabled him to move to Paris to avail himself of a formal education. However, after the publication of *Avertissement aux proprietaries (Warning to Proprietors)*, the scholarship was withdrawn. In 1840, he published his most famous work, *Qu'est-ce que la propriété? (What Is Property?)*, which he dedicated to the Academy of Besancon. The success of this pamphlet made him famous and even more controversial with the authorities. During this time he was to continue to visit Paris often, where he met with the other revolutionaries of his generation, including Karl Marx, Michael Bakunin, and Karl Grun.

In 1846, he published *Système des contradictions économiques ou Philosophie de la misère (The System of Economic Contradictions or the Philosophy of Misery)*. In it, he outlined his philosophy, which had, by this stage, been influenced by his reading of Hegel, as well as his reaction against the utopian ideas of Charles Fourier and Henri de Saint-Simon, who had popularized such words as "socialism" and "communism." He was forced to flee to Brussels in 1849 after an attack on Napoleon III, which he was suspected to have helped instigate. He returned to Paris and was imprisoned. After his release he published his book *On Justice*. However, this book proved equally unpopular with authorities and Proudhon fled once again to Brussels.

Proudhon believed that authoritarian political organization should be replaced by social and economic organization, which had voluntary contractual agreements as its basis. His great interest was in what he called *progress*, which he defined as the march away from authority and toward a society created by reason. Proudhon thus rejected all forms of religion and all things that create and serve any form of centralized government. Instead he proposed a notion of economic progress in which workers would, through free association, work autonomously for themselves and their families without supporting the rich few. Proudhon is best known for his work *What is Property?*, and the form of anarchism that he forwarded became known as "mutualism." Mutualism stresses the social element of human behavior. It rejects all forms of violence as a way to achieve these goals. Instead, Proudhon stressed the reform of society through the spread of worker's federal councils:

> In place of laws, we will put contracts. No more laws voted by a majority, nor even unanimously; each citizen, each town, each industrial union, makes its own laws.[9]

This system seeks to maintain individual ownership of small farmland and small-scale production while large-scale industry is composed of voluntary organization such as worker's co-operatives to ensure that the workers get their fair share. However, Proudhon was careful to avoid the notion of large-scale organization, which would present the same danger to individual liberty that totalitarian or democratic governments did. Proudhon was different from Marx in that he did not see the future as a society belonging to the industrialized proletariat, but instead as belonging to the artisans and peasants. It was both the mission and duty of the workers to establish this new federalist-type society, thus, unlike in Marx's vision, this creation of the new society would not have to be violent.

Proudhon died in Brussels, in poverty, on January 19, 1865. While in Brussels, he wrote a number of pamphlets reacting against the state in the 1848 revolutions, and constantly suggested economic, philosophical, and theological systems of change.

One of Proudhon's ideas that attracted a lot of attention, particularly in the United States, was the People's Bank. Initially, Charles A. Dana, who visited Proudhon in prison in Paris, brought Proudhon's work to the United States. Upon Dana's return to the United States, he wrote a series of articles for *The Tribune* and later for *The Spirit of the Age*. In them, Dana proposed Proudhon's system whereby credit would be provided to all at a basic cost. The result of this would be to end poverty and unemployment, and to achieve social justice for all. Such was the influence of Proudhon and this series of articles that nearly a century later Benjamin Tucker re-printed them in pamphlet form as *Proudhon and His "Bank of the People."*

An irony of Proudhon 's philosophy is that while he considered property a form of theft, his vision of anarchy could not be called collectivism. He did not advocate the abolition of private property, but instead believed that the artisans and peasants should be in control of their own land. His notion was based on a moral right. Property should belong to those who have worked, as opposed to those who had birthright. Yet the non-violent version of anarchy foreseen by Proudhon would very soon be overshadowed by more violent possibilities proposed by Michael Bakunin (1814–1876) and Peter Kropotkin (1842–1921).

Michael Bakunin was born in 1814, in the central Russian state of Tver, into a rich aristocratic family. At age fifteen he was sent to St. Petersburg and five years later was assigned to a regiment in Poland. The method of the suppression of the 1830 resurrection in Poland distressed the young Bakunin, so he resigned his commission and went to Moscow to study philosophy. Impressed by the German philosophers Schelling, Fichte, and Hegel in particular, he left Moscow in 1840 so that he could study their ideas more closely. The same year he was to go to Paris to visit Proudhon and Marx. Like Marx and Engels, he was influenced by Ludwig Feuerbach and, in 1842, published his first major political article *Die Reaction in Deutschland (Reaction in Germany)*. Due to the government reaction to the article, Bakunin was forced to flee to Switzerland. Later extradited to Russia, he was imprisoned, first in the Peter and Paul Fortress, and later in Siberia. Bakunin finally escaped in 1861 in an American sailing vessel bound for Japan. From Japan he went to the United States and from there to London. Influenced by the Franco-Prussian War and later by the Paris Commune, by 1876 he settled in Berne, Switzerland, where he died.

Bakunin's legacy to the anarchist movement is complex. It was he who showed clearly the differences between anarchy and communism, which resulted in the split in the International Revolutionary Movement. It was Bakunin who linked the revolutionary movements in Russia with those in the rest of Europe. He also successfully forwarded the notion of the virtues of violence and wrote about terrorism for its own sake, an idea that impacted revolutionary groups all over the world, then and now.

Bakunin's philosophy was primarily one that focused on the notion of revolution. Bakunin saw history as destruction and so believed only those with nothing to lose could be truly called revolutionaries:

> Let us put our trust in the eternal spirit, which destroys and annihilates only because it is unsearchable and the eternally creative source of all life. The desire for destruction is also a creative desire.[10]

Like Proudhon, Bakunin linked reason and revolt, but unlike Proudhon, he saw the act of destruction as successful in itself. There was, according to Bakunin, a basic goodness in humankind, which would come to the fore once the act of revolution had taken place. Whereas Proudhon saw the ideal revolutionary as a self-educated peasant or craftsman willingly and voluntarily cooperating with his neighbor in creating the new society, Bakunin believed that the revolution would come from those with nothing to lose. He was not interested in social or economic change; his only interest was the very act of revolution. The contrast between Bakunin's theory of revolution and Marxism is obvious even at this stage, as Bakunin believed German Marxism to be centralist, disciplined, and bureaucratic, the antithesis of anarchy:

> I hate communism because it is the negation of liberty and because humanity is for me unthinkable without liberty. I am not a communist, because communism concentrates and swallows up in itself for the benefit of the State all the forces of society, because it inevitably leads to the concentration of property in the hands of the State, whereas I want the abolition of the State, the final eradication of the principle of authority and patronage proper to the State, which under the pretext of moralizing and civilizing men, has hitherto only enslaved, persecuted, exploited and corrupted them.[11]

Bakunin's form of anarchy became known as collectivism. At it simplest, collectivism can be described as a political philosophy that seeks to collectivize all property and industry. This action, according to Bakunin, has to be done by force. Bakunin specifically rejected any kind of individualism, insisting that anarchy was primarily a social doctrine and its basis must be collective responsibility: "Property will cease to be a right; it will be reduced to the status of a simple fact."[12]

Bakunin was above all a Russian nationalist and sought to promote its revolutionary future. He was anxious to keep in touch with the happenings in Russia and to promote and help the possible upcoming revolution. In 1869, he was introduced to Sergi Gennadevich Nechaev, a twenty-two-year-old Russian who arrived in Switzerland. Nachaev and Bakunin together drafted *The Revolutionary Catechism, Principles of Revolution,* and other manifestos, which they deemed necessary in any fight against any state, anywhere.

> We recognize no other activity but the work of extermination, but we admit that the forms in which this activity will show itself will be extremely varied – poison, the knife, the rope etc. In this struggle, revolution sanctifies everything alike.[13]

What is significant here is that this acceptance of violence for its own sake is something not found elsewhere in Bakunin's writings, suggesting the huge influence Nechaev had over him. Nonetheless, such was the impact and the legacy of this idea of *la propagande par le fait* (propaganda by deed) that it would become the mainstay of the anarchist movement from then on. Prior to returning to Russia, Nechaev went further, calling for acts of individual violence to be carried out in order to stir up trouble for the authorities.

This brief association of Bakunin and Nechaev was to cause long-standing effects for the anarchist movement. Now and forever the doctrines of anarchy and individual acts of violence would be linked. For some, these individual acts of aggression against a state would symbolize the possibility of coming revolution. The other reality was that these individual acts of terror would now be associated with some criminals who claimed that they acts they had carried out were done in the name of anarchist principles. The most immediate impact of the writings of Bakunin and Nechaev was that terrorism (as opposed to an organized revolution) now became an acceptable political weapon.

After Bakunin's arrival in Switzerland he became involved in the politics of the International Working Men's Association. Bakunin never thought that membership in one revolutionary organization precluded membership in another. Thus it is more than likely that he never thought that his membership in this international body would cause problems.

Bakunin's idea after joining the International seems to have been to create an organization that would train and produce "propagandists, apostles, and finally organizers."[14] These people would, it was hoped, be the organizing force that would mobilize the necessary revolutionary forces throughout Europe. To achieve this goal Bakunin organized this group of people into a body, which he called the International Alliance of Socialist Democracy. However, no matter what Bakunin intended this organization to be, it was soon looked upon as a rival organization within the International.

Though Bakunin was prepared to compromise and to dissolve the Alliance so that it would not even appear separate from the International, Marx by this time appeared to have decided to rid the International of Bakunin and all of his influence. The crisis came to a head at the congress of the International at Basel in September 1869.

During this congress, while Bakunin supported the General Council on many issues – including the proposal that their executive powers should be extended and that they have the right to suspend any section – he was seen to be acting in a manner against the spirit of the International.[15] Despite this, Bakunin and his group successfully defeated the General Council on the matter of hereditary property. For the General Council, this was a matter that would clear up as soon as the revolution had happened. Bakunin had for a long time held very definite views on this point. He argued that if hereditary property could be abolished, any state would have automatically taken a massive step towards its own destruction. Hereditary property for Bakunin was really the only thing that denied the possibility of equality between men.

Bakunin and his supporters carried the vote. Though neither Marx nor Engels were present, Marx soon after began a campaign of letters, pamphlets, and circulars claiming that Bakunin was leading a vast conspiracy against Marx and all revolutionary movements. At the same time Bakunin and his supporters were arguing more and more against the Marxist notion of a organized proletariat, which they saw as nothing more than another form of a centralized state.

In the summer of 1871, Marx called a conference of the International in London. None of Bakunin's close supporters attended. There, Marx proposed the formation of a working-class political party, which was to be the vehicle toward revolution. This class proletarian action was a slight against Bakunin, and so the second resolution, declaring the International Alliance of Socialist Democracy closed, was easily passed. While Marx had gotten these resolutions passed, he had yet to win the war, as such was Bakunin's influence in mainland Europe that the only country interested in forming a party of the proletariat was in Germany.

Determined to end Bakunin's influence within the International, Marx called another congress, this time in the Hague. It was expensive for Bakunin and his supporters to travel there, and so representing Bakunin was James Guillaume, a Swiss supporter. By the end of a bitter congress, Guillaume and his associates were expelled and the seat of the General Council was moved to the United States. Marx had won, but the International, facing its end, had lost.

The reasons behind the end of the International were many and complicated. In part, they related to the real philosophical and practical theoretical differences between the communists and anarchists, but they also related to the personality differences between Marx and Bakunin. For Marx, the revolution would come. The process would be historical and one of realization. For Bakunin, the revolution could be made to happen by a handful of leaders who would inspire and exploit the existing possibilities. The tactics foreseen by the two men were radically different. For Marx, secret societies, which were disciplined, were vital, while for Bakunin no hierarchical organization was necessary, for the means of revolution had to reflect the vision of the newly created post-revolutionary society. The result of all this was that, from this moment on, it would be impossible for the left to agree on anything. Like Proudhon, at the time of his death in 1876 Bakunin was destitute and stateless. He had given up politics in 1874 when he had been part of the failed insurrection in Bologna.

Peter Kropotkin was born into an aristocratic family in Russia. In 1857, he entered the Corps of Pages of the Emperor at St. Petersburg and was made an officer. Soon afterwards he went to Siberia, where he was to spend the next five years. During this time in Siberia he discovered a passion for geography, so he left the army and enrolled in St. Petersburg University to study mathematics and geography. On a journey to Asia, Kropotkin realized that professional people have no right to be praised for what they do while other people are starving. What he proposed, therefore, was a *social revolution*. In 1872, he made his first decisive visit to Western Europe, visiting James Guillaume in Switzerland. He was so impressed by the Swiss anarchist workers that he had to be persuaded to return to Russia; it was pointed out to him that he could be more useful to the revolution there. Upon his return to Moscow, he joined a small intellectual anarchist circle, which promoted self-improvement, recruiting students, and associating with the working classes. Soon afterwards Kropotkin was arrested and spent time in the Peter and Paul Fortress. While there, his health deteriorated to such an extent that he was sent to a military hospital, from which he was freed. He quickly went to England, and later to Switzerland, where he took the opportunity to read and write extensively. In 1881, he was expelled from Switzerland and moved back to London, and then to France, where he was arrested and imprisoned for five years. Under public pressure he was released early and moved back to England. During the First World War, many anarchists opposed him when he openly and enthusiastically supported the allied governments.

When the Russian Revolution occurred in 1917, he moved back to Russia, delighted with, and full of praise for, the Revolution and those involved. As conditions in Russia deteriorated, and anarchists became more outspoken against the state, he was one of the few who the Leninist government did not dare to arrest or imprison, for fear of an international outcry. He died on February 8, 1921.

What differentiates the writings of Kropotkin from Bakunin and Proudhon is that, for Kropotkin, anarchy was a science. Heavily influenced by Darwin, he sought to discover new evidence for "the struggle for existence," which he saw as basic to Darwinian science. He found what he called a "theory of mutual aid," which suggested that societies were moving toward greater voluntary co-operation. Revolution was for him an act of justice establishing the working class as the creators of a new society. By the time Kropotkin was ready to write about his political version of mutual aid, he was living in England. The impetus to make his theory better known came as a reaction to the publication of T.H. Huxley's work "The Struggle for Existence" in the London periodical *The Nineteenth Century*. The crux of Huxley's argument was that life is a continuous free fight. Progress happens when competition between animals of the same species occurs. The strongest lives to fight another day and so there is no need for the spectator to give his opinion – it is not asked for nor needed. Kropotkin was horrified by Huxley's version of Darwinism. He replied to Huxley in a series of articles that appeared in *The Nineteenth Century* between 1890 and 1902 and were later brought together in his book *Mutual Aid*.

For Kropotkin, Huxley's concept of evolution was a distortion of Darwinism. Kropotkin did not deny that struggle played a part in life, but he could not accept the emphasis placed on competition and conflict. Kropotkin pointed out that Darwin himself, in *The Descent of Man*, acknowledged the importance of mutual cooperation. Kropotkin therefore argued in his articles that mutual aid has been "the chief factor of progressive evolution." Using an abundance of examples from both the animal and human world, he pointed out that survival is based on mutual help toward adaptation and survival.

Kropotkin admitted he was not blind to the very real negative side of human behavior. While man's natural instincts were cooperative, competitiveness was by no means lacking. What was more important was to discourage that part of men that made them "induce man to subdue other men in order to utilize them for his individual ends." Instead the prime objective of man should be to:

> Induce human beings to unite for attaining common ends by
> common effort: the first answering the fundamental need of
> human nature – struggle, and the second representing another
> equally fundamental tendency – the desire for unity and
> mutual sympathy.[16]

When it came to history, Kropotkin argued that it was cooperation rather than conflict that formed the basis of historical change. The rise of centralized states were the exception that proved the rule, as he noted that, even throughout this time, voluntary association of all sorts continued to look for ways to meet the various needs of humankind. Society was indeed looking to the past to go forward so that people could develop their faculties and skills.

The important question for the revolution was how the past was going to transform itself into a society of the future. In his book *The Conquest of Bread*, first published in 1892, Kropotkin outlines his doctrines. The model used by Kropotkin was loosely set on the Paris Commune. Here he explains how the revolution happens and how a society is transformed from the ground upward. What Kropotkin does not attempt to do is to detail each event that must take place, preferring instead to speak of the necessary social doctrines which already exist in all societies, and which are then necessary for these massive changes to occur.

What Kropotkin does do is to take Stirner's individualism, Proudhon's mutualism, and Bakunin's collectivism, and then move toward the notion of "anarchist communism." Under this system private property and ownership of goods would no longer be necessary; these would be replaced by the free distribution of goods and services. Unlike either the Marxists', or indeed Bakunin's, systems, these goods would not be distributed according to performance. This Kropotkin regarded as the wage system under another name. Instead, these goods would simply be given to all.

The revolution would create a three-fold outcome, which would free the toiling class; it would free them as producers from capitalism, from the government, and from religious morality. Unlike Bakunin, Kropotkin spent little time on how this society was going to happen; instead, he preferred to concentrate on his vision of the society that would come about as a result of the revolution.

Only one question remained: how was this society to be realized? Kropotkin was never afraid of the idea of revolution, and a revolution would indeed be necessary to create this new version of an older society. Yet he did want it to be as humane a revolution as possible. Kropotkin realized, perhaps more so than other philosophers of revolution, that the means of revolution would have a great deal of influence on the society created by the revolution. Kropotkin, therefore, while not totally opposed to a degree of violence, did condemn individual acts of terror. Violence was only useful if it served all of the people and a greater good. What Kropotkin gave to the anarchist movement was the idea of libertarianism – a free, and equal, society based on mutual aid, overseen by all. It would never be overrun by a few and it would be achieved with the highest of principles and ideals by those who understood that creating a positive and equal future meant being very careful with its creation.

Despite all these philosophical differences and theoretical methods of inception, popular culture, governments, and police the world over have focused on the perceived close association between anarchy and violence. Yet of its three core philosophers – Proudhon, Bakunin, and Kropotkin – that only Bakunin supported individual acts of violence and terrorism. To understand how, when, and where violent acts became acts of anarchy, it is vital to first look at the notion of "propaganda by deed."

The original notion seems to have been that of the Italian revolutionary Carlo Piscan (1818–1857). In 1857 he wrote:

> The propaganda by deed is a chimera, the education of the people is an absurdity. Ideas result from deeds, not the latter from the former, and the people will not be free when they are educated, but will be educated when they are free. The only work a citizen can undertake for the good of the country is that of cooperating with the material revolution; therefore conspiracies, plots, attempts, etc., are that series of deeds by which Italy proceeds to her goal.[17]

Nevertheless the popularity and common usage of the phrase is more associated with Michael Bakunin who, in 1870, declared that the time had come (during the Paris Commune) to spread the notion of revolution not by word but by deed. After this, anarchists noted that they could force a degree of change, if not indeed revolution, through individual acts of terror. As philosophical anarchy continued to persuade a few, forced philosophical and practical change became more appealing.

When many saw that the revolution was not going to occur easily, they instead proposed that in the meantime that they could make major propaganda-like advances by taking part in acts of violence, which would, at the very least, bring attention to their cause. Thus what became more important than the immediate revolution was that attention be brought to the cause. The result was an increase in demonstrations, and later an increased use of assassination. One of the obvious examples of this was the murder in Dublin, Ireland, of Lord Frederick Cavendish, in 1882. Appointed by the then-British Prime Minister William Gladstone as Lord-Lieutenant of Ireland, Cavendish went for a walk in the Phoenix Park on the afternoon of his arrival. He was attacked from behind and stabbed to death by a group who called themselves the Invincibles. The British government, nervous that this was the beginning of more severe attacks on British officials living in Ireland, allowed certain land reforms to pass through parliament, in an attempt to appease the Irish. This onetime act of terror had resulted in reform.

Anarchy and the revolution necessary for its creation, had quickly moved from philosophical argument to violent practical means. The cost of violence was high – the Invincibles were hanged – but it helped popularize anarchy's ideal of a new society: one in which the individual was cared for without being ordered about.

There is a real world and a philosophical world, and in the perhaps mythical, sometimes historical, world of heroes, heroes have one value, one cause, one belief to which they dedicate their lives. Everything else comes second to *the cause*. Emma Goldman discovered much to her frustration and disappointment that she was all too human: she felt loss, pain, and the cold weather. She did not like being hungry; she needed money, medical care on occasion, and new spectacles very often. She wanted to be just like those great mythical, mystical people, like Vera in Nikolai Chernyshevsky's *What Is to Be Done?*

When all was said and done, her autobiography reveals a seamstress, a worker. And she was a good worker who knew her material, what matched and what did not. She knew about conflicts, the practical, the obvious, and the shades of nuances which might not seem to make a great difference to some, but to the trained eye meant everything.

Emma Goldman was made up of differing different skeins; different shades of beliefs; she changed her mind on issues, she saw complications, and she saw her needs and the needs of others change. She was dedicated to, but not blinded by, ideals. Her world was a practical working-class world, where survival was *the* guiding practice.

Goldman knew this was complicated. In her autobiography she writes about a moment of absolute clarity:

> Later Robert Henri asked me to sit for my Portrait. I was very busy at the time; besides several people had already tried to paint me, with little success. Henri said he wanted to depict the "real Emma Goldman." "But which is the real one?" I asked; "I have never been able to unearth her.[18]

But other people, then and since, have thought and still think they understood her, and as a result, some created a character called "Emma Goldman." Indeed, there have been so many of these personalities produced that Bonnie Haaland, among others, has referred to the "cult" of Goldman. There are many, many "Emma Goldmans" out there; they dance and sing in operas and rock bands; they sell on eBay and have shows on Broadway; they appear on T-shirts and mugs; and they even appear on TV and in film – Maureen Stapleton got an Oscar for her version of Emma Goldman, in *Reds*.

So after I spent years looking at all these different Goldmans, seeing what they had in common, I had questions to which I could not find answers:

- Who are these Goldmans?
- Who created them?
- When?
- How?
- Was there a purpose in the construct?
- Do any of them at all relate in any way to the woman who lived between 1869 and 1940?
- And perhaps most importantly, was it possible that there are any "missing" Goldmans?

So the next issue became methodology. How was I going to tackle this issue? Was there a blueprint out there, a multiple-character-historical-construct, that picked and chose an Emma Goldman depending not only on the author's personal views, but also on the cultural and political circumstances of the time?

At the beginning of my research I was given two hints by Alice Wexler, Goldman's most published biographer. In 1992, having finished two substantial biographies of Goldman, she wrote an article called the "Emma Goldman and the Anxiety of Biography" in which she commented that what was necessary was for Goldman to be placed within a theoretical, particularly feminist, perspective, which may cause new questions to be asked about her and help to explore new answers.

In the same article, Wexler noted that while Goldman was writing her autobiography, she had also been writing fairly constantly to Theodore Dreiser; Wexler wonders if he had any impact on Goldman's writing.

Well, like all enthusiastic history students, I had a challenge: find the letters, find the link, find the context.

And I did.

This finding led me to other letters, and diaries, and notes, and people, and what I eventually found questions Emma Goldman's self-creation, which was published in two volumes in 1931 as *Living My Life*.

Emma Goldman was dramatic in everything she said and did – so she claims to have begun writing her autobiography on her 59th birthday and hoped to be finished by her 60th. The reality is that while she may have begun her official writing process in 1928, the unofficial process of talking out, planning, getting advice, opinions, etc., had been going on for years. As early as 1926, and even before that, her writings contain some very clear points:

a. Sex and sexuality are personal, not public, issues.
b. Loyalty to anarchism means any criticism is done inside the organization and never done in print or in public.
c. Violence will never be a means of success, but it is an under-standable sign of frustration.
d. The organization has really achieved very little, but the hope is in a continued struggle and protest movement, and so successes must be counted and people's loyalty is vital.

Being now aware of these factors, I had to consider what this meant. Would my looking differently at her life and her writings, specifically her autobiography, involve a different approach to understanding Goldman? The key was her autobiography and its construct. I had questions again.

• Why was writing an autobiography so important to her?
• As she wrote, what was the process?
• Who helped her?
• What was the result?
• How should we look at *Living My Life*?
• Why is her autobiography so important?
• How should we view her autobiography now?
• How does this approach help other studies?
• What is worth revisiting?
• What is the impact for biography? For history? For academia in general?

This approach to the study of Goldman will, I hope, give a different and more complicated picture of her and of other working class and politically active men and women. It will take us away from the single factory, union, town, and city, and into the realm of national politics, which will also give us the chance to study what it took for minorities to break through on a national level and what the costs were. There is also a need for academia to look again at radical female political activists at the beginning of 20th century America. Unlike striking unionists, they had more than one cause, were usually chased not just by factory owners and local police, but also by state and, much more importantly, federal authorities. This federal incision into the lives of Goldman, Bonnie O'Hare, and others makes their lives more susceptible and fragile.

So this book is the study of a woman, a book, and other books in the hope of getting to understand the complications of world politics. Simple, really!

CHAPTER ONE

An Exceedingly Dangerous Woman

We piled into taxis and drove straight to Ellis Island. There Sasha and I
surrendered, while Henry Weinberger prepared to demand the return of
the thirty thousand dollars deposited as our bond.
  "That is the end, Emma Goldman, isn't it?" a reporter remarked.
"It may be only the beginning," I flashed back.[1]

Early in the morning of Sunday, December 21, 1919, Emma
Goldman, Alexander Berkman, and 247 other so-called radicals
imprisoned on Ellis Island were suddenly awoken and hurried on
board the *SS Buford*: destination unknown. The United States federal government was not taking any chances with this group, as the
249 so-called dangerous radicals were accompanied to the ship by
250: one per prisoner. Despite the headlines of the day, the ignored
truth was that only fifty-one were actually anarchists; 184 were
members of the Federation of the Union of Russian Workers (in
other words, their "crime" was being Russian), while fourteen were
considered morally dubious persons: prostitutes and drug-dealers.
Nevertheless, *The New York Times* reported the event and concentrated on just two people: "the sweet sorrow of parting at last with
Emma Goldman and Alexander Berkman, for a generation among
the most virulent and dangerous preachers and practicers of the
doctrines of destruction."[2] This summarized public perception of
the event: Emma Goldman was finally deported. The public was
given every possible detail to assure them that they could sleep easier this night and every night from then on:

> Under the guns of Fort Wadswoth the leaden-colored trans-
> port *Buford* loomed vaguely in the beginning of yesterday's
> dawn, her port holes blinking out one by one as light came
> on. Shortly after 6 o'clock, splashing and rasping in the silence
> of the empty bay, the anchors came up to the bow, the

Buford's prow swung lazily eastward, a patch of foam slipped from under the stern and 249 persons who didn't like America left it.[3]

Goldman's memory of the events, recounted years later in her autobiography, *Living My Life*, describes her shock, though with typical Goldman flair for exaggeration, she juxtaposes these events with the Statue of Liberty and all these events and feigns disbelief, wondering if all this happened in the United States or Tsarist Russia, as she describes the inhumane conditions:

> We were led into a cabin. A large fire roared in the iron stove, filing the air with heat and fumes. We felt suffocating. There was no air nor water. Then came a violent lurch; we were on our way.
>
> I looked at my watch. It was 4:20 AM on the day of our Lord, December 21, 1919. On the deck above us I could hear the men tramping up and down in the wintry blast. I felt dizzy, visioning a transport for politicals doomed to Siberia, the *etape* of former Russian days. Russia of the past rose before me and I saw the revolutionary martyrs being driven into exile. But no, it was New York, it was America, the land of liberty! Through the port-hole I could see the great city receding into the distance, its skyline of buildings traceable by their rearing heads. It was my beloved city, the metropolis of the New World. It was America, indeed, America repeating the terrible scenes in tsarist Russia! I glanced up – the Statue of Liberty.[4]

The New York Times report of the day emphasizes her surprise differently as they report, "the countenance of Emma Goldman lost some of its color," as the other two female prisoners "sat with emotionless faces."[5]

Whatever Goldman's physical reaction to her deportation, the delight of the American press and government is obvious. *The New York Times* sums up the feeling of all Americans: "Americans know the revolutionary aliens now. They are determined that these soldiers of disorder shall be driven out."[6] A cartoon published that day shows both the relief experienced by all Americans. But it also enforces the moral correctness of the act, emphasized by the biblical language used – "It is better to give than receive" (Acts 20) – a comment on this event as well the recently changed immigration policy. While the illustration shows Uncle Sam enjoying the moment, he had no choice, and he stands staring out at the ship, satisfied by the day's work; America had to be protected – specifically from Emma Goldman.

By 1919 Emma Goldman was considered to be the most dangerous woman in America. She had been arrested sixteen times in the previous sixteen years on a variety of charges ranging from inciting a riot, to being a suspicious person, to conspiracy charges against the government and inciting the assassination of the president. *The New York Times* described her as "advocating a 'reign of terror,'" the woman leader of the Anarchists in this country, whose fiery teachings it was charged by many, incited Leon Czolgosz to the assassination of President McKinley." Goldman was the "most notorious anarchist in the United States" and "a firebrand of disorder and sedition."[7] She was feared by the mainstream press, accused of being a traitor by the government, and even used as a means to scare young children into going to bed early!

1919: THE YEAR OF FEAR

But why was Goldman deported in 1919? What had happened to make this the year that the federal government got involved in each case dealing with Goldman? 1919 was a year of fear, chaos, and change. When it came to disastrous events that year, Murphy's Law applied. Cultural icons such as baseball players were found to be corrupt, soldiers returning from war brought disease, letter bombs to the homes of prominent politicians terrorized people, and eventually Emma Goldman became the focal point of this fear.

While the First World War had been won and the troops were coming home, there was still an air of uncertainty surrounding everything in the United States. The Russian Revolution in October 1917 and the subsequent decision to agree to the Treaty of Brest-Litovsk signaled an outbreak of a new, intense fear. President William Howard Taft, in a speech in Chicago on February 21, 1918, days before the Treaty was officially signed, warned of "whispering traitors" who doubted whether America should be in this war. Taft insisted that Americans had to ignore this kind of conversation and be convinced that such people "cannot lead a moral people like us to give up a moral fight like this."

One way to halt or at least control fear was government-organized morality. So lawmakers began 1919 with the introduction of prohibition. The Eighteenth Amendment was ratified in January 1919, through the political impact and constant work of mainly Protestant evangelical churches. Drink, and because of it sin, was destroying the American working class, which they insisted needed to be saved, and prohibition was the solution. Billy Sunday, the best-known preacher of the day, spoke of the positive impact of Prohibition: "The slums will soon be a memory; we will turn our prisons into factories, our jails into storehouses and corn cribs, our men will walk upright. Now women will smile, children will laugh, hell will be for rent." Mark Lender, in his book *Drinking in America*, notes the calm that followed the passing of the Amendment: "The demon, in fact, died a largely quiet death on January 16, 1920. As notable a newspaper as the *New York Times* saw no reason to give its demise more than a single column."[8] The reason for such a silent death was, according to Lender, that banning alcohol was then seen as part of the patriotic war effort. The advocates of a ban on liquor

> fought the brewing and distilling of grains into beverage alcohol as emergency food conservation measure (the Lever Food and Fuel Control Act). And antiliquor forces happily watched the public turn even more strongly against the brewers – most of whom had German names – in the new wave of war-inspired emotionalism.[9]

So even though the war was over in 1920, the notion of protecting America still reigned.

However prohibition was not the major issue for the Bostonians in January, when, on the 15th, a tank of molasses exploded and swept through the streets of Boston's industrial north, destroying everything in its path until it finally landed in Boston Harbor. The huge tank, filled the day before with over two million gallons of molasses, exploded and began moving down Commercial Street in Boston's Little Italy, at an estimated thirty-five miles an hour, swallowing all before it. Twenty-one people died, 150 were hospitalized.

Stephen Puleo describes the events: "Midday turned to darkness as the 2.3 million gallons of molasses engulfed the Boston waterfront like a black tidal wave, 24 feet high and 160 feet wide at the outset."[10] He goes on to describe its slow but devastating trail:

> Molasses inundated cellars of businesses and residences along Commercial Street and in the freight sheds on the wharf, smothering men who were working below ground level. Electrical wires were torn down from their poles, smoking and sputtering, until they sank into the molasses. A one-ton piece of the steel tank sliced through a column of the elevated railroad, causing the tracks overhead to collapse nearly to the street. Thousands of rivets that fastened the steel plates had torn away as the tank collapsed, becoming deadly projectiles that sprayed the waterfront like machine-gun fire – the *rat-tat-tat* sound McManus heard – ricocheting off brick and stone and embedding themselves in wood buildings. In minutes – in *seconds* – the landscape in the North End inner harbor resembled a bombed-out war zone.[11]

But while Boston struggled to recover from the Molasses explosion and its devastation, it, along with the rest of the country, was still living in fear of the Spanish influenza, which was sweeping everywhere. An estimated 28% of all Americans were infected. Six hundred seventy-five thousand died because of it, ten times more than were killed in World War I. The average lifespan in America was depressed for ten years. As the flu continued its pounding impact across the country, there were reports of people just dropping in the streets and dying within hours. Reports of couples meeting for dinner and then dying later that night increased the already fearful state in which people lived. There was a shortage of doctors and medical personnel because so many were still in Europe, having gone with the troops to war. Soon there was a shortage of morticians, coffins, and gravediggers too. People were afraid to bury the dead, so bodies were thrown into the street where trucks came and collected them, dumping them into mass graves. Fear continued to be everywhere. You couldn't trust your friends or colleagues not to pass on the flu, nor could you trust authority figures to be there for you if you needed them. Anyone, everyone, might be infected. Such was the cultural impact of the flu that a common playground ditty sung to jumping rope was: "I knew a bird. Its name was Enza. I opened the window and in-flu-Enza."

Chaos soon turned from personal to political. From April to September 1919, newspapers were filled of accounts of riots and strikes all over the country. The race riots, which occurred in the spring and summer months all over the United States, increased anxiety and made people think more and more that a revolution was not just possible but probable.

In May, 1919, riots broke out in Charleston, South Carolina, killing one man and causing the city to be put under martial law for a week. In July, riots broke out in Washington DC; six people were killed and approximately 150 were injured. In late July and early August, some of the worst riots were in Chicago, at the end of which thirty-eight people were killed, over 500 hundred injured, and hundreds of homes destroyed by fire. Claude McKay, in his poem "If We Must Die," first published in *The Liberator*, the magazine founded by Max Eastman and his sister, Crystal, after their previous magazine *The Masses* had been shut down for its anti-war stance, urged the African-American community to stand up for itself. Not only were riots common, but the number of lynchings increased from thirty-six in 1917 to a reported seventy-six in 1919. The average number of people lynched, from 1910 to 1919, was sixty-two.

> If we must die, let it not be like hogs
> Hunted and penned in an inglorious spot,
> While round us bark the mad and hungry dogs,
> Making their mock at our accursed lot.
> If we must die, O let us nobly die,
> So that our precious blood may not be shed
> In vain; then even the monsters we defy
> Shall be constrained to honor us though dead!
> O kinsmen we must meet the common foe!
> Though far outnumbered let us show us brave,
> And for their thousand blows deal one deathblow!
> What though before us lies the open grave?
> Like men we'll face the murderous, cowardly pack,
> Pressed to the wall, dying, but fighting back![12]

Change and fear of change seemed to be the main motive behind these riots as over one million African-Americans from southern rural areas migrated to various cities. The African-American population in Chicago increased by 148% between 1910 and 1920, in Cleveland it rose by 307%, and in Detroit by 611%. In 1917, after the Supreme Court had declared municipal resident segregation ordnances unconstitutional, many cities and neighbourhood adopted restrictive covenants – whereby white property owners in certain neighborhoods agreed to a formal deed restriction. These agreements bound owners not to sell their property to African-Americans. Breaking this agreement meant they could be sued by the other owners in the neighborhood.

Claude McKay was clear that his theme of fighting back did not just apply to African-Americans, but also to oppressed people all over the United States. 1919 saw a rise in the cost of living and as unions tried to gain an increase in wages to make up the difference, the all-too-familiar impasse between worker, union, and employer occurred. But in 1919 strikes seemed even more dangerous. 1919 was a mere two years after the Russian Revolution, all unions were considered communistic, and all organizers of unions and strikes anti-American Communist spies. The Seattle General Strike, from February 6 to 11, was indicative of the discontent felt all over the country, and typical of government reaction to strikes.

Initially, the unions called for a rise in pay for the unskilled workers in the shipyards, which was refused and countered with an offer of a rise in pay for the skilled workers – a common enough tactic to divide union membership and so minimize any union effect later. Instead, the whole shipyard voted to go on strike. After a threat sent by Charles Piez, head of the government's Emergency Fleet Corporation, a wartime company set up to supply the Armed Forces with supplies, to the shipyard owners which stated he would withdraw the contract if any rise in wages was agreed to, one hundred more unions went on strike. The Mayor of Seattle, Ole Hanson called on the people of the city:

> The time has come for every person in Seattle to show his Americanism. Go about your daily duties without fear. We will see to it that you have food, transportation, water, light,

gas and all necessities. The anarchists in this community shall
not rule its affairs. All persons violating the laws will be dealt
with summarily.

The strike ended quickly, however, as the executive of the union
voted to end the strike when faced with federal troops being
brought in, as well as more police officers and other law enforce-
ment agents. Nevertheless the thirty-nine IWW (Industrial Workers
of the World) members were arrested, with Mayor Hanson declaring that "Americanism" had triumphed over Bolshevism.

It was perhaps for this reason that unions and strikes were considered anti-American. It was the Boston Police Strike in September
that shocked people most, especially as the police force went on
strike to demand the right to form a union. For the police force, the
issue was simple; they had not received a pay raise at all comparable to the rise in the cost of living over the previous ten years, and
the numbers of police recruits were not enough to maintain law
and order in an ever-growing Boston. So on September 9, 1919,
after a vote of 1,134 to 2, the police went on strike.

Boston immediately plunged into chaos as looters took to the
streets, taking advantage of the fact that there was no one to stop
them. The Governor of Massachusetts, John Calvin Coolidge,
urged on by President Wilson to be firm in his handling of the
event, fired the strikers and hired over one thousand new recruits,
at the higher rate of pay demanded by those on strike.

Even sporting events, a safe haven and refuge in times of trial,
were blighted. First, the Stanley Cup Finals were cancelled because
of the Flu epidemic. The finals were played between the Montreal
Canadiens and the Seattle Metropolitans. The teams were even in
the series (both teams had won two, lost two and drawn one) when
players from both teams became ill. The National Hockey League
felt it had no choice but to abandon the games so no Stanley Cup
was awarded that year. Days after the series was cancelled, Canadiens player Joe Hall died from the flu. Later, manager George
Kennedy would also succumb.

But it was the Baseball World Series scandal that seemed to be
the final proof that American decency was indeed coming to an
end. The story, which was eventually to unfold, was that the
Chicago White Sox first baseman Arnold "Chick" Gandil organized disgruntled colleagues and persuaded them to throw the World

Series against the Cincinnati Reds. Newspapers reported on the misdeeds and while the public remained loyal to the game and players, even signing petitions urging Baseball Commissioner Kenesaw Landis to reinstate the players who had previously received lifetime bans after they had been found not guilty in their criminal trial. Nevertheless, even the pure, innocent sport of baseball was forever tainted.

But while baseball was now slurred, the blame soon rested on the shoulders of Arnold Rothstein, a well-known New York Jewish gambler and businessman. While the Grand Jury investigation never pressed any charges against him, Rothstein became the figure most associated with the scandal, as he appears as the character Meyer Wolfsheim in F. Scott Fitzgerald's *The Great Gatsby*, and in Damon Runyon novel *The Idyll of Miss Sarah Brown* as Nathan Detroit. His Jewishness is highlighted through stereotypes typical of the day, when Fitzgerald writes of Meyer Woldsheim, "As I shook hands and turned away his tragic nose was trembling."[13]

The physical anti-Semitic stereotype expressed here was an all too common sentiment in 1919. 1919 was when Henry Ford bought *The Dearborn Independent.* Here Ford had a place to publish his anti-Semitic opinions in articles such as, "Are the Jews Victims or Persecutors?" "Jewish Gamblers Corrupt American Baseball," and "Jewish Degradation of American Baseball." Considering Ford's magazine had a subscription base of over 900,000, his diatribe had a following. During the war, the manual for instruction of Medical Advisory Boards warned, "The foreign born, and especially Jews, are more apt to malinger than the native-born." After protests were made to President Wilson, he ordered the deletion of "the unfortunate expression."[14]

While the flu, the molasses explosion, strikes, riots, and baseball scandals were each awful and impacted the lives of many individual Americans, it was the political bombings that caused massive political change in the United States – changes that most people were not aware of for a very long time. Particularly important was the coming to prominence of J. Edgar Hoover and the establishment of the FBI.

Between April and September 1919, a series of bombs were sent via the mail service to a variety of politicians all over the U.S. In April a bomb was sent to the Mayor of Seattle – it was defused. A few days later a bomb was sent to Senator Thomas Hardwick of

Georgia, and while the bomb missed him, it killed a servant and severely injured the servant's wife. Soon after, thirty devices, due to be sent to various politicians including John D. Rockefeller, were discovered by a postal worker. In June, eight much more powerful bombs were left at the houses of various politicians and judges: Boston municipal judge Robert Hayden; Cleveland Mayor Harry Davis; Massachusetts State Representative Leland W. Powers; New York judge Charles Nott Jr.; New Jersey manufacturer Max Gold; Pittsburgh judge William Thompson; and Attorney General Mitchell Palmer. The eighth bomb, for reasons still unknown, was sent to the Church of Our Lady of Victory in Philadelphia.

Mitchell Palmer had become Attorney General on March 5, 1919. Alexander Mitchell Palmer was born in May 1872, in Pennsylvania, into a strict Quaker family. After graduating with a law degree from Swarthmore College, he married Roberta Bartlett Dixon and set out upon a political career. A Democrat, he ran for Congress three times, winning each time, but the fulcrum of his political influence and success was his friendship with Woodrow Wilson.

When Wilson decided to run for President in 1912, he turned to his friend Palmer to run his campaign. When Wilson won, beating the incumbent President William Howard Taft, and former President Theodore Roosevelt, Wilson offered Palmer the cabinet position of Secretary of War. Palmer turned down the post, citing his Quaker pacifist background: "I could not, without violating every tradition of my people ... sit down in cold blood in an executive position and use such talents as I possess to the work of preparing for [war]."[15]

Over the next number of years nevertheless Palmer made himself available to Wilson to back, propose, and be part of various projects begun by the president. Palmer was a member of Congress when Wilson had the Federal Trade Commission, the Clayton Antitrust Act, the Underwood Tariff, and the Federal Farm Loan Act passed, and when Wilson established the Federal Reserve System.

In 1914, Palmer returned to Pennsylvania at Wilson's request to fight for an open Senate seat. Though Palmer lost, Wilson rewarded him by making him a judge on the U.S. Court of Claims. However, when the First World War broke out, Wilson had a new position for Palmer, one in which he thrived: Alien Property Custodian.

As Alien Property Custodian, it was Palmer's job to ensure that German-owned businesses in the United States caused no damage to the American economy and hence the war effort. Palmer began the job with zeal, seizing German firms, dollars, and patents. Once seized, Palmer in turn sold them to American owners at such low prices that suspicions of favouritism were whispered. The result of such a high-profile job was that his nickname in the American press was the "Fighting Quaker." The German press, for the record, named him the "Official American pickpocket."

With war at an end Wilson once again turned to his friend and offered him the position of Attorney General, as the previous Attorney General, Francis W. Gregory, had resigned amid allegations of an over-zealous department that arrested tens of thousands of people on little or no evidence. The result was a severe mistrust of the Department of Justice. Palmer within weeks had calmed the situation by recommending the release, pardon, and/or repatriation of some seven thousand prisoners.

On Monday, June 2, he was sitting at home in his town house on R Street, between Sheridan and Dupont Circles, an exclusive neighborhood that included such people as Franklin and Eleanor Roosevelt, William Taft, and Warren Harding. At around 11:15 PM, Palmer reported hearing a car pull up, footsteps, and then, "I heard a crash downstairs as if something had been thrown against the front door. It was followed immediately by an explosion."[16] His only child, Mary, was hurled from her bad and was crying hysterically in her room. His wife Roberta lay on the floor, bewildered. Palmer made his way downstairs, finding his house wrecked: stairs with broken steps, broken glass everywhere, cabinets thrown down and their contents broken, the front door was blown in, even the floor had been ripped up.

Franklin and Eleanor Roosevelt, who lived across the street, had been out for dinner. Franklin had just parked the car in a garage a few blocks away when he heard and felt the explosion. Franklin rushed back to check on his family. The explosion had broken windows in their house, so Franklin rushed upstairs to check on their son James, their only child at home that night. After finding him safe, Franklin rushed across the street to see the Palmers. He later reported to Eleanor that he found the Attorney General in a state of shock, reverting to the Quaker language of his upbringing, "Theeing and thouing all over the place."

Palmer and the police, sifting through the wreckage, found what remained of the body of the bomber, Carlo Valdinoci, and copies of printed handbills with the phrase "PLAIN WORDS" and signed "THE ANARCHIST FIGHTERS." The intent of this group of self-described "Anarchist Fighters" was clear:

> The time has come when the social question's solution can be delayed no longer; class war is on and cannot cease but with complete victory for the international proletariat ... There will have to be bloodshed; we will not dodge; there will have to be murder; we will kill because it is necessary; there will have to be destruction; we will destroy to rid the world of your tyrannical institutions.

The perpetrator of this bomb was quickly identified as being an associate of the Italian anarchist Luigi Galleani, who had arrived in the United States in 1901. Galleani, who was a resident alien, was deported back to Italy a mere three weeks after the event, on the grounds that as a non-citizen he had encouraged and taken part in the possible violent overthrow of the government.

When the riots and demonstrations had been occurring earlier in 1919, the press and public had been critical of Palmer and the Department of Justice for its lack of action. Ole Hanson, the outspoken Mayor of Seattle, charged that the Department of Justice was "weak, vacillating, and changeable." Hanson wanted Washington to "hang or incarcerate for life all the anarchists in the country."[17] New York State had decided to deal with its issue on their own by establishing a special Joint Legislative Committee to Investigate Seditious Activities under State Senator Clayton R. Lusk, thanks to the state's Penal Code, which allowed for such investigations in the case of suspected government overthrow by anarchists. It was the first time that such laws had been used since the assassination of President McKinley in Buffalo, New York, in 1902.

After the bombing at his home, and even despite the deportation of Luigi Galleani, Palmer was not satisfied, as he had decided that the communist threat was the most dangerous factor facing American life, and that the solution had two distinct parts: the short-term one (which he and others had to figure out) was how to solve immediate security problems in the U.S.; the long-term issue was how to ensure that all radicals were deported. In an interview given to various reporters from newspapers all over the country Palmer explained that something drastic needed to be done because "These bomb throwers will only increase."[18] Palmer met with Francis P. Garvan, former New York prosecutor, now Assistant Attorney General, and John Creighton, formerly of the War Trade Intelligence, now Senior Special Assistant, and the three decided that the best person to lead the Department of Justice's investigation was William F. Flynn. Flynn, known as "Big Bill," was the former chief of the U.S. Secret Service and the New York detective force. Flynn specialized in espionage. During the war he served as Chief of the United States Railroad Secret Service. In this position, he investigated plots to counterfeit millions of dollars and so undermine the economy, and another plot to blow up American ships in New York harbour. Flynn once claimed in a public speech that he had over fifteen thousand German agents under surveillance. Palmer boasted after appointing Flynn that "Flynn is an anarchist chaser. He is the greatest anarchist expert in the United States. He knows all the men in that class. He can pretty well call them by name."[19]

With these three now working with Palmer, and the press and public opinion firmly behind him, *The Washington Post* boldly declared, "Free Speech has been outraged long enough. Let there be a few free treatments in the electric chair."[20] Palmer set about finding out just how serious these issues were and what possible legal options they had.

The three quickly set up their short-term solution and within days of their first meeting, federal agents made arrests in around the country including Boston, Cleveland, New Jersey, New York, Philadelphia, and Pittsburgh. These raids were based on lists compiled by Flynn during the war, and though the authorities had no evidence to link anyone arrested to the June bombings, this was not a concern as Flynn described the arrests as "precautionary measures," explaining that these arrests were necessary to prevent further violence.

Palmer's long-term solution was to make use of the revised Immigration Act of 1918. The Act stated:

> ...that aliens who are anarchists; aliens who believe in or
> advocate the overthrow by force or violence of the
> Government of the United States or of all forms of law; aliens
> who disbelieve in or are opposed to all organized government;

aliens who advocate or teach the assassination of public officials; aliens who advocate or teach the unlawful destruction of
property; aliens who are members of or affiliated with any
organization that entertains a belief in, teaches, or advocates
the overthrow by force or violence of the Government of the
United States or of all forms of law, or that entertains or
teaches disbelief or opposition to all organized government, or
that advocates the duty, necessity, or propriety of the unlawful
assaulting or killing of any officer or officers, either of specific
individuals, or of officers generally, of the Government of the
United States or any other organized government, because of
his or their character, or that advocates or teaches the unlawful destruction of property, shall be excluded from admission
into the United States.

Under this act the government could deport any non-citizen
who was an anarchist, or who forwarded the idea of the violent
overthrow of the government. So Palmer proposed a massive deportation of all radicals back to Europe. In a speech at Georgetown
University, Palmer explained:

> There is no room and there is no need, in this country for peo-
> ple who resort to violence to impress their ultra-radical views
> upon the people or the Government. The Government propos-
> es to protect itself [and these radicals] should go back to the
> countries from which they came.

Palmer, with Congress's permission and money, then decided to
create a new office with the Bureau of Investigation under William
Flynn, but the person in charge would be given the title of Special
Assistant and would report directly to Palmer. The person in charge
of this new office was J. Edgar Hoover.

John Edgar Hoover was born in Washington DC on January 1,
1895, to Anna Marie Scheitlin and Dickerson Naylor Hoover, Sr.
He grew up seven blocks from Capitol Building, at 413 Seward
Square. Considered too small for the school football team, he
joined the Reserve Officers' Training Corps, excelling there and
enjoying the camaraderie he found. After school he enrolled at
George Washington University, lived with his parents and went to
law school at night. By day he worked at the Library of Congress.

He graduated from George Washington with both Bachelor and Masters of Law degrees, and while the young Edgar wanted to enlist and go to war, his father's illness meant he was financially responsible for the family, and so he needed a job. After having received a draft exemption from the Justice Department, he was hired to work for John Lord O'Brien who had recently taken charge of the War Emergency Division in the Justice Department.

Hoover was assigned to the Alien Enemy Bureau, a unit established to keep an eye on Germans in America. When the War ended O'Brien was returning to his private law practice in Buffalo, and since Hoover wished to remain with the Justice Department, O'Brien spoke to Palmer. Hoover soon had a job and the title Special Assistant. Hoover's work on Germans, radicals, and spies during the war, his intricate filing system – based on the Dewey Decimal System he had learned while working in the Library of Congress – and his huge capacity and enthusiasm for work meant that on August 1, 1919, Palmer gave Hoover his most important job yet. He intended to make a great success of it.

In the middle of all this chaos was Emma Goldman. And while her role in any of these dreadful events was nil, her reputation was everything. She was associated with an odd but dangerous combination of personal immorality and political chaos. Hoover's ambitions were soon to catch up with Goldman's reputation. It was Hoover who wrote a memo to John Creighton, in August 1919, referring to Emma Goldman and her longtime companion Alexander Berkman as "two of the most dangerous anarchists in this country." Deporting these two anarchists would establish his reputation and theirs forever.

CHAPTER TWO

New Americans and Anarchy

Emma Goldman and Alexander Berkman are, beyond doubt, two of the most
dangerous anarchists in this country and if permitted to return to the community will result in undue harm.
–J. Edgar Hoover

"A beast, a bloodthirsty monster!" I heard someone say: "she should have
been locked up long ago." "Locked up nothing!" another retorted; "she
should be strung up to the lamp-post.[1]

While testifying before Congress in 1936, J. Edgar Hoover was
asked about his investigations and arrest record. He specifically
mentioned his being in charge of the Emma Goldman and Alexander Berkman cases.

Senator McKellar: Did you ever make an arrest?
Mr. Hoover: No sir; I made investigations.
Senator McKellar: How many arrests have you made, and who
 were they?
Mr. Hoover: I handled the investigation of Emma Goldman and I
 prosecuted that case before the immigration authorities up to
 the Secretary of Labor. I also handled the Alexander Berkman
 case, and the case of Ludwig Martins, the former Bolshevik
 Ambassador to the United States.[2]

As Curt Gentry, one of Hoover's biographers, notes about the
importance of this testimony:

As his testimony before the Senate subcommittee indicated,
Hoover still considered the deportation of Emma Goldman
one of his greatest achievements. Although this had occurred

seventeen years earlier, to Hoover it was in no way ancient history: as far as he was concerned, it was still an open case.[3]

Twenty years after this, in *The FBI Story: A Report to the People* by Don Whitehead, Hoover notes that he was one of the last people to talk to Goldman before her deportation, and was there to see her thumb her nose at a Congressman who shouted "Merry Christmas Emma" to her from the dock.[4] This recollection, given in 1956, is all the more remarkable as Emma Goldman and Alexander Berkman were dead, but still they were important enough to Hoover to re-mention in order to keep his reputation intact. So the question becomes: why was Emma Goldman so important to J. Edgar Hoover? What did she do that she was considered so dangerous that J. Edgar Hoover was able to build up a fifty-three-year career with the deportation of Emma Goldman and Alexander Berkman as its founding stone?

EMMA GOLDMAN

Emma Goldman was born on June 27, 1869, in Kovo (now Kaunas), Lithuania. She was the first child of Abraham and Tuabe Bienowitch Goldman, though Tuabe did have two older daughters, Lena and Helena, by her first marriage. Abraham Goldman was an orthodox Jew, conservative and traditional in his views. The function of women, according to Abraham Goldman, was to get married and have children. The cultural and religious lack of importance for women, according to Abraham Goldman, was further highlighted as Emma Goldman always insisted that her father's disappointment at her birth was such that he never forgave her for her gender. "As long as I could think back, I remember his saying he had not wanted me. He had wanted a boy, the pig woman had cheated him."[5] It seems that even the birth of two sons, Herman in 1873 and Morris in 1875, did not change his mind.

Bad luck and little finances plagued the Goldmans. Soon after Emma's birth the family moved to Popelan, a small Baltic town, where Abraham worked as an innkeeper. However, in 1975, after the birth of Morris, Taube became seriously ill and Abraham suffered an accident, so the family moved again, this time to Konigsberg, where they moved in with Taube's wealthy family.

Up to this point, the young Emma had had little formal schooling. However, despite her father's reservations, with the insistence of
a Rabbi (a distant relative of the Goldmans), Emma was able to
obtain some formal education when she attended the local *Real-
schule*. While conditions at the school were harsh, with physical
punishment the norm, it was here that Goldman was taught to
understand and appreciate high German culture, French, music, and
opera, as well as many of the great European writers of the day.

Once again the Goldman family moved, this time to St. Petersburg. Taube had borrowed money from her family and Abraham
had set himself up as a grocery store owner. Emma Goldman's formal education continued for only six more months, as she, like her
sisters, had to help out in the family business.

The value of the education received by Emma Goldman in St.
Petersburg was not in the classroom, but in her awareness of political activists and literature, which opened to Goldman a new
approach as to how to change the status quo. It was during this
time that Goldman read Chernyshevsky's *What Is to Be Done?* The
impact of this book, not only on Goldman but on a whole generation of Russians and Russian immigrants, was, to put it simply,
enormous. Chernyshevsky popularized the ideas of the nihilist movement, which resulted in the movement in Russia gaining many
more followers.

The novel tells the story of Vera Pavlovna, a young woman
from a landed gentry family who expected her to marry and have
a family of her own. She, however, contacts the radical movement
and so escapes the life that would have been imposed on her. Vera
establishes a sewing cooperative and eventually falls in love with
Rakhmetov, a poor medical student, and her husband's best friend.
Her husband understands this relationship and leaves so that the
two can live happily together outside of the imposed constraints of
marriage. Vera's and Rakhmetov's relationship is equal in all aspects
and Vera is at all times free to search out any and all ideas. Vera
eventually decides to become a doctor so that she can help the poor.

The impact of this novel on Goldman was that it persuaded her
that the notion of family could be created by ideals rather than
duty, or tradition. The society in *What Is to Be Done?* is one of sexual freedom and personal choice, free of political and moral tyranny. It can be hardly surprising that, when Goldman met Alexander
Berkman and discovered that he too was greatly influenced by the
novel, she was immediately drawn to him.

In 1881, in Russia, Tsar Alexander II was assassinated by one of Russia's important terrorist groups, the People's Will or *Narodnaya Volya*. Alexander II had granted more religious freedom to the Jews in Russia and had emancipated the Serfs. Emma's mother, Taube firmly believed that these freedoms were the beginnings of total freedom for Jews in Russia, so when the Tsar was assassinated she was outraged. She regarded the nihilist People's Will as "cold blooded murderers ... who ought to be exterminated, everyone of them!"[6] Emma disagreed with her mother and when Emma heard that the nihilists had been executed she "wept bitterly over their fate."[7]

By 1882 Goldman's more immediate problem was that her father was attempting to find her a match in marriage. Instead of getting married, Emma begged to be allowed to continue her schooling. Her father instead got angry and refused:

> In a frenzy he threw my French grammar into the fire, shouting: "Girls do not have to learn much! All a Jewish daughter needs to know is how to prepare *gefullte* fish, cut noodles fine, and give the man plenty of children."[8]

Desperate to get away, she begged to go to America with her sister Helena. Their sister Lena was living there already. Initially, her father refused and Goldman had to continue working in a corset factory in St. Petersburg. However, after Emma Goldman threatened suicide, her father relented. Emma and Helena arrived in New York on December 29, 1884, on the SS *Geilert*.

The sisters' arrival to the United States was a mixture of great hope and utter frustration. Like most immigrants they looked out at that great symbol of the American dream – the Statue of Liberty – and thought that their troubles were over.

> The last day of our journey comes vividly to my mind. Everybody was on deck. Helena and I stood pressed to each other, enraptured by the sight of the harbor and the Statue of Liberty suddenly emerged from the mist. Ah there she was, the symbol of hope, of freedom, of opportunity! She held her torch high to light the way to the free country, the asylum for the oppressed of all lands. We, too, Helena and I, would find a place in the generous heart of America. Our spirits were high, our eyes filled with tears.[9]

The reality that was America quickly interrupted their thoughts and dreams.

> Gruff voices broke in upon our reverie. We were surrounded
> by gesticulating people – angry men, hysterical women,
> screaming children. Guards roughly pushed us hither and
> thither, shouted orders to get ready, to be transferred to Castle
> Garden, the clearing-house for immigrants.
> The scenes in Castle Garden were appalling, the atmos-
> phere charged with antagonisms and harshness. Nowhere
> could one see a sympathetic official face; there was no provi-
> sion for the comfort of new arrivals, the pregnant women and
> young children. The first day on American soil proved a vio-
> lent shock.[10]

They quickly left New York City for Rochester, where their older sister was living. Once again Emma was struck by the great con-trast between hope and reality, as her sister's house was small. She also noted that all day people came to visit them, saying that life in the new country was hard. She also notes the desperate irony that they still had a longing for a country that really was never theirs.

> All wanted to see us, to hear about the old country. They were
> Jews who had suffered much in Russia; some had even been in
> pogroms. Life in the new country, they said was hard; they
> were still all possessed by nostalgia for their home that had
> never been a home.[11]

Goldman soon understood many of the frustrations. There were jobs available, but they paid badly. There was as much discrimina-tion in Rochester due to her gender and religion as there had been in Tsarist Russia. Regardless of geography, she remained a Jewish woman, dominated by culture, tradition, and religion. Indeed, the conditions under which she was forced to work in Rochester were actually worse than those in Russia:

> Yet the work was harder, and the day with only half an hour
> for lunch, seemed endless. The iron discipline forbade free
> movement (no one could even go to the toilet without permis-
> sion), and the constant surveillance of the foreman weighed

like a stone on my heart. The end of each day found me
sapped, with just enough energy to drag myself to my sister's
home and crawl into bed.[12]

What Goldman had found in Rochester was a city where the
garment industry was run by the German Jews who, while they had
initially welcomed the Russian Jews and the cheap labour they provided, were by the 1880s less enthusiastic about the new arrivals.
Anti-Semitism was on the rise and non-Jews did not distinguish
between German and Russian Jews. Afraid for their own social and
economic positions, German Jewish factory owners treated the new
arrivals badly, trying not to encourage too many more immigrants.

Goldman quickly learned that she was a Russian Jew and would
always be considered inferior, even within the Jewish community in
Rochester. The irony was not lost on Goldman that her mother had
insisted that as a family they speak German and not Russian or
Yiddish. Yet it mattered for nothing. In Rochester the Russian Jews,
for the most part, joined the Knights of Labor, while the German
Jews were part of the Chamber of Commerce. Class distinction was
more important than any similarity of religion.

Proof of these differences became even more clear to Goldman
who had initially been optimistic about working for Leopold
Garson, Chairman of the United Jewish Charities of Rochester as
well as the owner of Garson, Meyer and Company, a supposed
"model factory." She was quickly brought to understand the harsh
reality; her pay of $2.50 a day was not enough to pay her various
bills nor at the end of the week to even enjoy a movie.[13] At this time
Goldman was giving her sister Lena $1.50 for room and board and
spending sixty cents in cab fare, which left her with only forty cents
for herself at the end of the week. Garson's reply was that
Goldman's tastes were extravagant and that, since all the other
workers seemed happy, she had better look for work elsewhere.
Goldman did leave and found a new job, working for a Mr.
Rubenstein, which paid four dollars a week.

Just a year after her arrival Emma Goldman married Jacob
Kersner, whom she had met in the new factory just four months
earlier. Kersner had come from an aristocratic family in Russia and
was well educated. He had been forced to leave Russia because of
the pogroms and, like Goldman, had come with the dream of a
much better quality of life. He too had read many of the same polit-

ical novels popular in Russian culture at the time, and this helped
them find common ground and interests. There was another reason
Goldman wanted to move out of her sister's house and this one was
practical: by 1887 her parents were living in Rochester, having emi-
grated from Russia. Probably pressured by the increasing number
of pogroms in Russia, Goldman's parents, her two younger brothers, and even Abraham's mother and sister all arrived. The life that
she had so desperately wanted to leave behind in Russia had simply moved to the U.S.

If initially Goldman thought that emigration to the U.S. would
free her from her family and cultural background, and give her
opportunities she had never had, she now knew she was wrong.
Her marriage to Jacob Kersner brought even less freedom. On their
wedding night Goldman discovered her husband was impotent. In
her autobiography Goldman is harsh in her description of Kersner;
he took a long time to seek medical help and did not seem willing
to continue with the treatment. Kersner also was insistent that, as
they were now married, Goldman should stay at home, and that
the factory was no place for a married woman. Kersner also developed a gambling addiction as Goldman complained that he spent
what money he did make – fifteen dollars – in card games. When
Goldman did decide to leave him, he threatened suicide, frustrating
Goldman and leaving her feeling more of a prisoner. In 1893, after
Goldman had left him for a second time and was living in New
York City, Kersner was sentenced to three years at Auburn Prison,
New York, for grand larceny. After his release from prison, Kersner
disappeared, only to happen into the life of Emma Goldman once
more, when he was found by J. Edgar Hoover, who persuaded him
to testify against his former wife.

While her marriage was causing her to sink into a depression, it
was the events of Haymarket in Chicago that awoke in Goldman
the same intense feeling she had in Russia when the nihilists assassinated the Tsar. The events and the aftermath of the Haymarket
Riot in Chicago became a moment of so-called spiritual awakening:

> The next morning I awoke as from along illness, but free from
> the numbness and the depression of those harrowing weeks of
> waiting, ending with the final shock. I had a distinct sensation
> that something new and wonderful had been born in my soul.

A great ideal, a burning faith, a determination to dedicate
myself to the memory of my martyred comrades, to make
their cause my own, to make known to the world their beautiful lives and heroic deaths.[14]

The Haymarket Riot erupted on Tuesday, May 4, 1886, in
Chicago, when a bomb was thrown by an unknown assailant at a
group of police officers who were trying to disperse a protest
march in support of workers who were on strike for an eight-hour
day. When the bomb went off, policeman Mathias J. Degan was
killed, and the police opened fire on the protestors, who had been
completely peaceful up to that point. What happened next is not
totally clear, but it seems someone shot back at the police.

This whole incident only lasted five minutes, but in the end,
seven police officers were killed and sixty were wounded, as were
as unknown number of civilians. The notoriety that followed seemed
to suggest that chaos and violence had taken place in Chicago, and
so in an attempt to calm public fears and to insist on a certain type
of justice, eight people connected with the rally were arrested and
tried for the murder of Officer Degan. They were August Spies,
Albert Parsons, Adolph Fischer, George Engel, Louis Lingg, Michael
Schwab, Samuel Fielden, and Oscar Neebe.

The trial began on June 21, and on August 19, the jury returned
guilty verdicts for all eight. Seven were sentenced to death, and one,
Oscar Neebe, was given a sentence of fifteen years. The cases were
appealed at the Supreme Court of Illinois, and at the United States
Supreme Court, where their attempt at review was refused.

On November 10, 1887, Illinois Governor Richard James Oglesby
commuted Fielden's and Schwab's sentences to life in prison. On
the eve of his execution, Louis Lingg committed suicide with smug-
gled dynamite. He died painfully from his wounds six hours later.
The next day, November 11, 1887, four were hung: Spies, Parsons,
Fischer and Engel. Six years later the three survivors were par-
doned by Governor John Peter Altgeld, who stated that Judge
Joseph Gary, who had been in charge of the trial, had conducted it
with "malicious ferocity," and further pointed out that there was
no evidence linking any of the eight with the bomb.

The problem with this incident was that everyone was aware of
the initial chaos, the fact that some policemen were shot through

friendly fire, and that those accused were organizers of the rally and had nothing to do with the bomb. Hence Goldman's emotional reaction.

The Haymarket Riot began with workers seeking the right to an eight-hour day. May 1, 1886 was set as the day when eight-hour day would become common. As the date approached and there was no sign of compromise from the employers, the Federation of Organized Trades and Labor Unions called a strike. Rallies were held all over the United States, with tens of thousands of workers turning out in support, particularly in New York, Detroit, and Milwaukee. But it was Chicago that saw the biggest reaction, as over forty thousand workers put down their tools and marched. One particular factory had a particularly uneasy employer-worker relationship: McCormick Harvesting Machine Company plant. Workers there had been locked out since February, and the owners had employed Pinkerton guards to protect strikebreaking workers who had been brought in, and to harass strikers.

August Spies, a union leader, had been insistent that non-violence was the vital approach, but on May 3, 1886, as protests outside the plant continued, shots were fired and six workers were killed. The killings caused outrage in the city and an anarchist group called for a demonstration to be held the following day at Haymarket to protest the deaths.

Initially the meeting was so peaceful that the mayor of Chicago, Carter Harrison, Sr., went home, having decided that there was nothing to worry about. August Spies, the first person to speak, urged the crowd not to overreact and to remain calm. As the meeting was drawing to a close, it began to rain and the crowds began to disperse. The evening had been completely uneventful. Then, when the last speaker for the evening, Samuel Fielden, was speaking, a contingent of police marched in and demanded the meeting be halted. Fielden pointed out that he was the last speaker and that nothing had happened up to that point. The police captain in charge was insistent.

At that moment the bomb went off. In the chaos that followed it seems that the police who were shot were actually shot by other police officers – friendly fire.

A telegraph pole at the scene was filled with bullet holes, all coming from the direction of the police. The pole was removed the next day and never recovered. Captain Schaack's [one of the officers in charge of the investigation] explanation that it had been 'very prosaically, and in the common course of business removed by the telegram company,' is unconvincing.[15]

Paul Avrich goes on to explain that Inspector Bonfield noted in the official report that the order had been given to cease firing as the police were afraid that they would begin to shoot one another, and that the *Chicago Tribune* at the time noted an anonymous source saying that the police were so afraid that they "emptied their revolvers, mainly into each other."[16]

Newspaper coverage, however, concentrated not on the numbers of civilians who were killed – even the police admitted it was greater than the numbers of police killed – but on the fact that the protest meeting was organized by a group of anarchists, who passed out leaflets before the meeting containing the phrase: "Workingmen Arm Yourselves and Appear in Full Force!"[17] The truth was that Fischer had put the leaflet together, but Spies had said he would not speak if the leaflet was distributed and so the leaflet was pulled. Nevertheless, a few hundred were distributed – a fact which would be hammered home at the trial.

Newspapers were full of stories of the anarchist menace. *The New York Times* led with the headline:

Anarchy's Red Hand
Rioting and Bloodshed in the Streets of Chicago.
Police mowed down with dynamite.
Strikers killed with volleys from revolvers.
The slaughter following an anarchist meeting-twelve policemen dead or dying – the number of killed or injured civilians unknown but very large – the bravery of the police force.[18]

The paragraph that began the story read:

Chicago, May 4 – The villainous teachings of the Anarchists bore bloody fruit in Chicago tonight, and before daylight at least a dozen stalwart men will have laid down their lives as a tribute to the doctrine of Herr Johann Most. There had been skirmishes all day between the police and various sections of the mob which had no head and no organization.[19]

In the trial that followed, the prosecution, led by Julius Grinnell, argued that the defendants were guilty as they were conspirators, since they had encouraged the bomb-thrower. The name of the bomb thrower was never offered or directly linked to anyone on trial.

The bias of the judge and jury was obvious to all and five were executed. The impact this had on working-class, union, and left-wing politics in America was immense, as many decided to get involved with Johann Most and others on the left.

At this time Goldman began reading *Die Freiheit* and was intro-duced to the ideals of anarchy as professed by Johann Most. She describes her reaction to this new world of ideas as something that "fairly took my breath away."[20] She describes devouring "every line on anarchism I could get, every word about the men, their lives and work. I read about their heroic stand while on trial and their marvelous defense. I saw a new world opening before me."[21] Soon after this Goldman made the decision to move from Rochester to New York City to work with the anarchist movement.

The truth seems to have been that there were many reasons behind Goldman's decision to leave Rochester. Her autobiography prefers to forward the more heroic notion of moving for the sake of anarchy: "I had definitely decided to go to New York, to equip myself for the work I had vowed to take up after the death of my Chicago comrades."[22] The truth seems to have been a complex mixture of high ideals and a family situation that was closing in on her. Goldman and Kersner had gotten back together in order to give their marriage another try. The main impetus behind this was the tightly-knit traditional Jewish community of which they were both a part. The marriage failed a second time and Goldman was ostracized by members of her own family, as well as by others in the community, for her decision to leave Kersner again: "I was immediately ostracized by the whole Jewish population of Rochester. I could not pass on the street without being held up to scorn. My parents forbade me their house."[23] Her sister Helena gave her money so she could go to New York City, where she arrived on August 15, 1889.

Even when she arrived at her aunt's and uncle's house in the Bowery area of New York City, their response illuminates the fam-ily's concern about the recent breakup of her marriage:

They asked me to make myself at home, gave me breakfast, and then plied me with questions. Why did I come to New

York? Had I definitely broken with my husband? Did I have money? What did I intend to do?[24]

Frustrated and tired she sought out A. Solotaroff, an anarchist whom Goldman had heard speak in New Haven. He quickly offered her a place to stay, and later on the same night in New York, Solotaroff brought Goldman to Sash's Café where she was introduced to Alexander Berkman and Johann Most. These three people would establish a philosophical connection that would last all their lives, complicated through sexual relationships and a changing degree of the espousal of the necessity of violence as a means of change.

JOHANN MOST

The importance of Johann Most in the history of anarchism is a much-debated point. His role and influence on the American left and on mainstream public opinion has been forgotten, if not dismissed, by historians. James J. Martin, in *Men Against the State,* writes of Most's role as being "exaggerated," insisting: "Most could reach a limited audience at best, since he was limited to his native tongue in directly communicating ideas."[25] Yet in 1886, a mere four years after his arrival in the United States, the *New York Times* ran an article describing him as "a man of such fierce thirst for carnage and conflict,"[26] while in 1891 *the Boston Globe* referred to him as "Herr Johann Most of New York, famous the world over as an anarchist."[27] After his death in 1906, the *New York Times* described him as "violent," "an agitator," "embittered" and "so violent were the doctrines he preached that he alienated some of his own followers."[28] Johann Most "was an enemy of the human race, a mere misanthrope, hating and envying whosoever was richer and happier or dissenter than himself. A human mad dog whose rabies was chronic."[29] On May 22, 1886, *Harper's Weekly* published a cartoon relating to Most. Called "When his skin is not in anger and when it is," it shows a well-fed man enraged, with a socialist flag in one hand and in the other a list, which states: "General devastation must be mercilessly proclaimed and carried into execution – *Freiheit* – I am not only there but very much there Herr Most." He stands there trumpeting these opinions, insisting everyone should listen. In the second piece there is the same man under the bed, face down, trumpet and demands dumped, just thrown aside. The only parts of him showing are his shoes, as in through the door has walked a policeman. All these opinions by important press outlets are hardly the impression left by a man with little influence on a small audience!

Johann Most (1846–1906) is a mythical character in U.S., and indeed European, radical history. Whipped by Emma Goldman on stage as he refused to condone Alexander Berkman's failed assassination attempt on Henry Clay Frick, he died alone and in poverty feared by authorities but very much ignored by anarchist America. His eldest son, John J. Most, in an interview with Paul Avrich in 1979, explained the very different opinions on his father and his lonely death as a result of his father being "a thousand years before his time, morally, mentally, and intellectually."[30]

Johann Most was born in the Bavarian city of Augsburg, to a clerk and a governess. His early life consisted of a number of painful incidents that were to scar him physically and emotionally all his life. First of all, he was an illegitimate child. His father could not afford the marriage license and, growing up, Most had to suffer through the moral righteousness of his neighbours. Most would later recount in his *Freiheit* newspaper: "When people said 'What you want is against the law, Jack,' Johann Most said, 'I was born against the law.'"[31]

Secondly, his mother, sister, and maternal grandparents all died during a cholera outbreak in 1856 when Most was ten years old. His father re-married a woman who hated Johann, and beat him and starved him. He was later to relate to Emma Goldman, "My whole childhood was a nightmare. My soul was starved for affection and my whole being was filled with the hatred of the woman who had taken the place of my gentle refined mother."[32]

The most important event in his life occurred on March 8, 1859, when he contracted an inflammation on the left jawbone. He was brought to a variety of quacks for the next five years who experimented on the young boy, inflicting nothing but pain on him. Finally, a real doctor, Dr. Agatz, saved his life by opening up the left side of his face and removing three inches of jawbone, which left him with a disfigured face. He later suggested that this face, the fear it brought other people, and the abuse he had to endure because of it was perhaps the reason he lived a life of protest against authority in any form.

Thrown out of school after he organized a strike of the students, his father found him an apprenticeship as a bookbinder.

Most soon moved out of the area, spending much of the next five years traveling. While in Switzerland, he met a group of young working-class socialist men who, for the first time in Most's life, showed him respect and friendship. Soon after he joined the Zurich section of the International Working Men's Association:

> From then on I began to feel like a real human being. A goal loomed before me, which went beyond the mere struggle for existence and the satisfaction of momentary personal needs. I began to live in the realm of ideals ... The cause of humanity became my cause. Each step that betokened its progress filled me with the greatest joy.[33]

In 1868, he went to Vienna where he was to be imprisoned for the first time. After his release from prison, he was banished, and he returned to Germany. Over the next seven years he was twice elected to the Reichstag, spent three years in prison, and was criticized by Engels for his publications. Prison had taken its toll:

> Imprisonment in Vienna and Suben, in Chemnitz and Zwickau, in Berlin and Plotzensee – not to mention sojourns in other dungeons – in short six years behind bars, eating at stingy tables.[34]

Rather than face an even longer period in jail, which had driven a number of anarchists and socialists to suicide, in 1878 he left Germany for England.

In January 1879 he published *Freiheit* for the first time while in London. Although he had few original ideas, his skill as a writer and editor made his publication both popular with his readers and with other writers. It was during this time in London that Most began to change his views from socialist to anarchist, calling for the violent destruction of all capitalist states and urging others to do as the Russians did by assassinating the Tsar. He was arrested in London. Upon his release he was invited to go to the United States for a lecture tour. He took up the invitation and on December 2, 1882, Johann Most arrived in New York.

Most was greeted upon his arrival as a hero who had been convicted unjustly by so many governments, and the press was also there to find out just who Johann Most was, what he thought, and just how dangerous he might be. Most answered their questions and the following day the newspapers were only too happy to relay his answers:

> "I shall, in this city and around this country, denounce the persecution of socialists and spread the truth of socialism."
> How did he feel about going to prison in Britain, for his article on the assassination of the Czar?
> "The Czar was a tyrant who trampled on the people. The British government was unfair to me. The abuse of me in Clerkenwell was more vicious than any of the dungeons of Austria and Germany."
> Had Clerkenwell changed him?
> "No, I outfoxed my keepers and published my beliefs. I'll continue to publish them. I'm more radical than ever."
> His beliefs – what were they?
> "Violence is justified against tyranny and tyrants. If society must be organized, communism is the way."[35]

After a brief rest and food, Most went to a meeting of supporters who were there to welcome him to New York. Most urged his audience that first night to get involved in the forthcoming revolution. From New York he proceeded around the country denouncing capitalism and urging an immediate violent revolution.

Johann Most became the face and the focus on this new anarchism in the United States. He brought with him his belief in "propaganda by deed,"[36] a distrust of trade unions, and his belief that "against tyrants all means are justified." In his *Freiheit* magazine, between 1880 and 1885, he published detailed instructions on bomb-making and other violent weapons that could be used against employers. In 1885, Most gathered much of this material and published a book called *Science of Revolutionary Warfare: A Little Handbook of Instruction in the Use and Preparation of Nitroglycerine, Dynamite, Gun-Cotton, Fulminating Mercury, Bombs, Fuses, Poisons, etc.* In this book, Most also published a list of people who should be assassinated, both individually and by type; the list included all state officials, clergy, and the majority of the police force. *Science of Revolutionary Warfare* soon became a relative best seller but succeeded in making Most and the anarchist movement better known to, and watched by, the police.

ALEXANDER BERKMAN

Goldman's multi-faceted, always complex relationship with Berkman was to develop as her primary relationship and was to last a lifetime. Her loyalty, love, guilt, and belief system revolved and evolved around him from the night they met and for the rest of her life.

Alexander Berkman was born in Vilna, Russia, in 1870, the youngest of four children in a prosperous Russian family. His father, Joseph Schmidt Berkman, a wholesaler in the shoe industry, had moved to St. Petersburg, while his mother Yetta came from a wealthy family.[37] Growing up in St. Petersburg the young Alexander experienced a life of certain privilege, as the family had servants and a summer home. Alexander was also formally schooled.

Alexander Berkman was attracted to the Russian radical movement through his older brother and his Uncle Maxim.[38] One night, soon after the assassination of the Tsar in 1881, Uncle Maxim was taken from their home, and later exiled to Siberia for his part in activities against the Tsar. While in Siberia he disappeared. Berkman recounts the family trauma upon finding out about Maxim's death in his book, *Prison Memoirs of an Anarchist*:

"Mama, what happened to Uncle Maxim?" I asked, breathlessly watching her face.

Her sudden change of expression chills my heart with fear. She turns ghostly white, large drops of perspiration stand on her forehead, and her eyes grow large and round with terror.

"Mama!" I cry, throwing my arms around her. Her lips move, and I feel her warm breath on my cheek; but, without uttering a word, she bursts into vehement weeping.[39]

The impact of this event became obvious afterward, when at the age of twelve Berkman wrote a school essay denying the existence of God and was immediately sent down to a lower grade. By age fifteen he was in further trouble for promoting revolutionary activity.

After his father's death, the family was forced to move back to Kovno, as the only way a Jewish family could live in such luxury was because of his father's status in business. Though now living within the Jewish pale, Berkman extended his circle of friends to

include some university students and even a local factory boy
whom Berkman had taught to read.

In 1888, with the death of his mother, from whom he was by
this time estranged, Berkman decided to move with his brother
Max to a university in Germany (Max had been denied entry to a
Russian university because he was Jewish). When Max decided not
to go to Germany, the young Alexander decided to travel first to
Hamburg and then to the United States. Once in the U.S., he got
various jobs working in cigar factories and printing shops.

What he really hoped for in the U.S. was a political freedom
where he could discuss the more radical ideas from the nihilists in
Russia. Disappointed with the lack of political and economic freedom he found in the U.S., Berkman decided to become involved
in the newly organized radical movement. He initially joined the
Yiddisher Arbeiter Verein (Jewish Workers Union) established to
help organize Jewish labour in the variety of sweatshops in the
major cities. Soon afterwards he broke with this group and helped
form the Pioneers of Liberty, an anarchist circle that followed the
teachings of Johann Most.

With the mixing of these three people anarchy in America was
changed forever.

THE LURE OF ANARCHY IN AMERICA

Anarchy was appealing to the newly arrived immigrant in the nineteenth century, as they, like many before them, hoped to find in the
United States a place where their American Dream could happen.
A popular Jewish lullaby sung during the nineteenth and early
twentieth centuries sums up the hopes and aspirations of all hoping to immigrate:

> Your daddy's in America
>   Little son of mine
> But you are just a child now
>   So hush and go to sleep.
> America is for everyone
>   They say, it's the greatest piece of luck
> For Jews, it's a garden of Eden
>   A rare and precious place
> People there eat challah.[40]

Instead, what they found was a country that, for many, was as bigoted and biased as their homeland, and a place where employment and fair wages were not guaranteed.

The situation seemed ready for anarchy. Paul Avrich has estimated that the International Movement (the new, all-encompassing movement of the left) had about five thousand members at the time, with about three times as many supporters.[41] The active members campaigned tirelessly, writing and publishing pamphlets and traveling throughout the country on speaking tours promoting more rapid social change. Membership numbers as collected by Avrich, have anarchists in as many as fifty U.S. cities and towns, concentrating on the Northeast, and Midwest, but extending as far south as New Orleans.

Anarchism soon became the favoured political stance of the skilled workers, who were in less and less demand as machines and huge numbers of unskilled workers became part of factory life. The only way for a worker to achieve a better life seemed to be to seek an end to capitalism and the establishment of a more caring, people-centred society. As Albert Parsons explained:

> We don't fight machinery. We don't oppose the thing. It is only the manner and methods of employing them that we object to. That is all. It is the manipulations of these things in the interests of a few; it is the monopolization of them that we object to. We desire that all the forces of nature, all the forces of society, of gigantic strength which has resulted from the combined intellect and labor of the ages of the past shall be turned over to man, and made his servant, his obedient slave forever. This is the object of Socialism.[42]

It was the May 4, 1886, events of Haymarket which moved the anarchist movement from the inside pages of the newspapers to front and centre. Immediately following these events, the American public and press reacted against all anarchists, declaring them to be non-American and dangerous, and forever linking them with terrorism and violence. The immediate impact for the workers was a worsening of conditions, as the employers, now with public support, were able to get legislation passed and could legally use the police as well as private security forces to end labour disputes.

What Haymarket did was to create in the U.S. the next generation of anarchists, inspired by martyrdom, willing to use violence, and anxious to change the conditions for workers in the U.S. and to create a more equal justice system. Goldman describes the moment for her as one of spiritual birth:

> I wish to say that the trial and death of the Chicago
> Anarchists decided my life and activities. In fact, the Chicago
> tragedy was the awakening of my social consciousness. I may
> also say that it had the same effect on hundreds, perhaps thou-
> sands, of people. I myself know a great many persons whose
> lives were molded by the judicial murder of martyrs.[43]

The speed of the trial, the obvious biases of judge and jury, and the executions that quickly followed created in Goldman what she later admitted to be an extreme emotional response,[44] but one which she insisted was necessary to create the soul of a revolutionary: "It is not enough to grasp our ideas; it is necessary to feel them in every fiber like a flame, a consuming fever, an elemental passion."[45]

ALL-AMERICAN ANARCHY

The irony of this passion and violence was that, for much of the early nineteenth century, the ideas behind anarchy in America were considered neither violent nor dangerous, and certainly not un-American. Anarchy was considered by some to be particularly American,[46] comparable with the ideas of Thomas Jefferson, who insisted on a form of government that governed least. Anarchy was romantic, agrarian, and rustic. Hardly surprising, then, that the most prominent original anarchists in America, Josiah Warren (1798–1874) and Benjamin Tucker (1854–1939), were white, male, and upper-class, from old Massachusetts families.

The so-called "Father of American Anarchy," Josiah Warren – referred to as "a remarkable American" by John Stuart Mill – was born in Boston into a long-established American family. Josiah's grandfather, General Joseph Warren, was killed at Bunker Hill while fighting the British. At the age of twenty, Josiah Warren joined Robert Owen's New Harmony community in Indiana. The experiment failed after two years and Warren left disillusioned with the concept of communalism.

What Warren decided as the reason behind the failure was New Harmony's insistence on authority and community ownership. As a replacement for these two concepts, Warren instead promoted the notions of individual initiative and responsibility. The individual in a capitalist society cannot become the master of his own labour, thus he could not get a fair price for his product. Warren thus proposed the setting up of a store based on the price per labour. Goods could be bought in this way with money or through a fixed price for their labour. The intention of the system was to get rid of profit. The constant exchanging of goods and labour, according to cooperation rather than supply and demand, would create a community where the value of each individual would be recognized.

This notion, borrowed in part from Owen, allowed the worker to work without having to cope with the high prices charged by the merchant, who worked only for profit. Though Warren did experience some initial success forcing down the prices in some nearby stores, his long-term project of setting up a village based on these ideas failed, as the villagers were forced to pay the high prices of the local merchants in order to get all they needed. Despite initial success and enthusiasm, in the end they simply ran out of money.

Warren outlined his ideas in the first anarchist American publication, *The Peaceful Revolutionist*. Warren argued that true freedom could only be found in individual sovereignty. The problem with society is that it demands that each individual surrender freedom for the sake of the community. Society must then be reconstructed so that each individual can enjoy true freedom. Society's demands made people conform while, instead, Warren insisted that people were capable of determining their own actions without interference from either church or state:

> Our surrounding institutions, customs, and public opinion call for conformity: they require us to act in masses like herds of cattle; they do not recognize that we think and feel individually and ought to be at liberty to act individually; but this liberty cannot be enjoyed in combinations, masses and connections in which one cannot move without affecting one another.[47]

This example of Warren's writings shows that important aspect of American anarchy: that belief in the right to individual ownership of property. This concept, which was the antithesis of European anarchy, was never seen by Warren as a means for the rich to remain rich and everyone else to remain poor. Quite the opposite. What Warren believed was that the only way for everyone to be equal was for everyone to have some ownership of property. This was the equalizing factor of the new society he hoped to achieve. By adopting this system of land ownership and his system of labour exchange Warren believed that individuals would succeed in raising each other to new and higher standards of living. The state has no role here, according to Warren. The state cannot force advancement; it cannot force the social order to exist. In short Warren did not believe that the state could do anything that a group of individuals voluntarily coming together could not.

Like many anarchists, education for Warren was the key to the creation of this new social order. Warren opposed the notion of Congress supervising education, arguing that all Congress would achieve would be to create a method that was dependent on a system, rather than one that would create a society based on respect and natural laws of harmony. For Warren, the only good government was one that allowed each person to rule herself, rather than forcing the individual to act according to the needs of the community.

The particular danger that existed in America, according to Warren, was that the needs of the individual would be placed in a secondary position to those of the state. For Warren this argument was nonsensical:

> ... I reply that there can be no greater than national happiness – that this, as I understand it, consists of the happiness of the individuals who compose the nation, and that individual happiness consists in nothing so much as the liberty of person and property. If this is unattainable in large masses, it shows us in one circumstance with which we have to contend, and proves that society will have to dissolve its *imaginary masses and combinations and RESOLVE ITSELF INTO INDIVIDUALS before liberty can be anything but a word.*[48]

The second major figure in American anarchy was Benjamin Tucker. Though by the time of his death he was largely forgotten, nevertheless what he gave to the American anarchist movement was an outlet for its ideas, as he also introduced to the American

movement many of the ideas that were more prevalent in Europe
at the time.

Benjamin Tucker was born in South Dartmouth, Massachusetts.
He came from a mixed Quaker and Unitarian background, which
afforded him the opportunity for free thought.

Tucker became involved in the presidential campaign of Horace
Greeley and so attended a convention of the New England Labor
Reform League in 1872. At this he met the then aging anarchists
Josiah Warren and William B. Greene. Soon after this meeting
Tucker bought Greene's book *Mutual Banking* and Warren's *True
Civilization*. Another person who was to have a major impact on
Tucker's thinking was the abolitionist and labour reformer Ezra
Heywood, whom Tucker also met at the same time.

Heywood was editor of the periodical *The Word*, and through
Tucker's reading of this magazine he got to know the works of
Herbert Spencer, Pierre-Joseph Proudhon, Max Stirner, and Michael
Bakunin, among others. Such was the impact of Proudhon on Tucker
that he began publishing *The Radical Review* in 1877. However, his
audience was too small and the money he used for this venture soon
ran out. Tucker then began working for *The Boston Globe* in 1878,
where he was to remain for the next eleven years.

In August 1881, Tucker published the famous *Liberty* magazine
for the first time. He managed to do this for the next twenty-seven
years, supporting this venture through a settlement left to him by
his family. *Liberty* was to become one of the most influential
mouthpieces of individualism in American history.

It was Tucker, through *Liberty,* who introduced the writings of
Josiah Warren, Michael Bakunin, Max Stirner, Stephen Pearl Andrews,
and Proudhon to a wider and enthusiastic American audience. The
list of contributors includes Lysander Spooner, Auberon Herbert,
Joshua K. Ingalls, and John Henry Mackay. George Bernard Shaw's
first original article for an American audience appeared in *Liberty*.
It was in *Liberty* that American audiences first saw translated ex-
cerpts of Nietzsche.

Through *Liberty,* Tucker outlined his own version of anarchy.
Here he affirmed his belief in Warren's emphasis on individual freedom and added to Warren by outlining his own emphasis on mutual banking. Following Proudhon, Tucker forwarded the notion that
the mainstay of capitalism, and hence the enemy of the individual,
was banking. If banking was controlled by the many, as opposed to

the few, interest rates would drop, the cost of living and banking would drop, and a better quality of life would be afforded to all. In fact, he even went so far as to point to the possibility that, without controlled banking, property would revert to the people, as opposed to interest groups, and rent-free property would become a reality.

Secondly, if workers were to have access to their own bank, interest-free loans would be possible and so society would change from one based on businesses run by few, where only the few gained, to a place where workers would be in demand and so their wages and quality of life would improve. Tucker's ideal society would then come into existence – one in which small business would have a non-exploitative relationship with others and one in which all would gain from whatever money was exchanged.

What Tucker suggested as a means of supporting this theory was a form of mutual banking. Industrialists with the sole purpose of making huge profits would no longer own banks. Instead banks would be set up in order to supply money, as the worker needed it. With more money in circulation, interest rates would have to drop and thus a society full of individual worker-owners of property and business would come into existence.

Tucker was certainly not in favour of violence to achieve this end. He did forward the notion that there existed in society a natural form of violence, which pushed society toward change. In this, Tucker was, like many Americans of his generation, highly influenced by the writings of Charles Darwin. However, his views on violence were to be severely tested with the arrival to the United States, in 1882, of Johann Most.

Thus anarchy in America, at that stage, was an individualistic philosophy of the educated, supported by those with a regular income, whose lifestyle involved a simpler way of living and usually the formation of agrarian communities. In short [American] "anarchy was individualistic, utopia, and peaceful."[49] How this new, peaceful, respectful society was going to be established was through "rational conviction."[50] These anarchists believed in persuasion and intellectual debate: no violence, no rapid change, and no class destruction.

Not only did these American anarchists (though utopian individualists may be a more apt description) have a peaceful strategy, the type of change envisioned by the Americans was not the final society expected by Proudhon or Bakunin. Instead, Josiah Warren, in *The Peaceful Revolutionist*, outlined his idea that an individual should still, within an anarchist society, have the right to private property. Equality for Warren came through a degree of ownership instead of non-ownership or any type of communal ownership. Warren supported a system of land ownership in which neither the state nor federal authorities played any role. The landowners (all people) would then choose to work together and would benefit from cooperation resulting in a rise of everyone's standard of living.

Warren tested his theory by setting up an experimental agricultural community in Ohio. However, an outbreak of cholera resulted in the closing down of the community. Nevertheless, Warren continued to promote his ideas through writing and lecture tours.

What existed in the United States, then, was a system of anarchy proposed by the established elite that would ultimately do nothing to change their position, place, or wealth. While it is true that many of the European anarchists were also born into the established classes, they left these groups to live and work as part of the working class. In the U.S. this was simply not the case. While Warren, Tucker, and others wrote of revolutionary ideas, they insisted that American society, for the most part, was something to which one should aspire, not destroy.

Pre-Civil War America was dominated by the notion of Romance, which meant stressing the inspiring beauties of nature, individual freedom, and the redemptive spirit of mankind as children of God. It was a time of departure from the earlier age of reason, which instead emphasized the significance of mankind's emotional capacities: moods, impressions, institutions, feelings, and aesthetic sensibilities. The Civil War involved mass slaughter for the sake of ideas and principles. It helped to create a society, which demanded an increased and quickened process of industrialization; it also created a society that now seemed more complex. Everything was now in a state of flux. Nothing was the way it used to be. The 1870s were a time of economic depression complicated by the beginning of the arrival of great numbers of immigrants from Europe, in particular socialists and other left-wing group members forced out of Germany by Bismarck's anti-socialist laws.

From 1890 to 1924 an estimated twenty-three million people arrived in the U.S. from eastern and southern Europe. Violent strikes and violent responses to them by the employers, aided by state and federal agencies, meant that the workers, along with the newer immigrants, began forming revolutionary, anti-establishment clubs. Albert Parsons was one new labour activist who saw too many analogies between the plight of the slaves in the South and the working classes after the Civil War:

> A great similarity between the abuse heaped upon these poor
> people by the organs of the rich and the actions of the Late
> Southern slave holders ... toward the newly enfranchised
> slaves, who they accused of wanting to make their former
> masters 'divide' by giving them 'forty acres and a mule.'

Parsons went further in explaining that the Civil War had achieved nothing. What it had only succeeded in doing to create a new kind of slavery, a new system of masters. This new system of 'wage slavery' was just the same as any other form. This new industrialized slavery was completed by two factors: the migration to the northern cities by the former slaves in the years after the Civil War, and the beginning of the mass arrival of immigrants from Europe.

The Social Democratic Movement that existed in 1876 was small; its membership was a mere 1,500[51] and only a fifth of those were born in the United States. Those who were American-born were deeply distrusted by the European-born members, in particular the Germans. All in all there was a severe shortage of English written books or pamphlets of any sort, which could have been used to persuade more people to the cause.[52] Despite efforts to bring about some form of unity to the variety of left-wing movements, each attempt met with failure owing to the distrust of each group for the other.

The railroad strike in the summer of 1877, however, brought a great many matters to a head. First of all, for the first time the general American public experienced a genuine fear of revolution and revolutionaries. Secondly, it frightened many institutions of the state to organize more and better, so that if such an event should even happen again, the next time they would be ready to deal with such a group more quickly and more violently. Thirdly, violence was now part of the labour movement in the United States. It was no longer a European (German and Russian) phenomena. It was now very much something to be used in the U.S. by Americans. Finally, the strike changed the basic belief of many Americans toward their own country. Whereas before they believed that America was different, that it was the land of opportunity where wealth was possible for everyone, now they believed that their country had the same basic faults within its state system, and so revolutionary changes to all sections of society were vital.

The practical consequences of 1877 involved the setting up of the Socialist Labor Party of North America, which had candidates running in a variety of elections across the country, winning a number of them. Another practical result was the number of publications in English that came about, including *The National Socialist, The Labor Standard*, and *The Socialist*. Such was the impact and popularity of all these events that in 1879 the Chicago Labor Movement, as part of its celebrations to commemorate the 1848 Revolutions and the Paris Commune of 1871, attracted a crowd of thirty thousand to the Lake Front. Yet less than two years later the Party was no longer considered a serious contender for public office, as its percentage of the vote dropped by 60%.

The reality was that, while public opinion was in favour of drastic change during times of economic depression, during times of economic growth the more socialistic solutions did not seem as necessary. As well, the labour movement was not an organized movement. It was disjointed, and was really composed of many different factions who saw many different solutions as a means of achieving their end. The biggest issue, over which there was disagreement, was the issue of violence.

Just as many police commissioners had begun preparing themselves for the next possible violent confrontation, many workers were equally determined that they would not be as easily hurt next time around. As early as 1875, a small group of newly-arrived German immigrant socialists had formed an armed group to protect themselves and their political friends against the police and other groups used by the owners to break the strikes and intimidate workers in general. Based on the German gymnastic association – *Turn Verein* – they called themselves *Lehr-und-Wehr-Verein* (Education and Defense Society).

According to their supporters, who included Albert Parsons, they were simply not willing to stand by any longer while they, their wives, families, and friends were being beaten or shot and killed by the police. This group was then not to be seen as plainly violent but simply as a self-defense move. Dressed in various uniforms representing the various nations that belonged (these included

Irish as well as German workers), they marched and drilled in the city streets until the Illinois legislature had enough and passed a bill outlawing paramilitary groups unless they were affiliated with the state.

The practical result of this law was that some members remained in the Illinois area and just remained underground while others went across the border to Missouri or Wisconsin. The philosophical result involved further splits and antagonism in the Socialist Labor Party. In 1878, the Executive Committee, headed by Philip Van Patten, insisted that the organization publicly disassociate itself from violence, declaring that the organization did not need it to fulfill its aims. On top of this, it gave the public a false impression of socialism and so the Executive Committee demanded that all members withdraw from any group that was involved with violence in any form. Van Patten went further the following year when he got a motion passed though Congress insisting that all members withdraw from groups that supported violence. In reality, all that Van Patten achieved was to antagonize the German socialists, who just ignored him anyway.

There was another issue that divided the SLP, and it was the question of cooperating with the Greenback Party. As was in keeping with the spirit and organization of the SLP, local branches had decided to form local coalitions with the Greenback Party. However, in 1880, the National Executive Committee decided that the party as a whole should support the Greenback-Labor candidate in the presidential election. Local branches were in an uproar. For the SLP, local autonomy was at stake. Much to the disappointment of the more radical elements in the party, the Greenback candidate was supported officially by the SLP. Though the coalition ended after the election, the whole notion was a disaster, as the SLP was more divided than ever.

Yet if the years 1878 to 1883 seemed a lean time in American anarchist history, they were also the years of growth, organization, and change. 1878 saw the arrival to the States of many German socialists. Forced out of Germany because of Bismarck's anti-socialist laws, they arrived determined to see a revolution and unwilling to compromise any part of their revolutionary principles for the sake of any type of parliamentary democracy. By 1880 they had formed themselves into the revolutionary clubs, which would within a short period of time form the practical basis of the new American anarchist movement. Though these groups were to call themselves social revolutionaries until the mid-1880s, their particular version of socialism was strongly anti-statist, anti-parliamentary, and anti-reformist. Their clearly stated ultimate aim was for a final and direct confrontation with capitalism, which would lead to its end.

Three other factors were equally important in establishing a populist anarchist movement in the United States: these were the London Social Revolutionary Congress of July 1881, the Chicago Social Revolutionary Congress of October 1881, and the arrival to the United States of Johann Most in December 1882.

The London Social Revolutionary Congress which became responsible for establishing what became known as the "Black International" – the much maligned and feared movement behind acts of terrorism the world over – impacted the left-wing movements in the United States as it pushed them once again toward organization. Thus various revolutionary clubs, socialists, and others gathered in Chicago in October 1881 in an attempt to re-organize themselves into a mass movement.

The newly-arrived anarchists and socialists heavily influenced this Congress. Benjamin Tucker sent a representative, Dr. Joseph H. Swain, while other native American socialists such as Philip van Patten refused to attend. Those who did go soon adopted a militant stance, denouncing private property and "wage slavery." They also upheld the notion of propaganda by deed and other methods of revolution. Indeed, by the end of the Congress, it founded a new party with an emphasis on revolution called the Revolutionary Socialistic Party. It was to be the first national anarchist party in the U.S., organized on those same lines that had been established by the London Congress previously: a loose confederation of autonomous groups linked to a main informational center in Chicago.

The importance of this Congress was that its message was revolutionary and violent and anarchistic in content. What did not happen, as a result of this Congress was an actual coming together of the various groups into a cohesive force. The person who would have to make that happen would arrive in the United States in December of 1882. That person was Johann Most.

The Congresses transformed the anarchist movement in the U.S. from an individualistic, intellectual, upper-class movement to an immigrant-dominated, working-class, violent revolutionary party. The discussion in London, and the need for one left-wing violent

movement, resulted in the various left-wing organizations and revolutionary clubs meeting in Chicago in an attempt to organize
themselves into one mass movement with clearly defined goals.
One of the more immediate outcomes of this meeting was that the
belief in propaganda by deed would now be part of the anarchist
movement in the U.S. Thus, the Chicago Congress became a meeting ground for the newly arrived, more militant revolutionaries,
who shunned the American version of anarchical individualism.

After Haymarket, "anarchy" and "anarchist" were the terms
used for "terrorist," "left-wing," "dangerous," "un-American,"
and "frightening" by the government, newspapers, and the general
public. Soon the term would have a person and name attached:
Emma Goldman.

CHAPTER THREE

Into the Public Eye

The story of dynamite – the actual stuff – in the United States, as a weapon of the have-nots in their war against the haves, dates from Most's arrival in the country.
–Louis Adamic, *Dynamite*

I was greatly disturbed. The charm of Most was upon me. His remarkable gifts, his eagerness for life, for friendship, moved me deeply. And Berkman, too, appealed to me profoundly. His earnestness, his self-confidence, his youth – everything about him drew me with irresistible force.[1]

The contrast between Johann Most and Alexander Berkman was clear to Emma Goldman soon after she met both in 1889. Most enjoyed nice restaurants, and drinking good wines, but for Berkman the cause was everything, and everything meant suffering and doing without. "The path of anarchism is steep and painful. So many have attempted to climb it and have fallen back. The price is exacting,"[2] Berkman insisted to Goldman in an early conversation. But the two confused Goldman:

> I was greatly disturbed. The charm of Most was upon me. His remarkable gifts, his eagerness for life, for friendship, moved me deeply. And Berkman, too, appealed to me profoundly. His earnestness, his self-confidence, his youth – everything about him drew me with irresistible force.[3]

Initially the lure of the great Johann Most was too much, though her first impression was confusing:

> Before long Johann Most entered. My first impression of him was one of revulsion. He was of medium height, with a large head crowned with bushy hair; but his face was twisted out of

form by an apparent dislocation of the left jaw, only his eyes
were soothing; they were blue and sympathetic.[4]

Soon the physical gave way to a more political, sexual, and almost
spiritual relationship: "I was dumb with excitement and nervous-
ness, full of the tumult of emotions Most's speech had aroused in
me."[5]

For six months after Emma Goldman arrived in New York,
Most, seeing her potential as a speaker, opened her up to a history
of anarchy and explained to her the potential that existed right
now for a revolution to occur. It was Most who taught her how to
speak; her aggression, her scorn, ridicule, and sarcasm were all
legacies of the teachings of Johann Most. Indeed, six months after
her arrival in New York, Goldman returned to Rochester, and was
to go on to Buffalo and Cleveland on a speaking tour. The tour surprised Goldman on two fronts: she was amazed at her own ability
to speak passionately, yet more importantly, she found her blind
obedience to Johann Most disconcerting when questioned after a
meeting as to why she was not supporting the eight-hour day.[6]

Confused by her insight, that day she was even more confused
when she returned to New York and faced Most's reaction. He did
not want to hear about the trip, instead preferring to see her as his
woman – "*Blondkopf, his little girl-woman.*"[7] Goldman got angry,
refusing to be thought of, or indeed be treated as, "a mere
woman."[8] Goldman's continued attempts to explain the reactions
to the trip were eventually greeted by Most's angry outburst: "whoever is not with me is against me."[9] Most had earlier disturbed
Goldman with an anti-Semitic outburst: "Here is my pound of
flesh you Shylocks!"[10] This outburst underlined Most's extremely
conservative views on women; he had wanted Goldman to marry
him and raise a family, and now Goldman was left feeling totally
betrayed and confused. Her sexual and philosophical relationship
with Johann Most was at an end. But their complicated political
and personal relationship continued until her death.

After breaking with Most, Goldman returned to Alexander
Berkman, with whom she had already begun a sexual relationship
at the same time she had been involved with Most. She also began
a sexual relationship with Modest Stein, Berkman's cousin.[11] Her
relationship with Stein, she explains in her autobiography, was very
different than her relationship with Berkman: "Fedya had no bear-

ing on my love for Sasha. Each called out different emotions in my being, took me into different worlds. They created no conflict, they only brought fulfillment." Berkman's acceptance of Goldman's relationship with Stein delighted her and soon the three of them, and Helen Minkin, decided to live together. Goldman during this period also had another sexual relationship Fritz Perter.[12]

These years were filled with delight for Goldman and she lived with the sexual freedom and political promise she had longed for in Russia. Berkman and Minkin both worked in factories; Berkman in a cigar factory, and Minkin in a corset factory. Goldman made silk waistcoats from home, while Fedya painted. Goldman was living the idea of marriage outside the legal and socially-accepted system, living finally as Vera in sexual freedom.

During this time Berkman, in particular, argued with everyone there – with Goldman he insisted she was not dedicated enough to the cause, that she was not prepared to give up luxuries, such as flowers, music, and the theater. Goldman saw Berkman as harsh, and rigid, and while she insisted that any revolution meant the individual could choose and enjoy, for Berkman it meant poverty and only needing the basics. For this reason Berkman also fought with Fedya, who, according to Berkman, spent too much on food.

The three, without Helen Minkin, moved away from New York City to Springfield, Massachusetts. After a failed attempt at setting up a photographic studio, the three were soon successful in establishing an ice cream parlour that within a short time was economically profitable. In an attempt to ease their conscience about making a profit, the three declared that they were earning much-needed funds for the movement.

The political events in 1892 in Pittsburgh would change their quiet revolution into a public one, and change their lives forever as Emma Goldman and Alexander Berkman became front-page news.

HOMESTEAD, HENRY CLAY FRICK, AND THE COST OF VIOLENCE

The news of the Homestead strike on Berkman, Stein, and Goldman was tremendous. Goldman later exclaimed, "To us it sounded the awakening of the American worker, the long awaited day of his insurrection."[13] In *Living My Life,* she vividly describes the moment:

Sasha was the first on his feet. "Homestead!" he exclaimed. "I must go to Homestead!" I flung my arms around him, crying out his name. I, too, would go. "We must go tonight," he said; "the great moment has come at last!" Being internationalists, he added, it mattered not to us where the blow was struck by the workers; we must be with them. We must bring them our great message and help them see that it was not only for the moment that they must strike, but for all time, for a free life, for anarchism. Russia had many heroic men and women, but who was there in America? Yes we must go to Homestead, tonight![14]

Berkman's memory of the event is also extremely detailed and powerful:

Clearly every detail of that day is engraved on my mind. It is the sixth of July 1892. We are quietly sitting in the back of our little flat – Fedya and I – when the girl enters. Her naturally quick, energetic step sounds more than usually resolute. As I turn to her, I am struck by the peculiar gleam in her eyes and heightened color.
    "Have you read it?" she cries, waving the half-open newspaper.
    "What is it?"
    "Homestead. Strikers shot. Pinkerton have killed women and children."
    She speaks in a quick, jerky manner. Her words ring like the cry of a wounded animal, the melodious voice tinged with the harshness of bitterness of helpless agony.[15]

Homestead in 1892 was the site of a massive dispute between the Carnegie-owned steel plant and the Amalgamated Association of Iron and Steel Workers. Previously management and workers had agreed to a contract for all the members of this union, all highly-skilled workers, that gave them what were considered to be decent wages and working conditions. However, as a new contract was about to be negotiated, management proposed to cut wages and introduce an open shop policy, which meant that non-union members could get jobs. Negotiations became more tense and awkward. The union, which was negotiating with Henry Clay Frick (as

Carnegie was in England), was holding out for a better deal, and
Frick was under pressure from Carnegie, as Carnegie wanted to get
rid of the union.

Negotiations, which began in January, were stalled by June
when Frick announced management would no longer bargain with
the union and would instead deal with workers individually. The
union still expected talks to continue, initially thinking this was a
negotiation tactic or threat, but instead, on June 25, 1892, Frick
locked out the workers and closed the plant. The workers in turn
declared a strike.

Frick needed strikebreakers and then needed guards to protect
the strikebreakers, so he employed three hundred Pinkerton guards
who, in the middle of the night, were towed up the Monongahela
River to Homestead to protect the strikebreakers the next morning.
The union members got wind of the plan and were waiting for the
guards. A battle of sorts began, which resulted in seven guards and
nine workers being killed.

The news of the strike, the battle, and the deaths reached the
front pages of newspapers everywhere and was even debated in
Congress. The general consensus was that workers' rights were
being trampled on by the use of the guards and so severe pressure
was being placed on Carnegie and Frick to stop their tactics and
give in to the workers.

Henry Clay Frick (1849–1919) was born in Westmoreland
County, Pennsylvania, grandson of Abraham Overholt, owner of
the Overholt Whiskey distillery. At the age of 21, Henry, with
some cousins, decided to set up a company to turn coal into coke
for use in the steel industry. In 1880, with a loan from Andrew
Mellon, Frick bought out his cousins and set up the H.C. Frick &
Company. By the age of THIRTY, Frick was a millionaire with
twelve thousand coke ovens and acquiring forty thousand acres of
coal.

By now, Frick included Andrew Carnegie among his friends and
business partners in various ventures. In 1881, Carnegie placed
Frick in charge of his steel plant. Both men opposed the unions and
were determined to break them. Carnegie, before the negotiations
began, ordered the Homestead plant to increase its output so that
it would have enough supplies to face a stoppage.

For Berkman in particular, this moment seemed to be the
moment of a workers' uprising, when even Congress was on the

side of the workers – all that was needed for the revolution to begin was "To remove the tyrant is an act of liberation, the giving of life to an oppressed people."

Goldman, Berkman, and Stein returned to New York, with detailed plans ready for their next move. They would issue a manifesto, which they would write in German and translate into English, but it would be printed with both languages side by side. Goldman and Berkman would go to Pittsburgh with the manifesto while Fedya Stein would remain in New York. However, they quickly decided that the time for words had passed when they found out that workers, and even children, had been killed in a battle with the Pinkerton guards.

> We were stunned. We saw at once that the time for our manifesto had passed. Words had lost their meaning in the face of innocent blood spilled on the banks of the Monongahela. Intuitively each felt what was surging in the heart of the others. Sasha broke the silence. "Frick is the responsible factor in this crime," he said; "he must be made to stand the consequence."
> It was the psychological moment for an *Attentat*.[16]

Berkman decided that Frick must be assassinated, after which he would commit suicide in what he described as the first voluntary act of "self-sacrifice" for anarchism in America.[17] Berkman placed himself within the violent Russian nihilist tradition of inflicting the most violence in order to achieve the quickest result. There was no question of immorality for Berkman:

> The question of moral right in such matters often agitated the revolutionary circles I used to frequent. I had always taken the extreme view. The more radical the treatment, I held, the quicker the cure."[18]

The mere decision to act brought Berkman closer to the heroes of Russia:

> Inexpressibly near and soul-kin I feel to those men and women, the adored, the mysterious ones of my youth, who left wealthy homes and high station to 'go to the People' to

become one of them, though despised by all whom they held dear, persecuted and ridiculed even by the benighted objects of their great sacrifice.[19]

In a final act of claiming dramatic Russian license, Berkman chose Rakhemetov as the name he would use. Rakhemetov was the revolutionary hero of Chernyshevsky's novel *What Is to Be Done?*

The initial plan was a bombing of Frick and his offices. However, despite following Most's directions in the *Science of Revolutionary Warfare*, the practice bomb failed to go off. Years later as Goldman thought about that week, it seemed like a farce, as she watched Berkman try to make a bomb. Both of them realized that if the bomb were too successful it could kill them and everyone else in the building. A second plan was soon devised: this time Berkman would go to Pittsburgh and shoot Henry Clay Frick.

There was, however, a stark reality of the revolution that had to be dealt with: first the monetary cost of getting a gun and then traveling to Pittsburgh. After arriving in New York, and buying what they needed for the now-worthless manifesto and later the bomb, the three would-be activists had fifteen dollars between them – not enough for all three to go and participate in the deed. Realizing that there was no one they could ask for help, Berkman went alone to Pittsburgh. Goldman made a halfhearted attempt at prostitution. (This time it was Sonya, Marmeladov's daughter in Dostoyevsky's *Crime and Punishment* who was Goldman's inspiration, as Sonya had to prostitute herself to support her brothers, sisters, and stepmother.) Goldman was paid by her one and only client, but told to go home, as she did not have the necessary "knack"[20] for prostitution. In the end, she wired her sister for the remaining money needed for Berkman to buy a gun.

On Saturday, July 23, 1892, Berkman entered Frick's office, posing as the head of an employment agency for strikebreakers, and attempted to assassinate him. Berkman shot twice, but after realizing that Frick was still alive he proceeded to stab him with a steel file. The attempt failed, as did Berkman's attempt at suicide. The police forced him to remove the capsule from his mouth.

Berkman's trial was unfair from the beginning. He was given no prior notice of the trial date and was therefore not prepared for the multitude of charges laid against him: feloniously assaulting Frick with intent to kill; the same for his alleged assault on John G. A.

Leishman, Vice-Chairman of the Carnegie Steel Company (who
had previously been to lunch with Frick and had followed Frick
into his office to continue the lunchtime conversation); feloniously
entering the offices of Carnegie Company on three occasions;
unlawfully carrying concealed weapons; plus three separate indict-
ments. By multiplying the charges in such a fashion, the usual max-
imum of seven years was circumvented. While Berkman made only
two objections – that he only entered the offices once and that the
lesser charges were all part of the attempt on Frick – his failure to
take formal objection meant that no appeal was possible. All the
evidence seems to point to the fact that Leishman lied – Berkman
made no attempt to kill him or to injure him in any way. The court
over-ruled Berkman's objections, and since Frick testified at the
trial, public opinion, which was never on Berkman's side, now
wanted him given the severest penalty possible.

Berkman, in one last attempt at drama and revolutionary impetus, decided to give a major speech to the court. However, as his
knowledge of English was not sufficient for such a detailed speech,
he decided to speak in German and have his speech translated to
the court. To Berkman's horror, however, his interpreter was a
blind old man who translated haltingly and badly (word for word),
thus any impact the speech could have had was lost.

Berkman was given the harshest penalty possible – twenty-one
years in Western Penitentiary and one year in the Allegheny
Workhouse, which due to the condition of these places was almost
a death sentence. Though Berkman insisted that he alone was
responsible for the attempted assassination, witnesses testified that
they had seen Berkman with Carl Nold and Henry Bauer, two
Pittsburgh anarchists, who were also later prosecuted.

The impact of Berkman's attempted assassination of Frick on
Goldman, individually; on the anarchist movement, communally;
and on the American authorities and public was to complicate all
their relationships. Berkman's attempt at a revolutionary awakening proved harsh for himself – he was now in jail for over twenty
years – and for Goldman, who never again forwarded violence as
a solution, but who would now be forever associated with violence.

Not only had Berkman failed to assassinate Frick, but the workers in Homestead were angry at Berkman for even attempting the
assassination. Public opinion moved away from favouring the
workers, especially when on August 3, Frick's baby son, Henry

Clay Jr., for reasons that had nothing to do with the assassination, died. Ultimately Berkman's attempted assassination would be described as one of the "most counterproductive acts of political martyrdom in history."[21] The workers were ultimately defeated in the strike, forcing Emma Goldman to have her first serious re-think about anarchism.

However, Goldman had a dilemma that was part political, deeply personal, and a matter of loyalty: would public condemnation of acts of violence mean she was also condemning Berkman? Therefore, it seems that she found it necessary, as a matter of loyalty, to maintain a public refusal to condemn violence, offering instead an understanding of the frustration of the perpetrator. In private, however, her attitude was different.

Goldman had learned quickly that violence achieved nothing. In a letter to Max Nettlau she explains:

> ...if you have read further in the book, you will have found that AB's act and his subsequent Calvary, have been my cross, and still are. That never again had I anything to do with an act of violence, though I have always taken my stand on the side of those who did. I have fought shy, all my life, from joining the cry of "Crucify!"[22]

Indeed, Goldman's anti-violent creed was evident earlier, when, in 1928, she wrote a letter to Berkman describing her autobiography. In this letter she extols the position in politics taken by Gandhi and wishes that she could follow such a creed:

> I feel violence in whatever form never has and probably never will bring constructive results ... I want the revolution to be understood as a process of reconstruction rather than what we believed it to be until now, a process of deconstruction.[23]

In the following letter to Berkman she goes further, explaining that violence in any form, even if it claims to be for the sake of revolution, is no good:

> If we agree that revolution must essentially be a process of reconstruction, destroying as little as possible – nothing at all in fact except such industries that make for war and disease –

if we can realize and boldly declare that the only purpose of
revolution must be transformation, then terror must go with
the rest and prisons and evil things of today must go with the
rest... If revolution cannot solve the need of violence and terror then ... I am against a revolution.[24]

Despite these private if definite reservations, Goldman's public
reputation was now firmly established. She was Jewish, violent,
brutish, European (non-American), and morally destitute, and
anarchy, her political philosophy of choice, was the political representation of this degenerate lifestyle.

The fact that Goldman was now the face of anarchy in America
was obvious when the first major interview with her was published
in *The New York World* in 1892, just a week after Berkman's failed
assassination attempt. The headline – "Anarchy's Den: Emma
Goldman, Its Queen, Rules with a Nod the Savage Reds" – and
opening paragraph set the scene of an opium den and brothel:
dank, dark, dirty, full of people who were not quiet human. In the
midst of these vicious, murderous types sits one woman: Emma
Goldman:

> In the far right-hand corner of the second room, near a dusty,
> cobwebbed window, sat a woman. Alone in that gathering of
> hard-faced, half clad men, enveloped in a dense atmosphere of
> choking smoke, she reclined in a barroom chair, reading. She
> seemed rather pretty. The back of her chair was tilted against
> the rear wall, and her left foot rested on the rung of a chair in
> front of her. A white straw hat, with a blue band streaked
> with dotted white, lay on the table at her elbow.[25]

The description of the charged atmosphere is emphasized
through a combination of skin, sweat, race, and colour. Goldman's
followers are described:

> One by one the swarthy, half-clad and grimy Anarchists in the
> front room had been coming near to where their queen sat.
> Some one of them probably gave her a sign to say no more. A
> dozen stalwart black and redbearded Anarchists stood a few
> feet back of the reporter.[26]

The masculinity of the room soon encompasses Goldman, as she is described as a hardened, damaged, ugly woman:

The mouth in repose is hard and sensual, the curves gross, the lips full and bloodless. A neck that once was rounded was still well poised, but as she turned her head the tendons bulged out into scrawniness, and blotches here and there added to the sharp disappointment one met after leaving the upper part of the face.[27]

After a few questions the reporter finished, and the interview was over. Goldman, in almost cannibalistic, fashion,

Smiled that hollow cavernous smile, her eyes shone behind her glasses. A glad and proud look was on her face, and while she made a faint display of quieting her slaves her pale face took on some color and she stood there wreathed in smiles amid smoke and beer fumes.[28]

By August 6, 1892, Goldman's growing reputation meant she was front and centre in *The New York Times*; in another article with similar themes, with her non-marriage to Berkman, her refusal to denounce him or his act of violence, and her firm belief in anarchism, Emma Goldman was now truly the face of anarchy.

While Goldman may have enjoyed some of the publicity she received, the same publicity resulted in her being evicted from her housing, and she found it difficult to find a new place to live. The eviction notice described the use of "some vigorous language" by the anarchists, and noted that "Miss Goldman had delivered a sanguinary address, and so had several others of the unkempt and unwashed."[29] She eventually found a room in a brothel, as no one else would even consider renting to her. In various reports, Goldman and other anarchists continued to be described not for their political opinions, but instead as unhygienic and unclean creatures.

Goldman's Jewish background also became part of the newspaper attack on her the following year, when she was sentenced to prison for the first time. *The New York Times* reported that there were a "number of frouzy-haired specimens of the tribe present," while the editorial the same day noted her sentence as a "wholesome and exemplary event." It went on to explain:

It is necessary that turbulent Europeans should be taught that
we do draw the line somewhere, and that though evil speaking
of dignitaries and institutions is permitted, it is not permitted to
make public speeches in any language known to police that
incite to criminal acts.[30]

Prior to her first sojourn in jail, Goldman's masculinity,
immorality, and violent nature were further intensified when, much
to the delight of the newspapers, Goldman horsewhipped Johann
Most on stage. Goldman later regretted this act, personally and
politically, and she admitted it was done at one of the lowest
moments in her life.

After the attempted assassination, Most attacked both Berkman
and Goldman in his magazine *Freiheit,* declaring that the whole
event was either fake and had been made up or was done to arouse
sympathy for Frick. Most then went even further by condemning
acts of violence in the U.S., declaring them unnecessary, and stating
there was no possibility of success through promoting or using violence. Goldman was horrified by Most. It had been Most, after all,
who was one of the main proponents of propaganda by deed, and
should surely have not only understood but also supported Berkman's (and her) plan.

There are a number of possible reasons as to why Most adopted such a position. The first and most obvious is the fact that at
that moment in U.S. history, he was the face of violent anarchy, and
if anyone was going to be arrested it would have been him. Despite
Most's bravado about time spent in jail, the reality was that he was
getting older and did not want any more jail time, in particular for
something he did not do! He had been released from jail, having
spent a year in prison for a speech given just after the execution of
the Chicago martyrs. As well, ever since Berkman and Goldman had
become lovers, Most had harboured a major resentment toward
Berkman and so he was never going to support anything Berkman
did. Finally, there was the fact that even Most had changed his
mind ofnthe usefulness of violence – violence simply would not be
a cause of change.

Goldman's fury could not be contained. She first demanded
through another anarchist magazine, *Der Anarchist*, that Most prove
accusations that the event had never happened. Most did not respond, so Goldman resolved to confront him personally.

At a meeting where Most was speaking, Goldman asked him to explain and prove any and all of his comments. He refused, instead making a reference to a hysterical woman. At this point Goldman took out a horsewhip from beneath her cloak, and proceeded to lash Most across the face and head, finally and dramatically breaking the whip over her knee and throwing the pieces at him.

This incident was not only to finish the Most/Goldman relationship, it caused rifts within the anarchist community that were never healed. Many years later, Most's son, in a conversation with Paul Avrich, reported the family's continued distrust and dislike of Goldman, clearly blaming her for the poverty and loneliness felt by Most and his family:

> Alexander Berkman was as phony as a three dollar bill. Father thought him a hypocrite; he called Berkman and Emma Goldman "financial anarchists," who made a living off the movement. He strongly disapproved of the three of them Berkman, Goldman, and their artist friend Modest Stein – living together as a threesome. "Degenerates," he called them. Emma had guts and brains but was lacking in character, he thought. He never forgave her.[31]

The reasons behind Goldman's attack on Most were, as always with Goldman, complicated. Later she did regret what she had done, realizing that they maximized the divisions in an already strained community.[32] In 1932, Max Nettlau, in a letter, told her that he had always suspected that the real reason behind the whipping was more personal than ideological. She did admit that she felt she had been wronged by Most: "I will say that he did slander me to a scandalous degree."[33] She nevertheless insisted that the cause of her action was ideological:

> That was not what impelled my action. I had so little personal life then that nothing anyone had done against me really mattered. But AB and his act mattered everything to me. You forget that Most's stand rent our ranks, the majority going with him, and only a few willing to stand by AB. In view of the fact that Most had always proclaimed acts of violence from the housetops, his attitude toward AB was too great a shock for me to reason about. You forget that I was only twenty-three,

then, with no other aim or purpose in life except the ideal.
One does not reason at that age, and that fervent stage, as one
does in maturer years; I admit that nothing Most, or anyone
else might have done, since 1892 would induce me to horsewhip them. Indeed I have often regretted to have attacked the
man who was my teacher and whom I idolized for many
years. But it was impelling to do so then.[34]

The press had a field day with Goldman's actions; here was the
proof they needed to denigrate Most and show to the world that
Emma Goldman was nothing more than a violent immoral, drunk
woman. *The New York Times*, on December 20, 1892, reported:

> The ill feeling that has existed between John Most, the leader of
> the conservative Anarchists and Emma Goldman, who drinks
> beer in Peukert's Anarchist saloon in Fifth Street and makes
> incendiary speeches, developed into an assault by that women
> upon Most on Sunday evening … No sooner had Most been
> introduced to the assembly than Emma Goldman, who had
> acquired notoriety as the champion of Berkman, the would-be
> assassin of H.C. Frink, stepped forward whip in hand, flour-
> ished it in Most's face, and administered a lash accompanied by
> select Anarchistic billingsgate epithets.

The report was clear: Emma Goldman, drunk, violent, fre-
quenter of immoral establishments, was even worse than Johann
Most, an anarchist.

CHAPTER FOUR

Words and Deeds

We are revolutionists not from love of gore but because there is no other way to free and redeem mankind. History has taught that. No use of trying to reform. The Gordian knot can be cut only by the sword, and within a few years the masses will write the history of the world.

–Johann Most, in Alexander Berkman's *Prison Memoirs of an Anarchist*

I feel violence in whatever form never has and probably never will bring constructive results. But my mind and my knowledge of life tell me that changes will always be violent. At least I want to eliminate as much as possible the need for violence. I want the revolution to be understood as a process of reconstruction rather than what we believed it to be until now, a process of destruction.[1]

From the moment Alexander Berkman decided to assassinate Henry Clay Frick, Emma Goldman felt forced to take a position maintaining that violence was a legitimate form of protest. Any other position for her would have meant turning her back on Berkman, and her guilt over his twenty-two year prison sentence would not allow this. In her book *Emma Goldman: An Intimate Life*, Alice Wexler states Goldman could never sort out her ambiguity about Pittsburgh. Initially she was very careful to deny any involvement or even knowledge of the event. A year after Berkman was sentenced, Goldman was in court for the first time and during her trial was clear in her answers that, while she did respect Berkman as a person, she by no means approved of his actions.[2] Even her friends, Hippolyte Havel and Frank Harris, who wrote biographical portraits about her, both claimed it was the police who tried to implicate her in the events, insisting that the police "exerted every effort to involve Emma Goldman in the act of Alexander Berkman."[3] Berkman, in his autobiography *Prison Memoirs*, stated that while she knew of the act, she did not take any role in it. It was simply too dangerous for Goldman to openly state she had played an active role, and indeed would have been in the room when Berkman shot Frick had money allowed. That would have certainly sent her to jail for a very long time.

There was also some dispute between Berkman and Goldman about the fact that Frick lived. Goldman and Fedya Stein had at one stage hatched a plan to blow up the Allegheny Courthouse if and when Berkman was condemned to death. When it was clear that Frick was going to live, Goldman was relieved, as Frick's living meant Berkman would be saved, and Goldman and Stein could then abandon their ill-conceived plan. Stein, even prior to sentencing, had arrived in Pittsburgh, having decided to assassinate Frick. However, it seems that his plan became known to the police, and he decided not to even try and to quickly leave Pittsburgh.

In a letter to Goldman from Berkman, sent just a month after his sentencing, he chastises her for her looking at the attempted assassination as a failure:

> I sense bitterness and disappointment in your letter. Why do you speak of failure? You, at least, you and Fedya, should not have your judgment obscured by the mere accident of physical results. Your lines pained and grieved me beyond words. Not because you should write thus; but that you should even think thus. Need I enlarge? True morality deals with motives, not consequences.[4]

However, there is no doubt that Goldman was overwhelmed at times by the guilt she felt as Berkman spent years in jail. She "yearned to give up my freedom to loudly proclaim my share in the deed."[5] Goldman told Theodore Dreiser in a letter in 1929 that she "regretted ever since that I did not share the consequences with him – it would have been easier than it was being on the outside."[6]

THE ASSASSINATION OF PRESIDENT MCKINLEY

Yet as careful as Goldman and others around her were in protecting her from severe jail time in the Frick case, Goldman inexplicably was full of bravado and would not be protected when it came to the much more serious issue of the assassination of President William McKinley in 1901. While there is one obvious difference here – neither Goldman nor Berkman were at all involved in the McKinley assassination, nor was anyone from her circle of friends or acquaintances – nevertheless it seems almost unbelievable that Goldman failed to understand thatm in the court of public opinion, she would be then and forever associated with the assassination of a president.

William McKinley (1843–1901) was the twenty-fifth president of the United States, elected to office for the first time in 1896 and then for a second term in 1900, with Theodore Roosevelt as his vice-president. In September 1901, President and Mrs. McKinley attended the Pan-American Exposition (World's Fair) in Buffalo, New York. The World's Fairs, since their inception in 1851 at Crystal Palace in London, had provided each country with an opportunity to show off their modern, specifically technical, advances.

On the first day of the fair, the president gave a speech explaining his position on tariffs and trade. On the second day, the president was due to meet the public at the Temple of Music. Leon Czolgosz waited in line with the rest of the public and as the president offered his hand, Czolgosz swept it aside, produced a .32 calibre pistol and shot the president twice, once in the chest and once in the stomach. As McKinley staggered, the Secret Service guards and other people jumped on Czolgosz, beating him severely. The Secret Service quickly brought him to a Buffalo jail, where he was asked two questions by James Vallely, a local Buffalo police officer: "Why did you shoot the President?" To which he responded, "I only done my duty," Vallely then asked, "Are you an anarchist?" Czolgosz responded, "Yes, sir." Later the District Attorney, Thomas Penney, officially questioned him:

> "What is your name?" "Leon Czolgosz."
> "Did you mean to kill the President?" "I did."
> "What was the motive that induced you to commit this crime?" "I am a disciple of Emma Goldman. I killed the President because I done my duty. I did not feel that one man should have all this power while others have none."[7]

Leon Czolgosz was born in about 1873 in Alpena, Michigan. His father had come to the United States as an immigrant from Prussia around 1871, fleeing the harsh new rules of Otto von Bismarck. His wife followed some months later and Leon was their first child born in the United States. Paul Czolgosz worked at a lumber mill, which would have probably given him a yearly salary of under $700, which meant that, like a number of nineteenth-century families, the children became a vital part of the family financial survival plan. Leon was sent to work initially at a glass factory in Pennsylvania and then he returned home to work in a wire mill in Ohio.

Czolgosz shot McKinley on September 6, but McKinley lived for eight days, dying on September 14. The official cause of death was given as gangrene. In truth, his whole medical treatment was highly questionable and even incompetent. First the president was brought to a local hospital, one without an X-ray machine, while another hospital only fifty miles away had an X-ray machine, which they could have used to show exactly where the bullets were lodged. Second, a gynecologist, Dr. Mathew Mann, with no experience with gunshot injuries, treated McKinley, and finally a bullet was left inside the president, as the doctor explained he could not find it.[8] During the surgery one of the issues had been the lack of lighting; this despite the fact that the nearby Exposition boasted new electric lights. Even after McKinley died, and an autopsy was performed, the bullet could not be found. After four hours, the family finally requested that the doctors "not injure the corpse any longer."[9]

But if the president lasted eight days, Czolgosz's trial lasted a mere eight hours, twenty-six minutes, and it took the jury only thirty-four minutes to return a guilty verdict. Just a month later, on October 29, Czolgosz was executed by the electric chair; eerily, it was filmed by Thomas Edison. Czolgosz's body was buried in the prison yard, though his family had asked for its return. They were told that the mobs would tear it apart, so to ensure the complete decomposition of the body the prison warden had acid poured over it.

McKinley was the third American president assassinated in fifty years – Abraham Lincoln had been assassinated in 1865, and James Garfield in 1881. On September 14, 1901, *Harper's Weekly* published a drawing entitled "At the Threshold" characterizing the shock and mood of the nation: North and South, shown as two grieving women joined together in bringing McKinley into the "Hall of Martyrs," where the entrance is adorned with busts of Lincoln and Garfield on either side. The woman with the headband marked "South" can herself barely stand, her head in her hands, visibly grieving. From the doorway McKinley is greeted by an angel, hand outstretched with a crown for the new prince of peace.

Czolgosz's statement that he was a follower of Emma Goldman immediately and obviously made Emma Goldman the most wanted person in the country. Goldman had been traveling in September 1901 and on September 6, she was in St. Louis. She heard about the assassination from a newsboy on the street corner. The following day the headlines changed to "ASSASSIN OF PRESIDENT McKINLEY AN ANARCHIST. CONFESSES TO HAVING BEEN INCITED BY EMMA GOLDMAN. WOMAN ANARCHIST WANTED."[10]

The same day *The Chicago Tribune* published an illustration of Emma Goldman entitled, "Emma Goldman, High Priestess of Anarchy Whose Speeches Inspired Leon Czolgosz to His Crime."

The blame for the assassination is clearly placed on Goldman. Even the devil in the illustration is horrified at Goldman; her eternal destiny is set as she is surrounded in fire! A bomb is in the centre place beneath her, and beside her two daggers show what kind of a person she is.

Goldman's recklessness and flair for the dramatic immediately sprung to the fore. She told her friends that she wished to go to Chicago as some of her friends, including Hippolyte Havel, were being held without bail until she was found. In St. Louis other friends persuaded her not to surrender to the police until at least she could give an interview to *The Chicago Tribune* giving her side of the events. The newspaper was willing to pay $500, which would be needed for her defense fund. Goldman agreed. She traveled to Chicago by train in a disguise, and after her arrival was hidden in the house of J. Norris, when the police raided.

Initially Goldman had the police fooled by pretending to be the Swedish help. However, once the police found a fountain pen with her name on it ,they were determined to simply remain in the house, so Goldman surrendered.

While the police in Buffalo, New York were working on Czolglosz to get him to implicate Goldman, Goldman herself was given the "third degree"[11] in an attempt to get her to confess. She was kept in a small airless room, without water, shouted at and pushed around. At one stage a police officer hit her in the face, knocking out one of her teeth. The following day harsh lights were used to keep her uncomfortable. From the outset of her questioning, Goldman had no contact with anyone, not even a lawyer. At night, the only notes passed to her were threatening ones, probably from the guards, which read, "Murderous Emma Goldman, you will burn in hell-fire for your treachery to our country." Another: "I wish I could get at you. I would tear your heart out and feed it to my dog."

While it became more and more clear in Chicago that Goldman was not involved and the police planned to release her, in Buffalo the police were working tirelessly on Czolgosz, determined to get him to name Goldman in the assassination. Czolgosz, however, kept insisting that he had seen Emma Goldman at the Franklin Liberal Club, where she said:

> she did not believe in voting and did not believe in govern-ment. Said all government was tyranny. She said she believed in Anarchy. I am an Anarchist. Anarchy as I understand it means self-government. That time in Cleveland was the only time I saw Emma Goldman.[12]

After further questioning Czolgosz admitted he had also seen Goldman in Chicago but had not talked to her.

The Buffalo police, led by Superintendent William S. Bull, had already decided that Goldman was involved and were determined to find the evidence necessary to link her to the event. Having dis-covered that Goldman had spent a vacation in Buffalo earlier that year, the police brought in her former landlady, Hattie Lang, for questioning. All Lang was able to tell them was that Goldman, with her friend Dr. Kaplin, had visited the Exposition and had seen Edison's Tower of Light. They then turned to Goldman's family, most of whom were still living in Rochester, New York. Since the assassination, the Goldmans had suffered taunts and snide remarks from people in the area. Goldman's nephews and nieces had suf-fered in school, while her father had lost a number of customers from his furniture store. Now Goldman's niece Stella Cominsky was brought in for questioning. For two days she was interrogat-ed, all the while maintaining her aunt was innocent.

Bull would not give up, and he sent a detective, Mathew J. O'Loughlin, to Cleveland to find out more about Czolgosz and his links with Goldman. O'Loughlin returned with the story that Czolgosz had become her follower and traveled with her. He even contacted George E. Corner, the Cleveland Police Chief, who kept a very close eye on radicals in his city, who insisted that Czolgosz could not be linked with the radicals there.

The final attempt made by the New York police was requesting the extradition of Goldman from Illinois to New York to face charges related to the assassination of the president. The District Attorney, Thomas Penny, affirmed that there was sufficient evidence to warrant him to bring Goldman to Buffalo for trial "for conspiracy to assassinate the President." The extradition attempt failed, mainly because it was opposed by Chief O'Neil of the Chicago Police force. Why he opposed this remains a bit of a mystery. Goldman in her autobiography notes that when he finally questioned her, he was convinced of her innocence, and her conditions improved greatly afterwards. There is also the theory that O'Neil was trying to weed out corruption within the Chicago force at the time; he knew that some police officers were trying to use the capture of Goldman to take some of the pressure off themselves, and he was determined not to allow that happen. Whatever the reason, Goldman was released from police custody, much to her delight and to the amazement of her friends.[13]

Goldman's release was irrelevant to her reputation; she was now enshrined as foreign and anti-American, and there would be a popular push throughout the country to get Goldman and other anarchists out of the country, while at the same time halting immigration of those deemed undesirable.

A frenzy swept the country after the assassination. Even Alexander Berkman, in a letter from jail to Goldman, commented, "The whole country seemed to be swept with the fury of revenge."[14] Johann Most was arrested for selling a copy of the *Freiheit* that contained the fifty-year-old article "*Der Mord*" (Murder). He was tried and sentenced to a year in Blackwell's Island. A mob of New Yorkers attacked a group of so-called anarchists in Paterson, New Jersey, burning their houses, after a report in the *New York Times* said anarchists there had been part of the plot,[15] and even in New Mexico an anarchist was killed by a mob, simply for being an anarchist.

The country seemed convinced that something drastic needed to be done to halt the anarchist menace. Even before McKinley had died, Roosevelt had written in a private letter to Henry Cabot Lodge:

> We should war with relentless efficiency not only against anarchists, but against all active and passive sympathizers with anarchists. Moreover, every scoundrel ... who for whatever

purposes appeals to evil human passion, had made himself
accessory before the fact to every crime of this nature and
every soft fool who extends a maudlin sympathy to criminals
has done likewise ... Tolstoy and the feeble apostles of Tolstoy
... who united in petitions for the pardon of anarchists have a
heavy share in the burden of responsibility for crimes of this
kind.[16]

On December 3, 1901, Theodore Roosevelt delivered his first
message to Congress as president. After his eulogy for the late
President McKinley, Roosevelt declared that the anarchist "is in no
sense, in no shape or way, a product of social conditions." The
anarchist is one

> ...whose perverted instincts lead him to prefer confusion and
> chaos to the most beneficent form of social order. His protest
> of concern for working men is outrageous in its imprudent
> falsity; for if the political institutions of this country do not
> afford opportunity to every honest and intelligent son of toil,
> then the door of hope is forever closed against him.[17]

Anarchists, in the view of Roosevelt and most Americans at the
time, could not be "American," because anarchists opposed and
openly sought to destroy the democratic foundations of the U.S.
    Newspapers and politicians showed their agreement, urging the
deportation of these dangerous elements, who now were a moral
and physical danger to society. Henry C. Payne of the National
Republican Committee, stated:

> The attempt upon his life [McKinley had not died yet] was
> not because he was William McKinley, but because he was
> President of the United States, and I believe is only the carrying
> out in one detail of a general plan upon the part of the
> Anarchists to kill the rulers of the leading nations of the earth.[18]

On September 8, the headlines went further, insisting, "City
Magistrates Declare that Enemies of Society Should Be Expelled
from the Country." Justice A. Gigerich stated, "The sooner Anarchy
and its supporters in this country are stamped out the better for the

civilized world."[19] Letters poured into *The New York Times* demanding the exclusion of anarchists and the expulsion of those already in the U.S.: "Exclusion is the safeguard that first suggests itself, and it is the most practicable. In fact we ought to shut out a considerable part of the immigration that flows to our shores."[20]

The result of this was the 1901 exclusion act, which would in turn form the basis for the 1918 act. The 1901 Act, officially listed as An Act To Regulate the Immigration of Aliens into the United States, was passed on its last day of session, March 3, 1903. It was the first act of its kind passed since the Alien and Sedition Acts of 1798, which permitted questioning the political beliefs of people entering the U.S. The act specifically denied access to anyone who

> ... disbelieves in or who is opposed to all organized government, or who is a member of or affiliated with any organization entertaining or teaching such disbelief in or opposition to all organized government.

The first person arrested under the terms of the act was John Turner, a Scottish anarchist, who was found with a copy of Johann Most's magazine *Free Society*, and a copy of his speaking schedule, which included a memorial for the Haymarket martyrs. Goldman immediately organized for the lawyers Clarence Darrow and Edgar Lee Masters to be his defense. However, despite trying to rally public opinion behind Turner, the country was still shocked by McKinley's assassination. *The New York Times* editorial declared it was "right – in the belief of Congress and of many, probably of most, Americans, it makes it our duty – to exclude him."[21]

In court Darrow and Masters argued that Turner's beliefs were philosophical and so under the Bill of Rights were protected. However, Chief Justice Melville Fuller, writing the majority opinion, held that the Bill of Rights did not apply to aliens, that Turner had no expectations of those rights, and that the government had the right to deny anyone who was perceived as a threat. John Turner became the first person deported under the act.

The truth was that Goldman played no part whatsoever in the planning or the actual assassination of President McKinley, and she would have saved herself and the anarchist movement a great deal of effort in their denials had she said so in public more often. But instead Goldman refused to condemn Czolgosz, and the question remains: why?

Goldman met Czolgosz on two occasions. The first was in Cleveland in May, 1901, where during an intermission of a lecture on "Anarchism" delivered to the Franklin Liberal Club, a young man "looking over the titles of the pamphlets and books on sale"[22] asked her for suggestions for reading. Goldman suggested some material and recalled that "his striking face remained in my memory."[23]

Goldman's always-precarious health gave out at this stage due to the summer heat and she went to Chicago to spend time with Abe and Mary Issak, editors of the radical *Free Society* magazine. As she was packing to leave Chicago, to go to spend time with her family in Rochester, she received a phone call from someone called "Nieman" who wanted to talk to her. Goldman explained that she was going to the station, and if he wished he could go with her to the station. She recognized him as the young man from Cleveland. He explained his doubts about the socialist club to which he belonged and she listened, then asked Hippolyte Havel to look after him. She then continued her journey to Rochester.

During her time there she read a piece in the Issaks' magazine, published September 1, in which they warned that a young man was trying to get involved in anarchist circles and had aroused suspicion. *Free Society* warned he could be a spy: "The attention of the comrades is called to another spy. He is well-dressed, of medium height, rather narrow shouldered, blond and about twenty-five years of age." He was "of the usual sort pretending to be greatly interested in the cause asking for names, or soliciting aid for acts of contemplated violence." The piece finished: "the comrades are warned in advance, and can act accordingly."[24] From the description, Goldman realized the paper was talking about "Nieman." She contacted Abe Issak, demanding he issue a retraction, as she insisted that there was no evidence to suggest anything of the kind. Issak initially argued that someone trying to get involved and talking openly about acts of violence was suspicious, but he gave into Goldman and the following month printed a retraction.

The next time Goldman came across "Nieman" was his photograph in the newspaper as the person who had assassinated the President. Czolgosz had begun using the name "Nieman" in 1885, after he and fellow workers at the Cleveland Rolling Mills had gone on strike and been blacklisted. However, while their names were listed, no one remembered their faces, so many simply changed their names. Czolgosz took the name Fred Nieman. "Fred" was the nickname his family used for him and "Nieman" means nobody in Polish. It was effective, as Fred Nieman was employed at the Cleveland Rolling Mills.

In 1901, Goldman's own views on violence were confusing and blurred. In an interview given to the *New York Sun* in January she insisted that acts of violence were done by "utter fools." The following month, in an interview in *Free Society*, she insisted that she had "never opposed force or propaganda by deed," and insisted it was vital not to judge the result but the cause. After her arrest, *The New York Times* printed a report in which they quoted Goldman as emphatically stating that "no Anarchist ring" was part of the assassination, and that Czolgosz had "planned the deed unaided and entirely alone."

THE ALIENTISTS AND THE ANARCHISTS

At the time of the assassination, Czolgosz's mental state was a subject of much debate; after all, many simply surmised that you would have to be insane to kill the president. But some wondered if it was moral to impose a harsh sentence upon him. Others took the view that this was a man totally responsible for his actions, legally, morally, and psychologically, and therefore he deserved no sympathy of any kind. For others in society another argument broke out: new immigrants had now shown themselves not only not to be Americans, but were dangerous to the safety of the United States, and so not only should immigration be halted, but all these dangerous Americans should be deported.

When Czolgosz's initial statement was taken by Buffalo lawyer, James Quackenbush, Czolgosz had insisted that he understood what he had done and why. Yet his stepmother at the time of his trial insisted that he was insane and his father added that when growing up Leon had been a strange child, always afraid and alone in life. There were other stories, which circulated for years after his execution, that Czolgosz had syphilis, but no proof of such has ever been found.[25] As the numbers of rumours grew about Czolgosz, and as the pre-trial issues became more medically and politically difficult, the District Attorney, Thomas Penny, took the advice of the Buffalo Police Surgeon, Dr. Joseph Fowler, and had Czolgosz examined by a group of alienists.

The study of insanity was relatively new, and its use in the courtroom was even newer and certainly controversial. The notion of doctors being "experts" in this area was cause for a lot of doubt. In 1888, while some judges allowed so called "expert testimony" by the medical profession, another case the same year favoured the testimony of the non-medical person over the doctor. Another reason why the decision was made in Buffalo to introduce alienists to examine Czolgosz may have been due to the fact that, in 1900, F.L. Oswald had written an article for *The North American Review* in which he argued that anarchist beliefs belonged to a "mental pathology."[26] So Dr. Fowler was joined by two experts, both from the University of Buffalo, for his examination: Dr. Floyd D. Crego, Professor of Insanity and Brain Diseases, and Dr. James W. Putman, Professor of Nervous Diseases.

For days the three doctors listened to everything Czolgosz said. They even tested him by sending in a person who pretended to be a friend. They spoke gently to him and then shouted at him and even threatened him. At the end of their study they noted:

> He is not a case of paranoia, because he has not systematized delusions reverting to self, and because he is in exceptionally good condition and has an unbroken record of good health. He is the product of Anarchy, sane and responsible.[27]

The defense, in an attempt to give Czolgosz some chance, asked Dr. Carlos F. MacDonald, Professor of Mental Diseases and Medical Jurisprudence at Bellevue Medical College in New York City, to examine him. MacDonald's medical views were known to favour a broader definition of insanity, which was vital if the defense had any hope.

Throughout his arrest and trial, and then as he awaited execution, Czolgosz was surrounded by other doctors. Dr. Gerin, the prison doctor, gave him a detailed physical when he arrived in prison, and along with Dr. Carlos F. MacDonald, he also examined Czolgosz before his execution. After the execution, MacDonald and Edward A. Spitzka undertook the autopsy. After the autopsy, Dr. Walter Channing and Dr. Vernon Briggs assessed all the information, and then began an investigation of Czolgosz's mental state.

The proof of the interest in Czolgosz for the medical community can be seen in the number of articles published in medical journals in the two years after Czolgosz's execution, and in the fact that on January 28, 1902, two alienists, Walter Channing and Vernon Lloyd Briggs, held a conference, where they explained to a large group of medical professionals the conclusions they had reached after reviewing all medical files on Czolgosz and interviewing family and friends.

All medical articles comment on anarchism, and all of them state that Czolgosz's link with the anarchist movement was mainly in his mind, as no one in the anarchist movement knew him, or had anything to do with him. During the time that Briggs and Channing were investigating for themselves any possible medical cause for Czolgosz's act, Goldman wrote to Channing to explain her thoughts. In his article, "The Mental Status of Czolgosz, The Assassination of President McKinly," published in *The American Journal of Insanity* in 1902, Channing was critical of the conclusions reached by Fowler and the other doctors. Channing pointed out that their study was done in a very short space of time and that they lacked any real knowledge of Czolgosz's previous life. Channing did, like all the other alienists, discuss anarchy, but was specific in his conclusions that Czolgosz did not know enough about anarchy to be able to declare himself an anarchist. Channing quoted an unknown anarchist saying Czolgosz was more likely a socialist than an anarchist. Channing also noted specifically: "Even Emma Goldman herself writes me that she was not well enough acquainted with his political views top know whether he was an anarchist or not."[28]

Channing's conclusions were that Czolgosz was indeed mentally ill and delusional; that at the time of his trial, it was impossible in such a short period of time to accurately diagnose him; and that, since no research had been done, and no interviews with family of friends were conducted, Czolgosz's doctors did not have the full picture when they reached their conclusions.

Channing's medical conclusions would seem to clear Goldman and the anarchist movement from any association with the assassination. So why, then, did Emma Goldman insist on constantly linking anarchy and the deeds of other anarchists with Czolgosz?

CZOLGOSZ AND GOLDMAN: VIOLENCE UNDERSTOOD

Goldman's sympathy for Czolgosz seems to have been tied up in her complicated understanding of her support for Berkman, who in 1901 was still in prison. In October 1901, she published an article in *Free Society,* entitled "The Tragedy at Buffalo." Attacking the American public, Goldman states, "Never before in the history of governments has the sound of a pistol shot so startled, terrorized, and horrified the self-satisfied, indifferent, contented, and indolent public." She goes on to explain that such an act of violence has to be understood as a reaction by "the sturdy sons of America [who] were sacrificed on the battlefield of industrial war, and the daughters outraged in corrupt factory surroundings." Czolgosz, she insists, only acted out of desperation as he realized that "his youthful dreams are but a farce." Such a reaction is normal just as "resistance against force is a fact all through nature," and so until government changes "force begets force."[29]

While in the same article Goldman explains that "Anarchism and violence are as far apart from each other as liberty and tyranny," she nevertheless insists that violence is the most understandable result of greed and big business.

But Goldman never made a point once if it could be made twice, and later in her 1911 essay, "The Psychology of Political Violence," she compares the acts of Angiollillo, Bresci,[30] Berkman, and Czolgosz, insisting that they have been misunderstood by the public, and that instead these men shared what she describes as a "supersensitiveness to the wrong and injustices surrounding them which compels them to pay the toll of our social crimes." Any new belief system, Goldman points out, comes not through "peace, but a sword." Violence, she says, needs to be understood as an act not just of violence but of despair.[31]

What is most amazing about all this is that, while Goldman continued to defend violence as an acceptable, if desperate, act by the impoverished, Berkman is always clear in his letters to Goldman that he considered the act useless and saw her views as "too sentimental."[32] Berkman explained in a letter to Goldman that "POLITICAL acts of violence are not in place in the U.S., but that only ECONOMIC acts could be understood and justified etc."[33] In another letter soon after, he reminds her of a letter he sent her just after the assassination pointing out that "at 30 one is not so reckless, not so fanatical and one sided as at 20." Even then, he wrote to her, "I cannot agree with you regarding the social value of Leon's act." According to Berkman, for violence to be worthwhile, it must have community rather than individual value, it must be directed against a real enemy, and the public must understand and accept it.[34]

The debate between Berkman and Goldman about the value of Czolgosz's act would continue for the rest of their lives. While this conversation would continue in private, in public Goldman's continued support for violence meant that from, 1901 until her deportation in 1919, Goldman's reputation became even more entrenched as *the* key figure of anarchism in America. She was portrayed as immoral, rude, crude, masculine, sexually promiscuous, bomb-throwing, evil, and dangerous.

Goldman was feeling extremely lonely and disillusioned by the end of 1901; she even had trouble finding a place to live, as no one would rent to people who had assassinated the president, so she went quietly back to New York City and rented a room under the name of Miss E.G. Smith. She returned to nursing, a career she had trained for during her first prison term in 1893. She shared her living space with her brother Moishe (Morris), a medical student, and a friend of his, "Dan," who was a lover of Goldman's for a time. She was lonely and decided to spend her time working in the Lower East Side tenements.

CHAPTER FIVE

Ideas, Life and Deportation

When in the course of human development, existing institutions prove inadequate to the needs of man, when they serve merely to enslave, rob, and
oppress mankind, the people have the eternal right to rebel against, and overthrow, these institutions.
–Emma Goldman, Declaration of Independence, *Mother Earth*, Vol. IV, no.5,
July 1909

I like the free spontaneity of a child who knows nothing, better than world-
knowledge and intellectual deformity of a child who has been subjected to our
present education.[1]

Goldman spent the months between October 1893 and August
1894 in jail, on Blackwell's Island, New York. Initially Goldman's
time in jail had provided her with a time for penance – she could
also suffer like Berkman – yet it also provided her with a time to
reflect upon her almost total reliance on Berkman and Most. Up to
this time she was torn between Most and Berkman, physically and
philosophically. Her time in jail also gave Goldman a break from
having to constantly choose between them as men, and between
their philosophies. Once released, Goldman chose neither by denying the validity of violence, and instead began her own type of revolution.

In an article published in *The New York World* in 1894,
Goldman summarized her time in jail as a "school of experience
[which] made me more of an anarchist than ever ... [I am] increas-
ingly determined to use every means in my power to spread my
doctrine among the people."[2] Later, she noted in her autobiography:

And yet more than all else, it was prison that had proved the
best school. A more painful but more vital school. Here I had
been brought close to the depths and complexities of the

human soul; here I had found ugliness and beauty, meanness
and generosity. Here, too, I had learned to see life through my
own eyes and not through those of Sasha,[3] Most[4] or Ed.[5] The
prison had been the crucible that tested my faith. It had helped
me to discover my strength in my own being, the strength to
stand alone, the strength to live my life and fight for my
ideals, against the whole world if need be. The State of New
York could have rendered me no greater service than by sending me to Blackwell's Island Penitentiary!"[6]

Another important change that occurred during Goldman's
time in jail was that she gained both notoriety and popularity, becoming *the* anarchist personality in the U.S. By the time of her
release, she was thirty years old, and her opinions were as sought
after as those of Most. Goldman had become part of the middle
class's and the educated class's cultures. Goldman and her version
of anarchy had moved away from the factory floor and the radical
coffee houses, into the dining rooms of the intelligentsia. If at the
time of her sentence, Goldman had been a relatively little-known,
Yiddish-speaking, Jewish, working-class anarchist, at the time of
her release, she was a well-known, English-speaking, much-sought-
after American figure.

Goldman's time in jail not only gave her a necessary break from
her lovers; it also proved to be great preparation for the next stage
in her public life, in that it provided her with a place where her
English language skills greatly improved. In jail she read extensively in English, and as a result began to appreciate for the first time
the particularly American version of anarchy that already existed.
Such was the impact of her contact with Justus Schwab, who was
a prominent socialist in New York, and John Swinton, editor-in-
chief of *The New York Sun* and who was also active in insisting on
the rights of the new European immigrants, as well as her readings
of Emerson, Whitman, Thoreau,[7] and Hawthorne in particular,
that she came out of jail determined to devote herself to promoting
the ideals of anarchism to a specifically American audience. Her
reasons were simple. She had been wrong in her assumptions about
America and Americans: "John Swinton made me see that
Americans, once aroused, were as capable of idealism and sacrifice
as my Russian heroes and heroines. I left the Swintons with a new
faith in the possibilities of America."[8]

Upon her release on August 17, 1894, Goldman delivered a

speech to a crowd of supporters at the Thalia Theater at Bower Street in New York. She was greeted with a long and loud ovation and spoke in both German and English. telling her audience that she was imprisoned for her ideas and for defending her right to free speech.

If Goldman's time in prison had made her think more about what role Americans should and could play in the revolution, the need for a revolution remained of crucial importance. Such was the need, according to Goldman, for change that she wrote her own version of the Declaration of Independence for a competition sponsored by *The Boston Globe* in 1909. She explained why the United States had lost its own ideals and argued that they needed to be re-established:

> The history of the American kings of capital and authority is the history of repeated crimes, injustice, oppression, outrage, and abuse, all aiming at the suppression of individual liberties and the exploitation of people ... The reign of these kings is holding mankind in slavery, perpetuating poverty and disease, maintaining crime and corruption ...[9]

Thus to overcome this tyranny, to achieve liberty,and the equal rights of "all human beings, irrespective of race, color, or sex"[10] a revolution was necessary. Once out of prison, the questions became just how this revolution should occur, what method would best suit the United States, and how to ensure the revolution would have a lasting impact.

One of the most important aspects of Goldman's jail experience was the fact that she worked as a nurse. This position provided her with the opportunity to help those who were sick and impoverished. It also gave her opportunities to continue to take on the state administration by pointing to the scams that were taking place at the prisoners' expense.[11] Goldman was also able to see firsthand how the various prostitutes coped with their lives through their addictions to various drugs. Seeing these women detox was a practical education for Goldman, as she saw the reality of their world:

> The sight of their suffering was heart-breaking. With the strength of giants the frail creatures would shake the iron bars, curse, and scream for dope and cigarettes. Then they

would fall exhausted to the ground, moaning pitifully through the night.[12]

Out of prison and having to finance her revolutionary work again, nursing proved to be invaluable. Nursing also allowed her time to think and write about changes that were needed in society, and it allowed her to work among the people she described as the "unfortunates."[13] The prison doctor who had provided her with her initial training also provided her with her first nursing job outside prison, at the Nurses' Settlement on Henry Street. Goldman was highly impressed with the women who worked there, giving as much medical care and information as they could to the poor of the city:

> [These women] were among the first American women I met
> who felt an interest in the economic condition of the masses.
> They were genuinely concerned with the people of the Lower
> East Side. My contact with them, as with John Swinton,
> brought me close to new American types, men and women
> of ideals, capable and fine, generous deeds.

Soon it became obvious to Goldman that, if she were serious about nursing, she would need to be trained. She had an offer to train in the U.S., but what appealed to her more was to travel to Vienna, where it was possible not just to train as a nurse, but also to learn more about anarchy. From prison, Alexander Berkman wrote to her, agreeing with her and urging her to go to Europe so that she could be "better equipped." So on August 15, 1895 Goldman sailed for England to begin a trip to Europe that would be part-official study and part-lecture tour.

THE DEVELOPMENT OF IDEAS

Margaret H. McFadden, in her book *Golden Cables of Sympathy: The Transatlantic Sources of Nineteenth Century Feminism*,[14] notes that there existed a system of communication and influence between women, socialists, and radicals in general that extended between the United States and Europe. McFadden notes in her study that this system of communication and exchange of ideas began to develop due in part to the rise and ease of communication, specifically the telegram, and the already-existing communities of radicals, which has begun to develop strategies to strengthen their own communities. The women's suffrage movement was in reality an international organization fought by women in individual countries. But each of these individual groups had strong and regular links to movements in other countries, which allowed for women to discuss practical tactics such as demonstrations, and later, more violent protests.

Ease of communication brought something else to the world: news of change, potential change, or even change that was being demanded. Daniel Rogers, in his book *Atlantic Crossings: Social Politics in a Progressive Age*,[15] points out that the social policy changes taking place in Europe became known to all in the United States through the news media, and impacted all aspects of American life, intellectual as well as political. Thus knowledge of Europe's changes meant that Americans were, for almost the first time in their relatively new history, being forced to realize the impact of social debates.

James T. Kloppenberg, in *Uncertain Victory: Social Democracy and Progressivism in European and American Thought, 1870–1920*,[16] goes further and actually states in his introduction, "Between 1870 and 1920, two generations of American and European thinkers created a transatlantic community of discourse in philosophy and political theory."[17] He goes on to explain that this new generation of thinkers depended not just on language and logic, but also on action. They struggled with the expansion of the state, and the decreasing importance of the individual within the state. They then thought up their own states until they eventually settled upon changing and refining the one that existed, creating the welfare state.

Most importantly, Kloppenberg notes that the theory of social democracy that emerged in the 1890s transformed socialist and radical doctrines. American social gospel movement followers combined with Fabians, French and German socialists, and other radicals to produce a newer blueprint of revolution. This new revolution would be based on experience, not solely on history. All involved shared an interest in the notion of equality. They wanted all of society to share in the benefits of the new wealth of society. Most importantly, they saw the notion of revolution as a process of

gradual change and reform. They no longer sought violent, immediate destruction and the transformation of the state and society.

Emma Goldman arrived in London in August 1895, lecturing
there, in Leeds, and in Glasgow, Scotland. She shared the platforms
with Louise Michel and other prominent European anarchists. She
met with Peter Kropotkin and Errico Malatesta. As well as being
impressed with Kropotkin's insights on the British working class,
Goldman was struck by the horrors of generational industrial
poverty and was determined to continue to work toward a more
equal society.[18]

In late September, using the name Mrs. E.G. Brady,[19] Goldman
set out for Vienna, to train as a nurse. During her time in Vienna,
while her training as a nurse was of the utmost importance, the
education of the radical Emma Goldman was equally important. It
seems worth noting that Emma Goldman had matured as a radical.
Prison was not something she aspired to just for show. She decided
to travel using Edward Brady's name to ensure that she could move
freely, be less obvious, and avoid problems with the police. She also
decided against making herself conspicuous while in Vienna, deciding not to get involved in protests, preferring instead to avail of all
the cultural and intellectual opportunities that Vienna had to offer.
So as well as attending classes for her nurse's training, she attended the opera and lectures, including those of Sigmund Freud. She
was in careful communication with Austrian anarchists, with whom
she discussed the various changes that were occurring in society.

In November 1896, now a qualified nurse, Goldman returned
to New York and at once began an exhausting schedule of working in the Lower East Side while lecturing around the U.S. As a
midwife Goldman was confronted by the horror of poverty and the
reality of so many women without access to birth control who were
forced into frequent pregnancies. So after two successful lecture tours
in 1897–1898 and 1899, Goldman decided to return to Europe in
November 1899, to pursue her dream of becoming a doctor so that
she could provide the practical help that was needed.

On her way to Zurich, Goldman stopped off in London, where
she spoke at a number of meetings against the Boer War, despite the
warnings of Kropotkin, who feared reprisal by the British establishment. It was in London that she met Hippolyte Havel, a Czech émi-
gré revolutionist, and the two soon became lovers and went to

Paris. Goldman's medical ambitions were quickly forgotten, as there she chose to continue her education, enjoying the variety of Parisian delights. Soon one of her sponsors wrote to her and pointed out that he was wiling to pay for her education as a doctor, not her life as a propagandist in Paris: "I am interested only in E.G. the woman – her ideas have no meaning whatever to me."[20] Goldman, furious, wrote back: "E.G. the woman and her ideas are inseparable. She does not exist for the amusement of upstarts, nor will she permit anybody to dictate to her. Keep the money."[21]

During her time in Paris, Goldman did attend a secret meeting of the Neo-Malthusian Congress, where she met Paul Robin, Madeline Verne, and George Drysdale. The information she learned here, she hoped, would be useful medically on the Lower East Side when she returned. She attended the opera and various concerts and plays while in Paris. She had also planned to attend the Anarchist Congress in Paris, but the French authorities forbade it, and though there were a few small meetings in the houses of a few individuals, the Congress was brief and almost non-existent. Running out of money rapidly, Goldman returned to the U.S. on December 7, 1900.

By the time of her return, Goldman's ideas had been well formed. She was no longer the pro-violent revolutionary that had entered jail in 1893, nor was she simply another revolutionary personality, intent only on creating a rumpus wherever she went. Instead by 1900 she had learned both formally and informally of revolution; she was well read both in American and European thought. She was also well aware of the social context in which she lived: America was full of potential as well as poverty, and America was a place where the potential for change was very real, as this was the land that created revolutionaries and therefore could do so again.

Goldman had no doubt that a revolution was needed in the U.S. Goldman had arrived back to the U.S. at a time of major economic depression. How this revolution was to occur was a bigger question, and it was her various trips to Europe that provided Goldman with the clarity needed to explain all of this.

What Goldman had learned in Europe she was to combine with the very American notion of individual rights, and Henry David Thoreau's notion that "government is best which governs not at all."[22] What she wanted to explain to her new American audience was that, while a revolution was necessary, it did not have to happen suddenly or quickly. Instead revolution could be eventual, evolutionary, and educational. It would create a society, rather than a state that would allow growth and freedom for each individual.

In 1911, Goldman wrote:

> Anarchism then, really stands for the liberation of the human mind from the dominion of religion; the liberation of the human body from the dominion of property; liberation from the shackles and restraint of government. Anarchism stands for social order based on the free grouping of individuals for the purpose of producing real wealth; an order that will guarantee to every human being free access to the earth and full enjoyment of the necessities of individual desires, tastes, and inclinations.[23]

The social change that she deemed necessary had to happen through revolution:

> No real social change has ever come about without a revolution. People are either familiar with their history or they have not yet learned that revolution is thought carried into action.[24]

The question for Goldman was not whether or not a revolution should occur, but instead what form this revolution should take: "I want revolution to be understood as a process of reconstruction, rather than what we believed it to be until now: a process of destruction."[25] Goldman had seen the high cost of violent direct action, and while she would not condemn those who felt this was the only way for change to occur, neither did she endorse it.

> I feel violence in whatever form has and probably never will bring constructive results.[26]

> I hope you know me well enough to know that I do not glory in violence. If I ever believed in taking a human life, no matter how dangerous, how evil, I was entirely cured from it after Sasha's act.[27]

Indeed, a year later Goldman had to go further to condemn violence, when she wrote:

You are right of course when you say that violence is contradictory to Anarchism. As a social philosophy, as a theory of
rights of the individual and the freedom of the collectivity;
Anarchism is the only philosophy, which does not propagate
violence.[28]

Since this new world would have a social order based on the
individual, the key to revolution for Goldman was the individual
with ideas. This individual could then choose to be part of a small
group, which would create a new society created through a new
and vital system of education. "It is only the individual who can
arouse and inspire never the mass."[29] She opposed the notion that
ideas would come from the masses and would be taken by an individual to create a new society. Goldman insisted that the masses
could not be trusted; after all, they were in favour of the vote,
which she insisted changed nothing and improved nothing. She also
noted that public opinion was taken into account by politicians,
particularly Roosevelt, and she insisted: "Public opinion is the
omnipresent tyrant."[30] In the preface to her collection of essays,
knowing that her lack of faith in the masses would be criticized, she
insists: "My lack of faith in the majority is dictated by the faith in
the potentialities of the individual." Later, in the essay "Minorities
Versus Majorities," she explains:

> As a mass its aim has always been to make life uniform, gray,
> and monotonous as the desert. As a mass it will always be the
> annihilator of individuality, of free initiative, of originality. I
> therefore believe with Emerson that "the masses are crude,
> lame, pernicious in their demands and influence, and need not
> to be flattered, but to be schooled. I wish not to concede any-
> thing to them, but to drill, divide, and break them up, and
> draw individuals out of them. Masses! The calamity are the
> masses."[31]

So the question must be asked: how will this revolutionary
change occur in society? After all, was it even possible to totally
change the whole of society, without violence? Goldman argued that
the only way to ensure a transformation of society was through a
slow but definite social process:

Of course you are right when you say social progress is slow. That is to say we think it is slow because we cannot perceive it with our naked eye. We see the progress only when the social forces break loose in a revolutionary manifestation.[32]

Education was the key through which this slow but definite change in society could take place. The fact that Emma Goldman placed the future of the revolution in the hands of education is not something that the press at the time, nor indeed many historians afterwards, have paid enough attention to. Alice Wexler, in her book *Emma Goldman: An Intimate Life,* notes, "Education, not dynamite would lead to revolution."[33] However, nowhere in this book, or indeed in any other, does Wexler expand on this aspect of Goldman's philosophy. Even Paul Avrich, in his book *The Modern School Movement,* notes the role and impact of the Modern School Movement, but somehow even he loses sight of the importance of Goldman's insistence on education as the key.

In that controversial essay "Minorities versus Majorities," Goldman clearly states:

> The living, vital truth of social and economic well-being will become a reality only through the zeal, courage, the non-compromising determination of intelligent minorities, and not through the mass.
>   This is the key "the intelligent minorities" which would band together, educate and then create a new society based on the notion of the rights and freedom of the individual as being of paramount importance.[34]

There was a very simple reason as to why education was the key to the creation of the new societal structure: "the child has no traditions to overcome."[35] As early as 1899, Goldman had spoken to an audience of Italian miners in Illinois of "the necessity of the unhampered development of the child,"[36] but it was her trips to Europe that firmed her belief in education.

Two people and one institution had influenced Goldman here: Paul Robin (1837–1912), Louise Michel (1830–1905), and the Modern School established in Paris. Her realization that education was the key component in any revolution was a position that

Goldman arrived at slowly. Goldman had been impressed by Michel's initial refusal to accept a position as a schoolteacher, as it would have meant that she needed to take an oath to Napoleon III. Instead Michel set up her own school, emphasizing the need for students to think for themselves. It eventually closed due to police harassment, and Michel later moved to London where she opened another school, only for it to be closed by police when bomb-making equipment was found in the basement. Michel was not implicated and continued a career of speech-making, urging the necessity of school reform as a means to revolution.

In 1900, Goldman visited the school established by Paul Robin and was impressed with the ideals Robin worked and lived under. Robin claimed that so-called facts taught to children under the guise of education were nothing more than the state's method of control.[37] He also insisted that the state continued that control of all people by ensuring that the only possibilities available to children were those available to their parents. The children suffered because of the so-called sins of their fathers. Yet while Goldman was thrilled with what Robin was trying to achieve, she was still critical of his insistences on using the regular textbooks in the classroom setting.[38] By contrast, Francisco Ferrer was later to produce 150,000 of textbooks, published specifically for his own schools. These books were designed to be both scientific and rational. Nevertheless it became clear that what was needed initially was a safe, healthy place where children could be given the opportunity to learn regardless of socio-economic background:

> Proper economic and social environment, the breath and
> freedom of nature, healthy exercise, love and sympathy, and
> above all, a deep understanding for the needs of the child –
> these would destroy the cruel, unjust and criminal stigma
> imposed on the young.[39]

It was in Paris in 1907 that Goldman became acquainted with Sebastian Faure (1858–1942). Goldman had heard him speak in 1900 on an earlier visit and was impressed with his personal decision to leave the church and "emancipate himself from all authority, whether in heaven or upon earth."[40] What Faure had succeeded in doing was taking twenty-four orphan children, discarding the more traditional methods of education, and replacing it with a system that emphasized the need for each child's opinion to be valued and for each question to be answered with honesty.

The result of this was remarkable to Goldman, and she noted the harmony that existed in the schools. Indeed, as Faure explained to her:

> It is surprising how frank and affectionate our little ones are to each other. The harmony between themselves and the adults at La Ruche is highly encouraging. We should feel at fault if the children were to fear or honor us merely because we are their elders. We leave nothing undone to gain their confidence and love; that accomplished, understanding will replace duty; confidence, fear; and affection, severity.[41]

Goldman remarked later:

> My visit to La Ruche[42] was a valuable experience that made me realize how much could be done, even under the present system, in the way of libertarian education. To build the man and woman of the future, to unshackle the soul of the child – what grander task for those who, like Sebastian Faure, are pedagogues, not by the mere grace of a college degree, but innately born with the gift to create, as the poet or artist is?[43]

With this new fervour, Goldman returned to the U.S., and in the April edition of *Mother Earth* wrote an essay entitled "The Child and Its Enemies." Here she outlined the variety of forces which come together to force personality, individuality, and thought from a child. All the child is taught are "Facts and Data."[44] The result of this is to continue a society where gradual but persistent destruction of the individual is prominent:

> Since every effort in our educational life seems to be directed toward making of the child a being foreign to itself, it must of necessity produce individuals foreign to one another, and in everlasting antagonism with each other.[45]

For Goldman, then, the solution was that education should insist "upon the free growth and development of the innate forces and tendencies of the child. In this way alone can we hope for a free community, which shall make interference and coercion of human growth impossible."[46] For Goldman all that the accepted system of education did was to maintain the existing "system of economic and political dependence ... by an inert mass of humanity, drilled and pounded into absolute uniformity, and that the school today represents the most efficient medium to accomplish that end."[47]

Goldman hoped that this new system of education would achieve the following in the United States: first she insisted it would draw out as opposed to drive in, a fountain of knowledge and curiosity; it would allow the child to learn and grown at his or her individual pace; and that the teacher would "channel" rather than dictate. Second, the new school system must be *libertarian*. By this she meant that there must be neither rules nor pressure of any sort coming from the teachers. Finally, the school must develop each individual in a harmonious fashion, so that the child can develop and blend freely with other people and with nature.[48] All of this would lead to a child-centred curriculum, in which morality was not imposed, but instead options were chosen and realized.

The person to whom Goldman would look to enable this revolution was Francisco Ferrer, described by Goldman in her article "Francisco Ferrer and the Modern School" as "a rebel."[49] Ferrer was born in Allela, near Barcelona, Spain in 1849. While his parents were practicing Catholics, his uncle, a freethinker, heavily influenced him, and soon Ferrer became involved in a failed coup and was forced into exile in Paris, France.

In France he became a Spanish teacher in a new form of libertine education being offered. One of his students, Jeanne Ernestine Meunie, died, leaving him a substantial amount of money, which convinced him to return to Spain. On September 8, 1901, Ferrer opened *la Escuela Moderna*. The aim of the school was to educate all classes of people in a rational, secular, and non-coercive setting. The purpose of the schools was "to create solid minds, capable of forming their own rational convictions on every subject."[50] One of the more important aspects of the schools was to make sure that there was no "duality of character in any individual – one which sees and appreciates truth and goodness and one which follows evil."[51]

These openly anti-clerical schools grew rapidly, and the Catholic Church in Spain grew more opposed to them. Pressure on Ferrer and the schools increased when one of the employees of the schools, Mateo Morral, threw a bomb at King Alphonso XIII's wedding party. Ferrer was arrested, and though he was later released due to insufficient evidence, the schools were permanently closed.

In 1909, political unrest in Spain increased, and the government's way of dealing with the protests was to introduce martial law. Ferrer was arrested, accused of conspiring against the government, and tried in a hurry, with false evidence and forced confessions being used. He was executed by firing squad on October 13, 1909.

What attracted Goldman to the ideals of Ferrer was his combination of ideals and action as he attempted to take education out of the control of the most powerful institution in Spain – the Catholic Church – secularize it, and allow children to think and evaluate for themselves. What Ferrer managed to achieve in a relatively short space of time was, according to Goldman and other anarchists such as Voltairine DeCleyre, to lay "the primary foundation for the overthrow of such portions of the State organization as exist by reason of the general ignorance of people."[52] De Cleyre continues, "The Social Order of Spain ought to be overthrown, will be overthrown; and Ferrer was doing a mighty work in that direction." It was the hope of Emma Goldman that Ferrer's school system, once established in the U.S., would achieve this dramatic end.

For an anarchist rebellion to truly become a revolution, what was needed for Goldman was "that the solution that evil can be brought about only through the consideration of *every phase* [italics hers] of life – individual, as well as the collective; the internal, as well as the external phases."[53] The reason that anarchy can succeed is that "Anarchism is therefore the teacher of the unity of life; not merely in nature, but in man."[54] What Goldman sought was a method of educating people wherein they would learn to think and discern for themselves the ideals of freedom and choice in every aspect of their lives. From this sort of system, which begins with teaching children, there would come a true American anarchist revolution. At the Second Anarchist Congress, in Amsterdam in 1907, Goldman declared her reason for needing to change schools:

> The Public School! The colleges and other institutions of
> learning, are they not models of organization, offering the
> people fine opportunities for instruction? Far from it. The
> school, more than any other institution, is a veritable barrack,

where the human mind is drilled and manipulated into submission to various social and moral spooks, and thus fitted to
continue our system of exploitation and oppression.[55]

Despite Goldman's initial feelings of helplessness upon hearing
that Ferrer had been executed,[56] she recovered and soon she was
organizing meetings and demonstrations against the Spanish government. By the spring of 1910, various peoples who had all been
deeply affected by the death of Ferrer had decided to come together to form the Francisco Ferrer Association. On June 3, 1910, the
first meeting took place. A variety of people spoke that night on
how best to commemorate Ferrer. Among those who spoke were
Alexander Berkman and Emma Goldman. Berkman had already
started the Modern Sunday school, the first Ferrer School in
America. He suggested that a man like Ferrer would not want a
monument; instead, he suggested setting up a series of Modern
Schools in the U.S. where children would be encouraged to self-
educate, "forming their own ideas and imbibing natural notions of
everything about them."[57] Berkman shared with Goldman a belief
that education was indeed a key:

> Just in proportion that the young generation grows more
> enlightened and libertarian, will we approach a freer society
> ... Can we indeed expect a generation reared in the atmos-
> phere of a suppressive, authoritarian educational regime to
> form the cornerstone of a free self reliant humanity?[58]

Of the twenty-two charter members of the Ferrer Association,
half were what Paul Avrich calls "active anarchists."[59] Emma
Goldman was not only the best known, but also the inspiration to
all and the most active. Indeed, Harry Kelly was later to write that
it was Goldman who "vitalized" the Association and ensured
whatever successes it did achieve.

Goldman was at the centre of all the initial protests to the
Spanish government against the arrest of Ferrer, and later at the
forefront of the protests against his execution. On her constant
tours, she spoke regularly and passionately about Ferrer, giving two
particular speeches: "Ferrer and the Modern School" and
"Francisco Ferrer: His Life and Work." She also persuaded audiences in all parts of the country to financially support the setting
up of Modern Schools in the United States.

The fact that a group composed mainly of anarchists got together to set up the Ferrer School in 1911 in New York is not a surprise. After all, Paul Avrich, in his book *The Modern School Movement*, notes, "No other movement assigned education a more prominent place."[60] Even William Godwin, the historical father figure of the modern anarchist movement, noted that the mainstream school system was "an instrument of domination in the hands of the ruling class."[61] Michael Bakunin insisted, "Children belong neither to their parents nor to society. They belong to themselves and their future liberty."[62]

The initial role played by both Goldman and Berkman in the Association was that of organizer. They were the people responsible for the finding the buildings, publishing the necessary books, and finding the pupils and teachers. Goldman had been particularly successful in raising money for the new school system by constantly lecturing on Ferrer on her lecture tours on the West Coast. Thus many of the people who were attracted to the school were initially drawn to the movement through Goldman.[63] For instance, the New York School's first director, Bayard Botesen, was enticed into the position through Goldman, despite her upfront warning that he could expect neither "salary nor glory."[64] Other prominent members of the school included Hutchins Hapgood and later Eugene O'Neill.

Establishing and opening a school was only part of the battle. What was more important to Goldman was how the school was set up, its everyday organization, and the main people involved with the students. It was also of vital importance to Goldman that the school not just be something that was used by day; instead she saw it as a centre of education. This was a place where adults, as well as children, from all walks of life could come to learn and discuss. This school needed to be a revolutionary centrepoint.

With this Goldmanesque philosophy in mind, the U.S. Ferrer Schools, for all their differences, had a lot in common. Firstly, local branches of the Ferrer Association administered them all, so each school's needs could be adapted to local needs and conditions. Secondly, teaching was through practice and not theory. So the emphasis was on crafts, physical education, and nature studies. Thirdly, all pursued the ideal of educating children as well as adults. Thus each school building could serve as a centre of radical social causes. Most had classes in Esperanto, the international language. Contacts between schools were frequent, with exchanges of

teachers occurring often. Ironically, just like Ferrer's school in
Spain, the Modern Ferrer Schools in the United States were heavi-
ly criticized by the churches, and in particular the Roman Catholic
Church.

What was needed from these schools to create a new and different American was an appreciation of American thinkers who wrote
in praise of the individual, particularly Emerson and Thoreau.
Goldman's friend John Dewey also influenced her. Dewey's attempts at educational reform have been described as "one of the
most significant cultural revolutions of the time."[65]

As well as the more obvious work done by Goldman, which
included raising money, she was also responsible for creating an
American anarchist educational organization, which included recent immigrants as well as Americans. This in itself was an achieve-
ment. Laurence Veysey, in his book *The Communal Experience:
Anarchist and Mystical Counter-Cultures in America,* notes that
Goldman in particular drew many of these native-born Americans
to anarchist culture.

What Goldman had successfully created was the ultimate anarchist hybrid organization. This was American anarchism, made up
of those American-born, upper-class, and well-educated. It was
also an organization that was made up of newly arrived immigrants, for whom anarchism was the only way to achieve their
dream of a stateless society where each individual was free to live
in harmony with nature and each other. American anarchy always
had a slightly disjointed appearance, in that it was made up of so
many who were so different in terms of class and religion. Nevertheless, the School was a real anarchist circle who wanted to
achieve the ultimate change in society, albeit through education
and not through the bomb. The impact of this new school and system of education was immediate. The school became a successful
centre of radical education, filled with radical ideas and people.

So once a system of education was successfully established – at
least in numbers, the Modern Schools were successful – the question then must be asked: what did the society that Goldman wanted to create look like?

THE NEW SOCIETY

Alice Wexler, in *Emma Goldman: An Intimate Life,* points out that
"the essential basis of [Goldman's] politics was opposition to the

state."[66] Wexler goes on to explain that, for Goldman, this meant opposition to any form of centralized authority, to all forms of big business, and to any laws made by governments that impacted people's day-to-day lives, including the draft and censorship.[67] Goldman opposed all forms of parliamentary democracy, as well as dictatorships. For Goldman, an individual's rights were lost in a parliamentary democracy as much as in any other form of government. To this end, Goldman urged people not to vote in elections, since "the vote was simply a means for the transference of the rights of the people to the control of the leaders."

> Education and agitation are the means. Whenever the people shall have arrived at a knowledge of the true principles governing harmonious social relations, they will put them into practice, without the ballot box ... correct ideas must precede correct action.[68]

Goldman opposed the ownership of private property by small owners as a way to create an ideal society, arguing that ownership was intrinsically evil. Goldman went so far in her opposition to centralized government as to oppose even a state welfare system for the poor, as well as nationalization of either land or property. Both of these, Goldman argued, would create nothing more than a stronger government. Goldman rejected parliamentary reform as a means to a lesser form of government; instead, throughout her life she insisted on complete and total revolutionary change. Yet the question remains" what did Goldman see in place of a parliament?

From Kropotkin, Goldman took the idea that human beings are naturally social. The problem for society and the individual is that man-made laws have taken away freedom from humankind. Removal of what Goldman referred to as "false forms of government" would allow the emergence of natural forms of social cooperation and mutual aid. This, in turn, would allow for the establishment of local organizations, which would set up schools, hospitals, libraries, and cooperatives. All of this would result in "a social order based on the free grouping of individuals for the purpose of producing real social wealth; an order that will guarantee to every human being free access to the earth and full enjoyment of the necessities of life, according to individual desires, tastes and inclinations."[69]

A second and equally important part of this local society as envisioned by Goldman was the absence of any type of organized religion. Alice Wexler goes so far as to describe Goldman's opposition to religion as "almost an obsession."[70] Indeed, after reading many of Goldman lectures and essays, this comment does seem valid.

Goldman lectured often on the moral, social, economic, and social benefits of atheism. She described Christianity as useful "in the training of slaves."[71] With heaven set out as the reward for the working classes, the notion of responsibility for the poor in present-day society is removed, as is the idea of paying workers fair and just wages. Nevertheless, Goldman's opposition to religion was not as simple as Wexler suggests.

Goldman's objection to religion was not an objection to the notion of believing, but to the notion of socially organized and rewarded injustice. Her own example of why organized religious practice equates with injustice is found in her essay "The Hypocrisy of Puritanism," where she explains that Anthony Comstock, the Postmaster General, was capable of "neither truth nor sincerity."[72] In the name of organized religion and moral guardian, he has, she states, declared himself to be the standard-bearer of American morals, sneaking into the private life of people and proving himself to be in the same league as the Russian secret police. The injustice is clear; he did away with many of the basic rights of the individual outlined by the Bill of Rights.

Religion, for Goldman, should not be the instigator of morals because those outside the accepted circles suffer, as do art and literature, which have to hold themselves to the false standards of those who know nothing about them. According to Goldman, women also suffer under religion. Single women are judged harshly for choosing to be sexually free, while married women are denied birth control and have to suffer physically and emotionally at the hands of their husbands. According to Goldman, the only thing created by religion is prostitution, censorship, prohibition, and generally unfair and ill-thought-out laws.

CRIME AND PUNISHMENT

One of the greatest questions anarchists faced was the notion of crime and punishment. After all if they really believed that human beings were intrinsically good, then there was no need for punishment, as there would be no crime. Such was the importance of this topic to anarchists that articles on this subject by Goldman, Berkman, and Kropotkin can be found, as can a series of letters between Berkman and Goldman.

In the August 1906 issue of *Mother Earth*, Berkman described prisons as revenge in an institution. He points out that those people being punished are taught nothing. Instead they are deprived of all human rights, with their natural impulses suppressed. The result of prisons is that people are outcasts, and ultimately the prisoners become merciless themselves. Prisons are expensive, and the fact that the number of people entering prisons is rising means prisons have failed, and will continue to fail.

Peter Kropotkin, writing in October 1913, describes prisons as "degrading," an "injustice," and as nothing but an institution seeking "revenge." So he asks, "are prisons answering their purpose, which is that of diminishing the number of anti-social acts?" His conclusion is a simple but definite no. The answer, he insists, is schools and universities.

Goldman herself wrote on this topic in 1911, in an essay entitled "Prisons: A Social Crime and Failure." Here she makes it clear that prisons are not a social protection. They teach nothing, she argues, except how to create more criminals. Society must, she insists, get over the instinct to strike back.

To halt crime, Goldman instead suggests the following. Firstly, she urges that we become aware of the potential for crime that is in all human beings. Then we will immediately begin to understand as opposed to condemning. Secondly, within prisons it is vital that prisons have the potential to earn a wage and to learn, and so to have skills on their release that can serve both themselves and society. She also insists that wages both inside and outside prisons be the kind that a person can live on. Otherwise, the prisoner, once released, will return to a life of crime, while the worker will soon feel that she has no choice but to choose a life of crime.

Ultimately for Goldman, there is no real way to solve the problem of crime other than to overhaul the whole of society and reform it in an anarchist way, so that justice for all is embedded within societal structures. However, it was never a debate that could be finished with so quickly. Faced often with man's inhumanity to man as a real part of life, this debate about where crime begins and what to do with the criminal was one that Goldman and Berkman continued with throughout their lives.

In 1928, while Berkman was in Paris working on a book he

hoped would explain "definite PLANS and SUGGESTIONS [capitals his] as to 1) how to bring about the revolution; 2) how to carry the revolution on; 3) how to develop out of the revolution anarchist conditions,"[73] he quickly became troubled by three complex questions:

> At this side I have come to problems that cannot be solved satisfactorily. For instance:
>
> (1) Has the revolution the right to defend itself? Then what is to be done to active enemies and counter-revolutionists? It leads logically to prison or camp.
>
> (2) If there is some trouble somewhere – a murderer or raper, etc., has been caught by the crowd – will you let mob spirit prevail? Or is it not better to create opportunity for a hearing for the accused? That means tribunes and courts and police. And what should the courts do? It is no use having them if they cannot restrain the further activities of the guilty man. It means prison.
>
> (3) Given an example – what is likely to happen: People starting to make a pogrom in Russia; or whites trying to lynch a Negro in America (this during the revolutionary epoch) – shall we let it go at that? Is not active interference necessary? By whom? By the "people"? But suppose those present are afraid to interfere. It means again that armed force is necessary in such cases, even against the mob. And the leaders of the mob who persist in exciting race or other hatred – should they be permitted to go on?[74]

Berkman goes on to express his frustration: " I fear there is no answer to these questions ... It comes to prison again. But once we begin with prisons, there is no end to it."[75]

Goldman's reply four days later shows her surprise and even her frustration toward Berkman, as she insists on reminding him of the importance of their work and their philosophical debate, and yet also reminding him that some questions simply have no answers. Nevertheless, she does insist that such are the importance of those three questions that they are worth answering. She insists that the revolution does have a right to defend itself. Though violence never solves anything – nor does it bring about what Goldman refers to as "constructive results" – violence will happen, and so a violent defense is fine.

True and real freedom of speech, Goldman insists, will solve the problem of so-called "active enemies." The only reason behind many acts of terrorism is that the "terrorists" lack a sufficient outlet for their complaints. So-called free societies like the U.S. do not really allow freedom of speech, and so frustration leads to violence and terror. In this new society, as envisaged by Goldman and Berkman, there will be no "active enemies," as their complaints will be listened to and dealt with.

Regarding criminals, Goldman responds: "if you are attacked by a robber and you have a weapon, you will use it. I see no inconsistency in that at all." While Goldman agrees that rape is a particular horrible crime and one that needs to be dealt with in a particular way, by setting aside a place and classes for rapists, nevertheless in no case must prison become a method used to deal with these or any other issues.

> I therefore say that you must set your face sternly against the very idea of prisons; the whole revolution would be utterly futile, if such terrible institutions as prisons, institutions which have proven a failure in the system we want to get rid of are again established.[76]

Yet as Goldman's ideas expanded, real life also had to be dealt with, and from her release in prison until her deportation in 1919, her personal life would cause her much pain and antagonism.

PERSONAL LIFE

Once Goldman was released from jail, she emerged as a personality. While working as a nurse on the East Side she was also a draw for the parties and evening companies of many of the families of established America. Goldman got involved in the theatre; at one stage she got the necessary financial backing for the Russian star Alla Nazimova to tour New York, Boston, and Chicago. This allowed Goldman to mingle "with Barrymore, Roosevelts, Harvard professors and well-placed Friends of Russian Freedom and periodically revealed herself to be the dangerous Emma Goldman, to the delight of her hosts."[77] These contacts and demands for speaking appearances in the drawing rooms of bohemian New York allowed Goldman to write, and to speak less about the revolution and more about drama, art, and literature. Her magazine *Mother Earth* differentiated itself from other left-wing publications at the time, as she encouraged contributions from prominent poets and writers, and it discussed issues of the arts, rather than issues with government.

When Goldman was first released from jail, she began an intense relationship with the Australian Edward Brady. He became a comfort zone for her after the pace of her relationship with Berkman. Brady, however, believed that a woman's place was motherhood. He even told her that her relationship with the anarchist movement was simply her searching for motherhood. As Goldman refused to give up anarchy, the two split in 1897.

While Goldman had a series of relationships, it was her relationship with Ben Reitman that helped her take advantage of the publicity surrounding her. Ben Reitman was born in St. Paul, Minnesota, in 1879, but grew up in Chicago. Having been a hobo, he returned to Chicago, where he initially worked at Polyclinic Laboratory, and then attended the College of Physicians and Surgeons in Chicago, where he received his medial degree.

As a doctor, Reitman became known as the "Hobo Doctor" as he provided medical care to the hobos, prostitutes, and homeless people of Chicago. In 1908 he and Goldman met, and the two began an intense relationship that, though it officially lasted eight years, had lifelong repercussions.

When Goldman met Reitman, it was two years after Berkman had been released from jail, having served fourteen years. Berkman and Goldman met in Detroit at the train station. Goldman was stunned, unable to move after seeing him. Just as Goldman's short jail term had changed her, Berkman's more considerable time had also changed him. He finally understood the reality of being poor, and the complex lives that people lived in order to survive, and just how complicated it was going to be to change anything.

While the political differences between Goldman and Berkman were many, the personal differences were more difficult and awkward. Berkman had spent long periods of time in solitary confinement; upon his release, he was severely traumatized, unable to spend any time in crowds without severe panic attacks. He had night terrors, and could not bear to share a bed, which put strain on his relationship with Goldman. Financially, he could not support himself; he tried to open a print shop, but he had to close it as he could not afford the union rates of the people who worked

there. He became frustrated when Goldman helped him financially, complaining that she was overbearing, and he hated being treated like a child. Goldman later wrote about the time as "the contrast
between his dream-world of 1892 and my reality of 1906."[78]

Goldman and Reitman met in Chicago after Goldman had been
banned from speaking by the police. Reitman offered her a place to
speak, saying that she would come on stage as an unnamed anarchist speaker. Reitman showed his colours and his liking of publicity early, and actually leaked word to the police and press that
Goldman was going to speak. The result was chaos that could have
been worse, had Goldman not urged the crowd not to react to the
physical tactics used by the police.

Reitman's role in Goldman's life, and the anarchist movement,
was established that night. It was Reitman who organized tours
and publicity for Goldman. He gave press interviews, charged for
meetings, and set out a schedule for her that was demanding but
raised an already high profile. What was different about Reitman-
organized tours is that he booked so-called respectable halls.
Instead of allowing publicity to happen through word of mouth or
the small left-wing press, Reitman advertised in the mainstream
newspapers, gave interviews, and persuaded Goldman to give interviews, not caring whether the reviews were positive or negative.
Reitman's ability to create publicity was noted during Goldman's
1910 tour, the first organized by Reitman, and her most successful
up to that point. She visited thirty-seven cities in twenty-five states.
She gave 120 lectures, sold over ten thousand pieces of literature,
and took in over three hundred subscriptions to *Mother Earth*
magazine. Goldman collected over four thousand dollars from admission tickets and over one thousand more from the literature
sold. For Reitman, publicity was all-important, and there was no
such thing as bad publicity. Even Goldman's talks changed; as well
as the fact that she now talked about a variety of topics, her
"warm-up" acts were no longer other speakers but cabaret. Then,
before Goldman spoke, Reitman went out and asked the audience
to give money and to buy anarchist (Goldman's) literature. Reitman saw anarchy as a business and he made it a successful one.

Ben Reitman was not always successful, though. Margaret
Anderson in *My Thirty Years War* describes Reitman as "the fan-
tastic Dr. Reitman (who wasn't so bad if you could hastily drop all
your ideas as to how human beings should look and act)."[79] He did

not see the need to bathe, and his nails and hair were a constant source of displeasure. He enjoyed shocking people, particularly through his telling of crude jokes. A bigger and more important factor, however, was that he did, on more than one occasion, embezzle funds. Goldman, furious, stopped him having anything to do with the financial aspect of the tours; nevertheless, she did not fire him as the two had already become lovers. Goldman declared that Reitman aroused a "Torrent of mental passion I never thought any man could arouse in me. I responded shamelessly, to its primitive call, its naked beauty, its ecstatic joy."[79]

Margaret Anderon was not the only person who objected to Reitman. Berkman quickly complained about the type of show Reitman created. He did not trust Reitman with the finances, with good reason, and hated what he was doing to the serious message of the revolution.

By 1911 Goldman and Reitman's relationship had begun to wane. Reitman was neither an intellectual nor an anarchist, and did not enjoy or want to have any part in Goldman's activism. While he enjoyed his share of the spotlight through his connection to Goldman, he remained a Christian, even having Sunday School classes in the same rooms as the anarchists held meetings, and was known to ask them to pray with him. While Goldman defended some of his actions through his right to free speech, it was obvious that the intensity of their relationship was ending, not just because of Reitman's many sexual encounters besides Goldman, but also because he wanted to marry and have a family. Reitman wanted a home for himself and Goldman alone. Goldman did not. At this point, they were sharing accommodation with many people from the organization and many others who just stayed for various periods of time. With Reitman threatening to return to Chicago, Goldman found a house that they could share, though finances were extremely tight. Within weeks the two were fighting even more, and Reitman left the house to return to Chicago to spend time with his mother. Once again, the two decided to join together to begin a lecture tour, but political events were drive them apart, then and forever.

On April 20, 1914, the Colorado Fuel and Iron Company, owned by the Rockefeller family, retaliated against striking miners by setting fire to a tent where their families were staying. The

National Guard, who had been brought in by the mine owners to deal with the strikers, killed twenty people, including eleven children. Known as the Ludlow Massacre, it sparked outrage in major cities throughout the United States. While some protests were organized outside the Rockefeller offices in New York City, a group of anarchists, including Alexander Berkman, decided to protest outside the Rockefeller home in Tarrytown. While there, they seem to have come up with a plan to blow up the house in retaliation.

What seems to have happened next is that, in its planning stage, the bomb blew up prematurely in an apartment in Harlem, killing three men and one woman. Goldman, who was on the West Coast at the time, knew nothing about the plan or the event. Berkman, on the other hand, does seem to have had some involvement.

While Berkman never publicly acknowledged any involvement or knowledge of the event, Avrich, in *The Modern School Movement*, makes clear that Berkman was involved, basing his conclusions from testimony gathered from associates of Berkman's at the time. Berkman organized the funerals of those killed, and in the July 1914 issue of *Mother Earth*, he explains again that, in certain circumstances, violence is necessary. This was one such moment for him, as "while labor gathers this power, its success will be hastened, its courage strengthened by tempering oppression with dynamite."[80] Alice Wexler finds "it difficult to believe that the older, more experienced Berkman – having lived through the disastrous plot of Homestead – would have masterminded a bomb plot that risked the lives of young inexperienced comrades while he himself remained in the background,"[81] Avrich, on the other hand, is clear in his opinion that, for Berkman, the Ludlow Massacre,

> with its Pinkertons and militia and killing of workers, was a repetition of Homestead, and Rockefeller another Frick. Although twenty-two years had since elapsed, all the indignation came rushing back, and all the determination to retaliate.[82]

The closeness of Ludlow and Homestead, the fact that Berkman never really got over his jail experience, and its apparent futility, his depression, and the reaction of people protesting on the streets of major American cites could have meant that he jumped into action, deciding that there would be public understanding of propaganda by deed in this case. The three people killed were probably putting the bomb together, and if Avrich is correct that Berkman was indeed the "Chief Strategist," it is possible that he was going to be the one who would bring the bomb to the Rockefeller household in Tarrytown. His silence about his own role was legally wise, and his lack of denial is perhaps his guilty statement.

In her autobiography, Goldman claims to have been horrified at the events, and equally disturbed by the editorials that appeared in *Mother Earth*. But when Ben Reitman wrote to Goldman and expressed his horror at the events, Berkman's eulogies, and the editorials in *Mother Earth*, Goldman defended Berkman, and even the actual act:

> I absolutely must insist that my position is not against violence and never will be unless I become weakminded. When I said the Lexington affair was to be regretted, I only meant that the place was ill and stupidly chosen.[83]

Reitman, though, was very uneasy about the events and the fact that his association with the anarchists implicated him. He had spent time in jail for various offenses, but never any long period of time, and he really did not want to spend any more time there. Reitman began to spend more and more time in Chicago, supposedly to visit his mother, but he had also began an affair with Anna Martindale, whom he had met the year before. For financial reasons, Goldman had begun searching for a much smaller place to live and to work, and for a time she and Reitman played the game of still being dedicated to each other. Eventually, in the summer of 1916, Reitman admitted to Goldman that their relationship was over, which was hardly a surprise to either of them. Reitman married Martindale soon after. Though Reitman and Goldman still communicated throughout the years and even collaborated on some political issues, particularly relating to birth control, the relationship was strained and would never recover, even to the point of friendship.

However, in 1916, Goldman's serious legal issues, which would eventually lead to her deportation, began. Like most anarchists and left-wing activists, she opposed the First World War, and so she was spending most of her time giving speeches dissuading young men from joining the army. Up to this point nearly all of Goldman's arrests had been for nuisance acts, such being a suspicious person and lecturing on birth control. However, on June 15, 1917, she was arrested on charges of conspiracy to violate the Draft Act, with the legal backing of the Espionage Act. She pleaded not guilty and was released on bail of $10,000. The newspapers were full of stories that this money had been paid by German agents, which was not the case.

She was found guilty and sentenced to two years in the federal penitentiary at Jefferson City, Missouri. Goldman appealed the case to the Supreme Court, but it failed and she was returned to Missouri to serve her sentence.

DEPORTATION

On Saturday, September 27, 1919, Emma Goldman left Missouri Prison. She signed papers at the Federal Building in Jefferson City and then proceeded to Chicago, accompanied by her niece Stella Ballantine, by train. It had been her fifteenth prison term. She was tired and needed rest, but what she did not take into account was the outcry among the American public for the deportation of radicals.

From Chicago, the two women traveled to Rochester where Goldman was able to meet with her mother. From there, Goldman, along with her sister Helena, Helena's daughter Minnie, and Ballantine, went to New York, where they met with Alexander Berkman. He had also spent time in jail, in Atlanta, and had at this time also returned to New York City. They all moved into Ballantine's Greenwich Village apartment, where Goldman and Berkman immediately tried to resume their political activities.

Personally, for each of the people, life was chaotic and crowded. Helena was still grieving after the deaths of her husband Jacob Hochstein and her son David, who had been killed in France during the war. Berkman's nightmares, which had begun after his first term in prison, had now returned, which made him restless and irritable. Goldman herself was suffering from severe dental pain, but felt she had to be the one looking after everyone else.

Throughout this time, Goldman and Berkman were under surveillance by federal officials who were looking for information they could use to deport her. As well as following her and taking notes at every speech she made, the Justice Department even managed to have an agent employed by Berkman and Goldman as a secretary. With the mountains of information the Department of Justice had gathered and with the 1918 law passed through Congress allowing for the deportation of naturalized immigrants on charges that they belonged to any organization that advocated revolution or acts of sabotage against the government, a hearing was set for October 27, 1919, which would determine Goldman's legal status in the country.

Goldman's and Berkman's immigration statuses were very different. Berkman had never become an American citizen, and so after a hearing held in Atlanta, and since he refused to fight for his right to stay in the country, his deportation was almost assured. Goldman, on the other hand, wanted to stay. While she had not applied for citizenship, she claimed that through her marriage to Jacob Kersner, who was a citizen, her status should have been automatic. Her father had become a naturalized citizen in 1894, but as Emma Goldman was already over twenty-one, that gave her no legal status. But there were two problems with her marriage to Kersner as the basis for citizenship: first, Kersner had been denaturalized in 1908, which invalidated Goldman's position, and second, there was a question as to whether or not their marriage had any legal standing. It had been a religious service, but it was unclear if the necessary civil paperwork had been filed.

Unknown to Goldman and her legal team, a young and ambitious J. Edgar Hoover had been planning and take care of details to ensure that Goldman and Berkman would be deported. It was Hoover who had organized the arrest of Berkman as he had walked out of jail in Atlanta, with Hoover even conducting some of the questioning himself. Worried that a St. Louis jury might be sympathetic to Goldman, he delayed her arrest until she got to New York City, where he felt a jury would be more than likely to deport her.[84]

When Goldman got to New York, all the legal issues were in place: she was arrested, she was not a citizen, she had been arrested just two years previously for obstructing the draft, and finally, Hoover had the edited version of the Czolgosz transcript ready for the trial. There was no legal means to keep Goldman in the United States.

On October 27, 1919, on Ellis Island, the hearing as to whether or not Emma Goldman would be allowed to stay in the United States began. The government offered forty-four speeches of hers as proof of her anarchist beliefs. Goldman was also questioned, but each time simply declined to answer.

That night she and some friends had a dinner at the Brevoort Hotel, where people paid just over five dollars to have dinner and listen to a speech given by Goldman. Goldman was determined to use the press to her advantage, issuing a statement insisting that these proceedings were no better than Tsarist Russia or the Spanish Inquisition. Knowing that there were Department of Justice spies at the dinner, Goldman promised, "To the Department of Justice men present I wish to say for their benefit that I am going to continue preaching revolution, as long as I am in the U.S. and out of jail."[85]

Hoover was furious after reading the report the next morning and after hearing that Goldman had planned a speaking tour before the end of the proceedings against her. He advised the Department of Justice to speed up the hearing and proceedings against her.

Goldman did manage to give speeches in the Midwest, but on November 26, her deportation was ordered and on November 29, Anthony Caminetti, the Commissioner for Immigration, Hoover's superior, denied any further time and ordered her deportation.

Goldman was not hopeful that any further appeal could be won and immediately began collecting supplies and money necessary for life elsewhere. On December 5, 1919, she and Berkman surrendered to authorities at Ellis Island. Goldman tried one last appeal, arguing that the denaturalization of Jacob Kersner was invalid as it had occurred after his death. The truth was that neither she nor any of her legal team had any proof of this, and it was quickly established that Kernser was, in fact, alive when the denaturalization happened. On December 12, the Supreme Court denied Berkman a stay, but Goldman was granted one week. She, in the end, declined the appeal and instead prepared to leave. She wrote letters to friends and consoled herself with the idea that "I go in the consciousness that I have done my work well or our enemies would not hate me so much."[86]

So early on Sunday, December 21, 1919, watched by Caminetti, William Flynn of the Justice Department, J. Edgar Hoover, and a host of people from the press, Emma Goldman, Alexander Berkman, and 247 others set sail for the Soviet Union, on the SS *Buford*. Hoover had now established his reputation within government circles as the person responsible for the deportation of Emma Goldman, and she had been forced out of the United States, to be allowed back only for a few weeks in 1933. Any attempt at her return was blocked forever by Hoover.

CHAPTER SIX

Nowhere and No One

The Jewish women who are "flame bearers" carry a hidden tradition that proposes to augment a patriarchal tradition by restoring spiritual authority to Jewish women. Believing in the power handed down to them by matriarchs, the young American women of the novel help one another to transmit it.
–Janet Handler Burstein, *Writing Mothers, Writing Daughters*, 172

To me one of the greatest delusions is the notion that writing is a joy. (It maybe to some as interjected by my impetuous secretary – damn her –but is not to most.) In fact, some of the greatest writers have suffered agony of spirit during the process. I may not have greatest in common with them but, by Jesus, I've got the agony.[1]

From the time Goldman was deported from the United States in 1919 to her decision to finally begin writing her autobiography in 1928, her life was a series of constant geographical changes, as well as idealism found, dismantled, and demolished. Along with the other deportees on the *Buford*, she arrived in Russia in 1920, hoping to take part in the new society being established there. Arriving there she was greeted a band, which played "The Internationale," and by various Bolshevik figures. Goldman declared, "This is the greatest day of my life. I once found political freedom in America. Now the doors are closed there to free thinkers, and the enemies of capitalism find once more sanctuary in Russia."[2]

While Goldman and Berkman lived in Russia for the next two years, their time there went from bad to worse. Initially, they believed the party line that food supplies and conditions for working people remained so poor because of the Civil War and the fact that the new government simply had not had a chance to work. As time went on and conditions stayed the same Goldman, became disillusioned, with food so scarce that the government placed guards at flour mills.

Lenin and others rejected any and all ideas proposed by Goldman and Berkman. Goldman was the first to speak out against what she saw. Berkman remained loyal to the possibility of a revolution for longer, but with the Kronstadt Mutiny in March 1921, both decided they had to leave and could no longer support the regime. In his diary, Berkman described his thoughts as he waited for the end to come:

> Days of anguish and cannonading. My heart is numb with despair; something has died within me. The people on the streets look bowed with grief, bewildered. No one trusts himself to speak. The thunder of the heavy guns rends the air.[3]

The two soon moved out of their official quarters and refused government rations, and moved into much smaller and more squalid conditions, closer to those of the average Moscowvite. By the summer of 1921, with the Bolshevik government arresting anarchists, Goldman and Berkamn had no choice but to leave. In December 1921, they crossed into Latvia.

Goldman was both furious and disheartened with Russia and wrote two books on her experiences: *My Disillusionment with Russia* and *My Further Disillusionment with Russia*. Goldman explains this frustration:

> I found reality in Russia grotesque, totally unlike the great ideal that had borne me upon the crest of high hope to the land of promise...I saw before me the Bolshevik State, formidable, crushing every constructive revolutionary effort, suppressing, debasing, and disintegrating everything. Unable and unwilling to become a cog in that sinister machine, and aware that I could be of no practical use to Russia and her people, I decided to leave the country. Once out of it, I would relate honestly, frankly, and as objectively as humanly possible to me the story of my two years' stay in Russia.[4]

Goldman left the Soviet Union in December 1921 and, while she hoped to be allowed back to the United States, the reality was that she began a nomadic lifestyle, constantly moving around Europe, staying in a country only until that government came under pressure to expel her. Friends eventually bought her a cottage in the

south of France, in the then-out-of-the-way village of St. Tropez.
But even there she was constantly fighting with the authorities to
allow her and Berkman to stay.

Her open hostility to the Soviet Union did not go unnoticed in
the U.S. *The New York Times* reported as early as 1920 that
"Emma Goldman Sees Tyranny in Russia." In 1922, another report
declared some communists were complaining that Goldman did
not understand what was happening in the Soviet Union. In 1924,
the *Times* noted that Goldman had a new role as she "Starts in
London her Campaign for Oppressed Russians Against the Bol-
sheviki." This distancing from, and fighting with, the left, while it
gave her some "good press" in the United States, also had the effect
of shrinking the circle of people willing to help her, financially and
legally. Goldman once again had become a distant, lonely figure –
her individualism had taken on a whole new meaning as she had
no real organization to depend on and no obvious chance of finding a place to live peacefully as she got older. It is in these circumstances that Goldman decided to write her autobiography. Goldman was initially hesitant to write her autobiography because she
felt that, "When one has reached a good philosophic age ... capable of viewing one's own life – one is likely to create an autobiography worthwhile."[5] For some time, the choice about writing was
further complicated by the lack of sources and available material.
In the introduction to *Living My Life* she explains:

> The great difficulty that faced me was the lack of historical
> data for my work. Almost everything in the way of books,
> correspondence, and similar material that I had accumulated
> during the thirty-five years of my life in the United States had
> been confiscated by the Department of Justice raiders and
> never returned. I lacked even a personal set of the *Mother
> Earth* magazine, which I had published for twelve years. It
> was a problem I could see no solution for.[6]

Persuaded by friends, their documents, and her own large collection of letters, Goldman eventually began her autobiography on
June 27, 1928, her fifty-ninth birthday. Though she had hoped,
with typical dramatic and theatrical Goldmanesque flare, to complete the project in a year,[7] it was not finished until January 1931
and not published until October of that year. The reasons for the

delays were many. First, writing was difficult for Goldman. Remembering was painful. In the introduction to her autobiography she admits:

> Writing had never come easy to me, and the work at hand did not mean merely writing. It meant reliving my long-forgotten past, the resurrection of memories I did not wish to dig out from the deeps of my consciousness. It meant doubts in my creative ability, depression, and disheartenings [sic].[8]

Indeed by the time Goldman began to write in 1928, her financial insecurity was causing her great worry. Her financial situation was such that she had to find a way to earn money quickly: her eyesight was failing, money from friends in New York was not as forthcoming as it once had been, and she saw the writing of her autobiography as a means to pay bills and allow her (and Alexander Berkman) to have the option to continue living in France. There was another, perhaps even over-riding, reason for Goldman to begin to write her autobiography in 1928: the slim hope that she might, in her old age, be able to return to the United States.

Neither Goldman nor Alexander Berkman could understand the forces at work determined to keep her out of the United States. In an October 1931 letter to Roger Baldwin[9] and Robert Reinhart,[10] Berkman writes:

> We have information from officials very high in the Ministry of the Interior that it is the US that is pushing the case against me. Details are of course almost impossible to obtain ... It is hardly probable that any private American busybody or some individual Secret Service man (as suggested by Roger) should have so much influence with the French Government. At any rate, it would be interesting to investigate this matter at your end.[11]

Neither Goldman nor Berkman could conceive of the power and influence of J. Edgar Hoover, whom Roger Baldwin had insisted was behind the effort. Goldman hoped that writing and publishing her autobiography presented her with what a chance for her to show the American people, and more importantly the American

government, just how American she was. Furthermore, she hoped
the publication of her autobiography would clarify just how much
she understood and appreciated the United States, and more importantly, what she would and *would not do* if she were allowed to
return. Goldman needed to appear in the autobiography to be
everybody's grandmother: calm, serene, maybe a little eccentric,
but mostly misunderstood. She could no longer afford to appear to
be violent, fiery, short-tempered, or critical, and certainly not a terrorist or dangerous. What Goldman set out to achieve was to produce a particular version of herself, useful to her and Berkman in
1928.

As Alice Wexler has commented, the final result of this writing
and reasoning was the production of a book, which was:

> Not a history of Goldman's life as she actually lived it, but a
> recreation of her life as she saw it at a particular moment,
> from the summer of 1928 to the spring of 1931.[12]

Reading *Living My Life*, some seventy-plus years after its publication, it seems exaggerated, almost mystical, and certainly theatrical. It describes days gone by, full of heroes and villains, those
who understood everything, and those who were always blind to
the truth. It is simplistic, dramatic, sometimes perhaps revolutionary, hardly ever critical, always surprisingly respectful, slightly conservative, and full of explanations.

That Goldman chose to write her autobiography in order to
persuade the American public of her gentleness, loyalty, and honesty, is indeed typically American, according to Robert F. Sayre. In
The Examined Self, autobiography, Sayre claims, has particular
social and cultural importance in America[13] as it assures readers
that individualism in America is alive, "rugged and rewarded or
repentant and resilient."[14] Thomas P. Doherty notes that autobiography is a style of writing which suits the "traditional American
self-image: individualistic and optimistic."[15] The purpose of
American autobiography for Doherty is that it reassures the reader
of the value of the individual, it points to the possibility of success,
and it affirms a faith in country.[16] Loving America and being
American, according to Sayre, means that autobiography explains
and helps readers to understand ideas as "they are embodied in
persons and their stories of their suffering, hope, strength, sacrifice,

and courage."[17] Albert Stone emphasizes the point, stating, "Autobiography indeed mirrors and creates the social, historical and aesthetic varieties of our [*American*] national experience."[18]

American autobiography, then, is not just the written memoirs of the politically important, or of the rich and famous. It can provide a way in which lesser-known people, and/or people outside of the accepted norm of the political sphere, can explain their acts, motivation, and even what Sayre refers to as their "changing self-concepts."[19] In other words, autobiography has another function in that it has become "essential reading for recovering or discovering the experience of Americans who were not part of our literary and cultural establishments."[20] Hardly surprising, then, as Linda Wagner-Martin notes, is that the numbers of autobiographies in the nineteenth and twentieth centuries written in the U.S. grew "with relish."[21] Autobiography fills a specifically American need.

By the nineteenth century, autobiographies had progressed from a series of memoirs, diaries, and letters to organized volumes of prose. Patricia Meyers Spacks notes that two-volume, thousand-page works were not uncommon during this period.[22] In the nineteenth-century United States, the function of autobiography had an added dimension: not only did it give an account of the life of the individual in America, it was also a means by which newly arrived immigrants could explain that they too had become Americans and should be counted as such.[23] As Sayre notes, what an autobiography does is provide an opportunity for the individual to defend herself, and then to establish the beliefs she has chosen to live by.[24] For immigrants in particular, at the end of the nineteenth century and the beginning of the twentieth, autobiographical accounts provided success stories on a number of levels. They gave accounts of harsh childhoods, hard work, and then successful economic endeavours. They also had another possibility: that of showing immigrants' loyalty to their new country, and proving that they wanted very much to be seen as proud and loyal Americans.

It is this aspect of the American psyche to which Goldman wanted to appeal. She wanted to write an American book, for an American audience, and when reading it, she wanted the reader to feel an American wrote it.

For American women and immigrant women in particular, the issue of autobiography was furthermore complicated not just by their newness to the United States, and their active political role, but also by a certain social risk attached to writing. In other words, who these women were, what they felt about whomever, whatever they gave up, and what they refused to surrender became secondary to the importance of the cause in their lives.[25] The public life subsumed the private and the personal. Many women autobiographical writers fail to emphasize themselves; instead the cause, whatever it was, becomes the all-important item. Even in re-counting their life stories, women lack what Spacks calls "any distinct sense of individual destiny,"[26] and "diminish the self in the reports of their cause."[27] This lack of self, this "silence" about themselves is what Tillie Olsen refers to when she first writes about the concept of silence.[28] For American women, autobiography is not just an adventurous success story; it depicts the roles they played behind the usually male-organized and dominated events of their lives.[29]

In emphasizing their public roles, women fail to mention their private lives: they omit details about their education, their beliefs, and the reasons behind any decisions they had to make. Instead we get a very definite and resounding silence. Ultimately the reader lacks an understanding of what and who makes the writer. In many cases, not only are life stories obscured, but also people who were very important in the lives of these women are ignored and forgotten. Jane Addams intimately lived with Mary Rozet Smith for forty years, yet her biographer chooses to record that "life eluded her [Addams]," because she never married.[30] Jane Addams' deeds have superseded her personal life; the accepted public record has subsumed the private.

For politically active women, the ideal is paramount; it is their life purpose. However, usually it is a more easily understood and accepted role, such as the wife of a politician, rather than that of leader of some sort, that is written about. Any role outside the accepted norm demanded a certain amount of "discretion," based on their public place. In the introduction to her first volume of the biography of Eleanor Roosevelt, Blanche Wiesen Cook explains her frustration that Eleanor Roosevelt left out so much in her own memoirs, as have many who wrote about her:

> Marriages hid romances; romances were discreet and buried
> in archives; archives were until recently closed. Although ER
> kept much of the historical record, the private details of her

life with others and with FDR were entirely obscured in three
volumes of memoir and several autobiographical essays ...
ER's memoirs were understated, self-deprecating, monuments
to discretion and silence.[31]

But what could Eleanor Roosevelt really reveal? What did she
want to reveal? After all, what was the purpose of her even writing
her memoirs?

The resulting text, in the case of Eleanor Roosevelt and other
women, is half-stories of half-lives that are at best half-true. So, as
Spacks points out, what we get through this type of history is a
series of events in which these women took part. They recount the
events, diminishing their roles, explaining away their parts, and
usually happy to state they were lucky to be there.[32]

This "silence" does not simply result in the reader not knowing
details; it results in the author hiding herself. Then, as Adrienne
Rich points out:

> Whatever is unnamed, undepicted in images, whatever is omit-
> ted from biography, censored in collections of letters, whatever
> is misnamed as something else, made difficult-to-come-by,
> whatever is buried in the memory by the collapse of meaning
> under an inadequate or lying language – this will become not
> merely unspoken, but unspeakable.[33]

In many cases, women who write about themselves seem to feel
that they do not need to explain how they coped with the number
of tasks society assigned to them: wife, mother, lover, and daughter. They seem to feel the need to not mention so much about themselves, socially and sexually. Many, like Emmeline Pankhurst, seemed
to subsume themselves to what she calls her "husband's beliefs"[34]
and in the end denies the existence of what Spacks calls her "private reality."[35] Instead, the emphasis in many sets of memoirs is on
the giving to the cause, the wish to do well, and to be seen as good.
This reasoning was the only valid motive for their lives.

As Emma Goldman began to write, the combination of the private
and public was inflammatory. The public Goldman was an already-
documented text dominated by violence and opposition. If Goldman
was to successfully write an American autobiography, she had to

somehow change the public view by allowing the private reality to appear, but only insofar as it would show her as part of a caring cause. The public, crusading Emma Goldman had to be curtailed.

The result of all this non-writing is that autobiography, as a means of knowing women, has to be historically doubted. How, then, is it possible to find any value in these writings? Rich provides a possible solution as to how we can correct this lapse: re-visioning.[36] This act of looking back in a new way, of taking not just a closer look at texts, but a deeper and different look at texts, will allow women to know the past and to allow past women to be more fully known.[37] Since a woman's life story is a process of coping with a "dialogue of domination"[38] as well as "a process of the construction of the self,"[39] women's stories need to be approached by looking for concepts of "authorship and authority," with "bonds and divisions," and then by examining "the divided selves" that result.[40] If one does not look more closely at the text, beyond the plain narrative account, one will only find in a woman's autobiography the life story of a wife, daughter, mother; society's reaction to unusual women; the struggle to be part of family and community; and finally, family demands at odds with individual's needs.[41] As Estelle Jelinek points out in *Women and Autobiography*, women generally do not reveal their more painful and intimate memories in their autobiographies.[42] The result of this simplified version of a life is a collection of portraits of friends and acquaintances. Yet even the values of these portraits of friendship are suspect, as Weisen Cook explains:

> Women's friendships were obscured and trivialized. Whether heterosexual or homosexual, the private lives of political women were declared beyond the acceptable boundaries of historical inquiry. As a result much of our history and the facts that define our heritage have been removed from our consciousness.[43]

Leaving out events means omitting the personal. That means friendships and relationships are obscured, lost, even ignored. The result is careful writing that at best is "detached," according to Jelinek, but in reality the result is more serious, as the omissions are critical:

The admission of intense feelings of hate, love, and fear, the
disclosure of explicit sexual encounters, or in the detailing of
painful psychological experiences, are matters on which autobiographers are generally silent.[44]

Goldman's writing reveals her decisions about what should be
included. In particular, sex and sexuality was not a subject about
which she was prepared to be totally honest, despite the encouragement of friends such as Frank Harris, who had recently published
his autobiography, *My Life and Loves*, which detailed his many
sexual encounters. In a letter to Goldman he explains his rationale:

> Furthermore, we want a woman's view of life and freedom in
> sex matters, want it badly: your life and mine will be the first
> chapters in the Bible of Humanity.[45]

Goldman, by way of reply, points out the need for caution, politically, socially, and psychologically:

> I realized at once how utterly impossible it is to be perfectly
> frank about sex experiences and to do so in an artistic and
> convincing manner. Believe me, it is not because I have any
> puritanical feeling or that I care in the least for the condemna-
> tion of people. My reasons for the impression regarding the
> facts of sex are that I do not consider the mere physical fact
> sufficient to convey the tremendous effect it has on human
> emotions and sensations. Perhaps it is because to woman sex
> has a far greater effect than to man. It creates a greater storm
> in her being and lingers on when the man is satisfied and at
> ease. At any rate, I feel that the effect of the sexual relation-
> ship is psychological and cannot be described in mere physical
> terms. I mean sex between two harmonious people, both
> equally intense.[46]

Goldman's admittance, even before she began to write, that she
was not going to tell her full story means that looking, reading,
studying, and exploring *Living My Life* must be done using Rich's
re-visioning techniques.

Women writing autobiographies, sharing information about
themselves, and explaining their roles and sometimes their deci-

sions to act are vital concerns for historians. But the fact is clear that these autobiographies begin, at least, as partially self-censored works, as the expectations imposed on women seem to be demanding. These limitations need to be recognized in order to evaluate the text. Goldman, for example, notes in the introduction that she did not write her account alone: Emily Holmes Coleman ("Demi") acted as her personal secretary, while Alexander Berkman took on the role of editor. When Demi left, Miriam Lerner took her position, and throughout this time Arthur Leonard Ross was giving legal advice to Goldman. This number and variety of people involved in the project means that when Goldman writes the word "I" it needs to be seen not as a personal pronoun, but a complicated collective pronoun, combining the beliefs and experiences of a wide variety of people.

The construct of "I" in this autobiography – perhaps in radical political women's autobiographies – is a tool, created, it seems, to subsume Goldman's gender and sexuality under a more easily understood purpose – being American. The question then becomes how to view the "I," de-construct the "I" in its various forms, and attempt to interpret and evaluate it.

The reason behind this censorship, as explained by Sidone Smith in *A Poetics of Women's Autobiography,* is that, while for the male rebel the validity of his belief system is found in his actions, for the woman, action, rebellion, and a personal set of beliefs result in her being cast out of society, and so she and her beliefs fail to be appreciated:

> The rebel whose text projects a hostile society, against which he struggles to define himself, if he is male, takes himself seriously because he and his public assume his significance within the dominant order: Only in the fullness of that membership can the fullness of his rebellion unfold. For women, on the other hand, rebellious pursuit is potentially catastrophic. To call attention to her distinctiveness is to become "unfeminine." To risk a voice and to authorize a public life are to risk loss of reputation. Hence distinctiveness may never be attractive in and of itself.[47]

So to re-vision successfully, to gather more knowledge, and to understand the life of Emma Goldman, it is necessary to begin with the notion of gender. Being a woman in society, writing about womanhood, and explaining how to cope with such a demanding ordeal is the first expectation as outlined by the Personal Narratives Group:

> Women's personal narratives are, among other things, stories of how women negotiate their "exceptional gender" status both in their daily lives and over the course of a lifetime. They assume that one can understand the life only if one takes into account gender roles and gender expectations. Whether she has accepted the norms or defied them, a woman's life can never be written taking gender for granted.[48]

The starting point for a study of Goldman involves not just realizing she is female but that she is a woman from an orthodox Jewish background. Remembering Janet Burstein's questioning ("As a child, I often wondered why my mother was angry at rabbis and their rules"[49]) and Cynthia Ozick's frustration ("My own synagogue is the only place in the world where I am not named Jew"[50]), this study must distinguish between being Jewish and non-Jewish in America. Goldman's coping and dealing with a general anti-Semitism that was systemic at the time, while not unique, is still particular to her method of writing about herself.

Burstein, in her introduction to *Writing Mothers, Writing Daughters*, writes of the need for Jewish women to understand themselves, to "stretch beyond the personal into collective social experience."[51] She goes on to explain the tangled makeup of identity:

> Thus the inward work of understanding my mother merged almost imperceptibly with questions about the extent to which other Jewish women understood their mothers, about the process that constructs us all as gendered and ethnic creatures – as American Jewish women.[52]

The difficulty lies in the complex relationship between being Jewish in America and being an American Jewish woman. Being Jewish seemed to mean not being American enough. As Andrew R. Heinze in "Adapting to Abundance: Luxuries, Holidays, and Jewish Identity" notes, some Jewish festivals were changed to show the delight and appreciation the Jewish community felt for the opportunity to live in America, and in an effort to prove loyalty.[53] Thus Chanukah was integrated into an American secular Christmas, Passover became a festival of appreciation of higher living in the U.S., while Sukkoth was adapted to the celebration of a new home in a new land.

Goldman, like many newly-arrived Jewish women immigrants, had been raised in an orthodox, male-dominated domain. Remember, Goldman had initially come to the United States after she had refused to agree to a marriage arranged by her father. "Girls do not have to learn much! All a Jewish daughter needs to know is how to prepare *gefullte* fish, cut noodles fine, and give a man plenty of children,"[54] her father insisted. His views echoed those of Rabbi Eliezer's statement that "whoever teaches his daughter Torah, teaches her obscenity,"[55] and the frustration forever enshrined by Anzia Yezierska in *Bread Givers* as she explains her father's view of women,

> The prayers of his daughters didn't count because God didn't listen to women. Heaven and the next world were only for men. Women could get into Heaven because they were wives and daughters of men. Women had no brains for the study of God's Torah, but they could be the servants of men who studied the Torah. Only if they cooked for the men, and washed for the men, and didn't nag or curse the men out of their homes; only if they let the men study the Torah in peace, then, maybe, they could push themselves into Heaven with the men to wait on them there.[56]

While a certain amount of factory work was financially necessary in Russia, ironically, once in the United States, Jewish women formed the backbone of the garment factory workforce and an important part of the financial stability of the family unit. Women were the workers. However, these jobs forced another irony to rise up. Goldman's Jewishness, like that of many thousands of others, was complicated by the fact that she was part of the later group of Jewish immigrants to arrive in the U.S.: working-class Eastern European and Russian Jews. Their arrival not only brought out an anti-Semitic feeling in mainstream America, but they also were frowned upon and discriminated against by the German Jews who had already established themselves in businesses in the various major cities. In the 1880s, German Jews owned 234 of the 241 clothing factories in New York City, and Goldman's expectations of a fair wage from fellow Jews were quickly dissipated. The reality for many, including Goldman, was that factory conditions in the United States were as bad, if indeed not worse, than the working conditions they had left behind. This irony meant further difficulties in the attempt of Russian Jewish women to integrate into American life.

Goldman had to force her way out of a world in which she was theologically and traditionally second class into a society in which she was legally a second-class citizen. If Berkman's and Most's rebellious natures were not accepted, Emma Goldman's attitude were deemed appalling on every level: culturally, traditionally, politically, and legally. Thus to re-vision means to begin a study of *Living My Life* with her attitude toward her life as it was, as it was seen by others, as was expected, and as she hoped. This process will then be used to explain why her autobiography was put together in such a format – to how many audiences did Goldman have to explain her life?

CHAPTER SEVEN

Writing an American Story

I want very much to have the memoirs done by June 1929. That year will
have deep meaning for me. In the first place I will have rounded out sixty
years – certainly the largest part of one's life. And I will have given forty
years to my ideas. I realize that most of them were spent chasing wind-
mills, in trying to present to the world an ideal which to me contains all
the beauty and wonder there is in life – the only raison d'être for my existence, and the world less than ever wants to know anything about it.
–Emma Goldman to Evelyn Scott, June 26, 1928

I was not hewn of one piece, like Sasha [Alexander Berkman] or other
heroic figures. I had long realized that I was woven of many skeins, conflicting in shade and texture.[1]

According to Albert E. Stone in *Autobiographical Occasions and
Original Acts*, "it is precisely the function of the autobiographical
act to convert historical events and psychological experience into
personal identity."[2] However, as Alix Kate Shulman suggests in
Between Women, difficulties exist in trying to know Emma Goldman through her autobiographical work. Schulman explains, "I discovered that I had to read Emma on two levels at once, observing
what she revealed consciously and again unconsciously."[3] But beyond this, *Living My Life* is more complex in nature than the conscious and unconscious, as its focus, purpose, and the dramatic
prose all hide, and at the same time partly display, not only Emma
Goldman the person, but also the political hopes and disappoint-
ments of Goldman and her generation of radicals. In 1931, just as
Goldman finished her autobiography, she wrote to Berkman,
explaining what she knew to be the reality of their life's struggle:
"we both know how little we have achieved in the past and how little we will leave behind when we go."[4] The honesty of this comment
is perhaps a reflection of Goldman having re-lived her life as she
wrote about her hopes and dreams over the previous years.

The purpose, then, of this chapter is to look closely at Goldman's autobiography, *Living My Life*; its inception, creation, and text; to investigate its language and meanings; to notice its edits, editors, and influences, what is said about whom, how it is said, and for what purpose. This chapter is about Goldman's construction of her life story, and ultimately the creation of a particular, political, new American woman.

As Goldman got older, she began to be more aware of her developing physical inabilities and she feared mental instability:

> I discovered, much to my discomfiture, that old age far from ripening wisdom and mellowness, is too often fraught with senility, narrowness, and petty rancor. I would not risk such a calamity, and began to think seriously about writing my life.[5]

Theodore Dreiser told her, "You must write the story of your life EG; it is the richest of any woman's of our century." Aided by Peggy Guggenheim, who donated five hundred dollars, W.S. Van Valkenburgh, editor of the *Road to Freedom*, and others who put together a basic financial package of $2,500, on June 27, 1928, her fifty-ninth birthday, Goldman began writing. She hoped to finish in a year, by her sixtieth birthday, described by Goldman as "the psychologic [sic] moment, as by then I shall have covered sixty years in this rotten world, out of which forty have been spent chasing windmills."[6]

There were a number of other less romantic, more practical factors that were instrumental in getting Goldman to begin writing. Though she and Berkman had been living in France in 1928, there was no guarantee the French government would let her stay. During the 1890s Goldman had been introduced to James Colton, a Welsh coalminer known for his rebellious attitude. When Goldman and Colton met again in 1925, Colton offered to marry her, so she could secure legal documents and a British passport. Goldman accepted his offer. The two were married in London in 1925. Goldman paid for his journey from Wales to London and gave him financial compensation for the two days of work he had missed. Later she wrote to him, thanking him for his act: "thanks to you my faithful comrade. I cannot find words to express my appreciation of your sweet solidarity."[7]

While the marriage did give her some legal security, she was constantly aware that a determined legal team could once again uproot her. She needed the financial security that she hoped the sales of the book would provide; this would give her money for food, medical needs, and if necessary a legal defense fund. However, much more importantly, she needed to appear to be much less politically controversial, so that she would be allowed to live out her old age in peace. As always, Goldman was aware of Berkman's needs as well as her own. Berkman was in dire financial straits; writing to Goldman, he explained, "We [Berkman and Emmy Eckstein] have been sitting here for almost two weeks without a cent. Some days we did not have enough money to buy food. Nor for a carfare."[8]

Before Goldman sat down to write, she insisted she was going to write "without gloves," writing "in my own way, no matter what the cost will be."[9] Yet in a letter to Alexander Berkman in 1927, she admitted her agenda:

> I am writing about the life of Emma Goldman, the pubic person not the private individual. I naturally want to let people see what one can do if imbued with an ideal, what one can endure and how one can overcome all difficulties and suffering in life. Will I be able to do that and yet give also the other side, the woman, the personality in quest for the unattainable in a personal sense?[10]

However, the reality was that physical and practical forces had already undermined such high ideals. First, Goldman admitted to Arthur Leonard Ross, who had become her lawyer, "My book is my first and last chance in life to get enough material results to secure myself for whatever few years there are left in me to live."[11] Second, she also knew that the goal of her writing had to produce something that would explain "the slice of American life I portrayed, and not so much my own private and personal experiences."[12] Goldman missed living in the United States. In a 1925 letter to Alexander Berkman she described her reaction as their longtime friend and comrade, Eleanor Fitzgerald, decided to return to the United States:

I was terribly affected by Frizie's[13] going back to the land that
has shut me out. I especially felt it when I got onboard the
"France." I would have given years of my life if I could have
gone along with her.[14]

Goldman began the project with typical gusto. On June 29,
1928, a mere two days after she had begun, Goldman wrote to
Berkman delighted with the progress: "Since I began writing at 9PM
Tuesday, I have written six thousand words."[15] Initially she wrote
for up to twelve hours a day, and within five months had completed nearly seven hundred pages of manuscript, but only reached the
year 1900. In his autobiography, Rudolf Rocker tells of his family's
visit with Goldman at this time. She would get up at six in the
morning, write, clean, eat, write, and finally eat again. Sometimes
in the evenings, as they sat together, she would read sections out
loud to whomever was there.[16]
     The autobiography was always going to be constructed around
Goldman's fierce loyalty to the anarchist cause. Criticism of anarchism or those closely associated with her philosophical viewpoint
was not an option. In letters to friends she explained she was not
going to use her autobiography to criticize other anarchists, and
warned them that when she wrote to them about certain subjects,
these comments were for them only. Loyalty to the cause was more
important than her reputation. In a 1930 letter to Ted McLean
Switz, Goldman clearly stated,

> I am telling you this not for publication but merely the to
> show you that with all the frantic efforts of your comrades to
> discredit my revolutionary zeal, I have the honor of still being
> considered very dangerous by every government.[17]

It is always vital to remember that for Goldman that loyalty to
the anarchist cause mean loyalty to Berkman, In a letter to Arthur
Leonard Ross, she explained that her relationship with Berkman
would be central to the story, since their relationship "is the leitmo-
tif of my 40 years of life."[18]
     While Goldman insisted she was writing "history," and so col-
lected a great number of pamphlets, books, and had letters to
friends and acquaintances returned to her to help ensure factual
truth, her method to ensure authenticity was "to transfer myself as

far as possible into the particular period described and my reactions at the time to whatever happened to me."[19] She was aware "that I have nothing left in terms of personal relations from all who have been in my life and have torn my heart."[20]

The reality was that such a sizable project quickly overwhelmed Goldman, and she was not sure where the actual book should begin. In a letter to Berkman she wrote about her fear and general indecision; she received a curt reply:

> I don't know why you have such difficulty in starting your work. Maybe you can't concentrate because of too many distractions and visitors. We had talked the first part over and came to the conclusion that you begin with your childhood. In any case you have a lot to write about your childhood and it should be done in a full reminiscent way. Or you begin with Rochester and your coming to New York and then review your early impressions as a strong influence in your development.[21]

Living My Life, as published, duly begins, as Berkman suggested, with Goldman's arrival in New York from Rochester and describes her initial impressions of the city and the anarchist movement to which she was introduced that day. While the influence of Berkman is there from the night of her arrival in New York City, another major influence on Goldman at the actual time of her writing was Theodore Dreiser, and in particular his novel *Sister Carrie*.

Dreiser and Goldman had been in fairly regular contact at this time. Dreiser was interested in finding out more about Goldman in order to write a short biography about her. In a fairly constant exchange of letters, while Dreiser attempted to understand her philosophy, motives, and actions, Goldman expressed her frustrations at his inability to understand her political non-violent philosophy. Nevertheless, despite the philosophical impasse, Goldman and Dreiser continued a dialogue.

Theodore Dreiser's novel *Sister Carrie* was a particularly poignant and personal novel for Goldman. Dreiser's novel is based on the life of Dreiser's sister Emma, who lived with L.A. Hopkins, a cashier in Chapin & Gore, a bar in downtown Chicago. What Emma Dreiser did not know was that Hopkins was already married. Nevertheless, when she did find out, she was still willing to elope with him to

Canada, though she was unaware that he had stolen $3,500 from the company before they left. Hopkins did eventually return most of the money and the couple moved to New York, where Hopkins spent most of his time unemployed. Emma Dreiser eventually left him, but chose to ignore Theodore's offer to live with him and instead moved into her own small Manhattan apartment.

When Dreiser wrote *Sister Carrie*, he based it on this series of events, but set it in initially in Chicago – the place Goldman considered her spiritual home – and then in New York, Goldman's actual home. When Goldman had trouble beginning her autobiography, she turned to the fictional Carrie (Emma) to help begin her life story.

A close comparison of each book's opening pages shows numerous similarities between the two:

Sister Carrie	*Living My Life*
It was August, 1889.	It was the 15th of August 1889.
She was eighteen years of age.	I was twenty years old.
… a yellow leather snap purse, contained her ticket, a scrap of paper with her sister's address in Van Buren Street and four dollars in money[22].	My entire possessions consisted of five dollars and a small hand-bag. [23]

Dreiser explains Carrie's attitude toward her old life using a clothing metaphor, as does Goldman:

Sister Carrie	*Living My Life*
The threads which bound her so lightly to girlhood and home were irretrievably broken.[24]	All that had happened in my life until that time was now left behind me, cast off like a worn-out garment.[25]

Why did Goldman choose to begin her autobiography at the same moment in time as Carrie Meeber? Goldman had always insisted that her moment of spiritual birth, her arrival, was the execution of the Haymarket martyrs, not when she first came to the

United States. If Chicago was the place of her spiritual birth, New York was the point of Goldman's baptism, and the opening chapter notes the date, the time, and place not just of this arrival but of all major arrivals in Goldman's life.

The arrival of each woman to the major cities was difficult. For Carrie, Chicago was "vast."[26] For Goldman, New York was "large."[27] But the men they met the day of their respective arrivals soon downsized the city, and changed the rest of their lives; for Carrie it was Charles H. Drouet, while for Goldman it was Alexander Berkman. The impact of these meetings is the constant theme for the remainder of both books.

There are other comparisons between Goldman and Dreiser's Carrie/Emma that also must have struck Goldman. Both the Dreiser and Goldman families spoke German as their first language. Emma Dreiser and Goldman each had four siblings. No one had any long-term formal education, which was something they were all conscious of throughout their lives. Both families were raised with particularly strict religious and moral regulations. With this strictness, which in both cases stemmed from their fathers, also came economic insecurity. The fathers of both families failed to provide for their families economically, which meant what should have been considered basic items, such as food and clothes, were actually luxury items. "Carrie Meeber," like Emma Dreiser and Emma Goldman, would revolt against this moral strictness and want to enjoy material goods. However, obtaining this standard of living was not easy for either woman. Familial and economic realities played a major part in their lives; Goldman, after her arrival in the United States, stayed with her sister and brother-in-law. Carrie did likewise after her arrival in Chicago. Despite all their ambitions, both women worked in squalid factory conditions forced on them out of familial duty to contribute to the household expenses, resulting in both of them having only fifty cents for themselves.

Neither woman fitted in with her family; each was frowned upon for being morally suspect. Emma Goldman eventually left her husband, much to the horror of her family and community, and Carrie chose to sit on the steps on her building and went for walks alone, acts that were frowned upon by her brother-in-law. Both left their families to enjoy their interests, which included the theater, and both women were involved in sexually active relationships outside marriage, deemed inappropriate by the standards at the time. These sexual relationships symbolized the revolt that both women

were involved in, and were an expression of their desire to establish their individual rights. With so much in common, little wonder
that, when Emma Goldman began to write, she, at least in the beginning of the book, took on the person of Emma Dreiser and the
character of Sister Carrie to help establish herself as this American
woman.

In a 2001 article entitled "Cultural and Historical Contexts for
Sister Carrie,"[28] Claire Eby explains that Dreiser's novel reflected
the drastic changes seen in the United States after the Civil War.
The country moved from an agrarian economy to an industrial
one, in which the pace of life transformed from slow to rapid, as
"speed became the order of the day."[29] However, two other factors
in particular must have appealed to Goldman: the impact of Darwin's evolutionary ideas on all aspects of society, and the notion of
personal gratification and desires. Darwin's theory of evolution
had impacted the anarchist writings of Peter Kropotkin. Goldman
had met and become close to Kropotkin while in the Soviet Union.
Dreiser's language references notions of competition, struggle, and
survival, of an evolving moral and social order, all of which would
have appealed to Goldman.

While the new American woman was a vital part of the workforce, she also wanted material possessions to show as her reward
for being part of the process. In a letter to Evelyn Scott, Goldman
explained that while "one wants to see the fruit of one's efforts,"
the reality is "that individual effort is really of very little consequence to the evolutionary forces in the world."[30] Goldman had
accepted that, despite her work, a revolution would only happen in
a slow evolutionary manner – neither her input nor that of anyone
else in the anarchist movement would change that scientific fact.
But Goldman was also interested in theater, food, and enjoyed
material and monetary rewards for her work. Goldman related to
this new American woman, who was showing herself not just capable of work, but deserving of rewards.

Along with Berkman and Dreiser, a third person was involved
in Goldman's writing process whose role remains somewhat
unclear, though it was surely substantial, was Emily Holmes
Coleman (Demie). Emily Holmes Coleman was born in Oakland,
California in 1899. She had initially written a letter to Goldman
after she married Lloyd Ring Coleman, a friend of Goldman's
nephew, Saxe Commins. Soon the two began a regular correspon-

dence. Later Emily and her husband moved to France, where Lloyd Coleman worked for *The Chicago Tribune,* and she began writing a novel, describing her time in a mental sanitarium, where she had spent some time after suffering postpartum depression after the birth of her son.

Demie Coleman's relationship with Goldman deepened when she organized a surprise birthday party for Goldman. Soon afterwards, Coleman became Goldman's secretary, specifically the typist for the manuscript – a vital position, as Goldman explained to Berkman:

> I have no idea whether the damned thing is good or rotten, whether it hangs together, sounds plausible, or whether it is chaotic or unreal. I will be able to judge better when the stuff is typewritten. This afternoon we begin with the job, I will dictate to Demie on the machine.[31]

If Coleman's role was simply that of typist, her practical influence would be unimportant; however, Coleman's influence extended beyond merely typing and proofreading. Goldman herself admitted Coleman was "no good" in various letters, that she "not only thinks while I dictate, but she corrects me every time I say anything she doesn't agree with."[32] At other times, Coleman went further, criticizing Goldman's writing style demanding a more detached manner: "Your whole trouble has been that you have been living this story as well as writing it."[33] A week after Goldman began writing, Evelyn Scott[34] tried to calm down her friend, saying, "I wish I had a secretary who, besides giving provocative hints of her own interesting self, could teach me how to spell."[35] Berkman eventually became concerned about how much control Coleman had over the manuscript, pointing out to Goldman that Coleman's ideas were so different than theirs:

> My only objection is your proposing to make Henry [Alsberg], myself and Demie [Coleman] the "executors of your mss." Demie does not belong there. She is a fine girl and all that, but you know that neither Henry nor I will agree with her on the question of the book and its contents. To appoint her together with us means only to create trouble. Better make it [Rudolf] Rocker in place of Demie.[36]

Thus from the beginning, indeed even before the project began, Goldman was always going to write this autobiography with other people's influence at the fore.

The initial years of writing for Goldman were 1928 through 1929; it seems that revisions and editing were done in 1930 and 1931. However, each year has a distinctive feel in regard to Goldman's emotional attitude toward the book, what she remembers, how she remembers, and ultimately what is written. With the opening sorted, Goldman wrote feverishly, obsessively describing her actions to friends as "a disease, a poison."[37] Berkman, in turn, described the atmosphere in St. Tropez, where Goldman was writing, as "oppressive," noting that "one is afraid sometimes to smile or laugh and often we do not exchange a word at meals because E. is in a bad humor generally."[38]

For Goldman, 1928 was an intense year for her writing. Her letters to family and friends are full of complaints, demanding more help, urging them to cajole her into continuing her writing, urging their support. Evelyn Scott wrote to her in 1928, assuring her she understood the pain Goldman was going through, and telling her that what she felt was normal: "Well as to the agony, I don't really believe anybody, making an effort to say honestly, with that exactitude which an aesthetic sense demands, really enjoys writing."[39] Goldman was also very aware that Berkman was writing a manuscript, later published as *What Is Communist Anarchism?*, at the same time, and assured him that she would not show him her book until he was finished. His book, like his life, was Goldman's priority.

> I have made up my mind not to let you see a line until you have finished your book. I simply won't let anything else take much of your time or interfere with your writing.[40]

By November 1928, Berkman was aware of both the struggle and the slow process Goldman was facing, and he tried to encourage her:

> I hope you continue well with 1900 and 1901. You really must bear in mind that you need not worry about how much you write up in a day, because I think you have done extremely well. In a few months you have written more than half of

your autobiography. It is from that standpoint that you must look at the matter.[41]

However, even though Berkman had not officially seen the manuscript at this stage, Berkman and Goldman corresponded almost daily, commenting and debating not only about anarchist philosophy but also about events. They still argued over their reactions. Berkman constantly insisted what he remembered and the way he remembered particular historical events were correct, and that Goldman's memories were flawed:

> Am glad to get your long letter. I cannot say that I agree with some of your points, but what is the use of discussing them? Each will remain with an old opinion, anyhow. I have come to think that views, opinions, etc. are less a matter of thinking than of temperament. So the more useless the discussion. I hold, however, that what I wrote in *Memoirs* is entirely correct in every particular, historically and psychologically.[42]

Later, in the same letter, he explains that he and others have evolved more than Goldman and that she must simply accept these facts as truth. Berkman refers to her reactions as "too sentimental," which he repeats later, and "too much," but this time adds they are also "womanish."[43]

Goldman's frustration increased as Berkman refused to budge on issues and continued to demand she accept his opinion. Berkman noted Goldman's attitude in his journal:

> Working hard, now, at nights at St. Tr. Sometimes she is worried, not satisfied with her work. But I think it will be OK after a lot of cutting and revision. She thinks I don't understand her struggle in writing and living through the past. It is no use arguing about it though. Our outlook is different. Her attitude to things is very feminine.[44]

Berkman wrote to Goldman that, while he understood her "nerves," it might be better "to skip some things, as much as possible and treat only of the most important events," and that this method "should apply to various experiences, personal as well as social."[45] The issue here is that Berkman was not at this stage officially editing Goldman's work, but in a letter to Goldman in April, 1929, he clearly stated, "I want to live long enough to help you revise your book, for I am vain enough to think that no one can do it as well as I."[46] His influence was tremendous, as each event was questioned, not only the rationale for them but the actual facts. Ultimately, Berkman used his biased, gendered perspective to explain away what he considered to be her inability to change her mind and agree with him.

The use of words such as "womanish," "feminine," and "sentimental" were harsh. On the other hand, Goldman's relationship with Berkman always had a critical side. In a 1925 letter, Goldman wrote to Berkman, wondering "if you and I will yet end up agreeing on most issues we fought so valiantly when we were young?"[47] Later the same year Goldman admitted, "There is certainly a community of moods and feelings between us."[48]

When Goldman and Berkman met in New York in 1889, he immediately took it upon himself to be her teacher, mentor, and lover. He opposed her love of the arts, theatre, and dance in particular (from which the "If I can't dance" slogan partly evolved[49]) when there was a revolution still to be fought and won. It is interesting to note that in *Living My Life,* when Goldman explains the reality of the revolution and how so many people thought so little of women, she does not mention Berkman as having any of these attitudes, and instead attributes that stance only to Johann Most, who was well known as having clear misogynistic attitude. On her return from her first speaking engagement in Rochester, she wanted to explain to Most her doubts about anarchy; Most did not seem to want to know:

> I [Emma Goldman] asked. "Don't you want me to tell you about that?" "Yes, another time." Now he wanted only to feel me near – his *Blondkopf,* his girl-woman.
> I flared up, declaring I would not be treated as a mere female.

Most treated her and other woman as objects, and he was not open to change. On the other hand, Berkman, she insists throughout *Living My Life,* was dedicated to the cause and was open to anyone who could prove their worth. According to Goldman's published autobiography, Berkman trusted and valued women in the same way as he valued men, but the severe use of gendered language in private letters by Berkman does suggest that many of his attitudes were edited out.

In early 1929, Goldman finally felt ready to show the whole manuscript to Berkman for comment and editorial help. Goldman spent the following day in bed. Berkman's reaction to Goldman is noted in his journal:

> E. was hurt at my opinion of her autobiography. Told her all must be reworked. Would take several months at least. Very strained relations. I am sure she thinks I've failed her, but the only way I could help is to take the whole mss and rework it.[50]

Goldman, in a letter the following month, reminded Berkman that "writing my book has proven the hardest and most painful task I have ever undertaken or gone through."[51] She went on to explain:

> It is not only the writing, it is the living through what now lies in ashes and being made aware that I have nothing left in the way of personal relations from all who have been in my life and have torn my heart. You have failed to realize the deeper current of my misery since I started and there is another year to go through with... I should have known it will be torture to revive the past. I am now paying for it. I am not holding anyone responsible. I am trying to explain why I grieved at your suggestion.[52]

Berkman's suggestion was that the whole manuscript needed to be revised. Berkman's help, however, was complicated by his refusal to leave his partner Emmy Eckstein, even for a short time:

> It goes without saying that I should like to have you help me with the final revision, but since you announced that you cannot be away too long from Emmy, and I certainly have no desire to induce you to, I don't see how you can help me. I confess if matters were reversed, no man could stop me from coming to your help, if the separation would mean for the rest of my life.[53]

Berkman, in his reply, dealt offhandedly with this whole issue, simply stating, "You will not agree anyhow, and I know you have always been prejudiced against Emmy."[54] The complicated history between Goldman and Berkman seemed to collide at this point.

Relations between Goldman and Berkman had been strained for some time, especially as Berkman claimed that Goldman had used his diary for her book *My Disillusionment with Russia*. Then, in 1823, Berkman met Emmy Eckstein, a young German-Jewish woman thirty years his junior. Eckstein's parents were furious at the relationship and even threatened to have her committed to an insane asylum if she did not break up with Berkman. Instead, she ran away to live with him in France.

Goldman and Eckstein were jealous of each other at various times.[55] Eckstein represented the future, and Goldman the past. Berkman's attempt to keep peace between the two involved him not seeing Goldman. Indeed, once, when Berkman and Eckstein did stay with Goldman, Berkman had to inform Goldman that he had gotten over his aversion to sharing space with others and would in fact share a bed with Eckstein. So when Berkman wrote to say he could not come to help her edit her manuscript, and that the reason for that was Emmy Eckstein, Goldman was understandably hurt.

In May 1929, Berkman attempted to ease the hurt felt by Goldman about his comments when he wrote:

> I need not tell you that I fully realize what you are going through with your book, my dear sailor girl. Even more, no doubt, than I did with my ABC. Do you know that I went through much worse sensations than with my *Memoirs*? The latter was bad enough, but the writing of ABC, the days when I could not continue and so on, gave me serious thoughts of suicide, of destroying the ms., and other such pleasant reflections. But your autobiography is far, far more rendering of course. So I know what it means to you, even if I seldom speak of it.[56]

As Berkman began the editing process, Goldman had to let the manuscript out of her sight; the tension between the two did not ease as the process continued. Berkman's constant and overwhelming corrections and changes at this stage were noted in his January 1930 journal entry:

> The Mss., after I correct it, looks worse than an ordinary battlefield. Some pages: half of it crossed out by me, on the other half every word, literally changed by me. I hope she'll never write another book. No such luck.[57]

By 1930, Berkman's revisions were done and the manuscript was nearing completion. 1930 proved to be legally chaotic as Goldman's and Berkman's ever-present precarious visa situations arose again, and Berkman was almost expelled from France. Goldman, in an April 1930 letter to Arthur Leonard Ross,[58] urged Ross to use the account of their expulsion from the States in order to persuade French authorities to allow them to stay, and in the hope that it might make public opinion in the U.S. more sympathetic to their case. By June 1930, Goldman knew that she was probably going to be allowed to remain in France,[59] however, Berkman's position seemed more uncertain. He had been deported to Belgium and was only allowed back to France through a combination of supporters that included Thomas Mann, Albert Einstein, and Bertrand Russell, among others. Even though Berkman was allowed back, he had no passport and no identity card, and there was still a French deportation order against him. In a letter to Michael Cohn,[60] in June 1930, Berkman outlined his fears and his demands for support when he declared, "I live in constant anxiety."[61] This visa issue meant that the final parts of the manuscript were slower to be revised and edited.

March 1930, Goldman's deadline with Knopf, had passed and she had only written up to 1919, the time of her deportation. In a letter to Harry Kelly she explained that she was emotionally and physically exhausted, and wanted to stop. Her publishers, however, reminded her of the contract, which had specifically stated that she would bring the autobiography up to date: 1929. They insisted that they were willing to delay publication until she had her story up-to-date. Forced to write the story of the deportation, Goldman added the necessary chapters. Goldman being Goldman, however, she complained bitterly about publishers, from then on equating them with the state.

Finally, in late February 1931, Goldman mailed the last part of the manuscript to Knopf in New York. With some typical (unedited) prose she wrote to Arthur Leonard Ross: "I am sending you a cable today conveying the great news that I have at last operated on the appendix of *Living My Life* and Jesus Christ and God know that no operation would cause anyone more agony or such struggle as the last six months have been."[62]

What was published in October 1931 was a nine-hundred-page, two-volume book that sold for $7.50. Goldman objected heartily to the price, which she said was way too high during the Depression. She also complained that Knopf had really got two books from her for the price of one very small advance.

The book begins with an "appreciation" in which Goldman writes of Berkman: "For eighteen months Sasha worked side by side with me as in our old days. Critical, of course, but always in the finest and broadest spirit. Sasha also it was who suggested the title, *Living My Life*." She also specifically mentions Demie, whom she describes as being "a wild wood-sprite with a volcanic temper." Goldman goes on to say,

> My world of ideas was foreign to her, natural rebel and anarchist though she was. We clashed furiously, often to the point of wishing each other in St. Tropez Bay. But it as nothing compared to her charm, her profound interest in my work, and her fine understanding for my inner conflicts.

In return, Berkman called *Living My Life* "a GREAT WORK, not merely interesting but fascinating, honest, powerful, gripping."[63] Critics hailed it. In *The New York Times Book Review* of October 25, 1931, R.L. Duffus wrote, "her autobiography is one of the great of its kind." It quickly became a bestseller because of its library sales in the first year. Goldman had a partial literary success.

Nevertheless, the question is just what Goldman, Berkman, and others created in 1931? Is *Living My Life* an account of how Goldman actually lived her life, as the title suggests, or is the book instead a story created to show and recount aspects of her life, one that is necessary to revisit and re-appraise? If the latter is the case, then *Living My Life*, described as "a testament,"[64] instead becomes a work destabilized by gender,[65] and needs to be seen as "theatrical"[66] rather than historical. In short, *Living My Life* becomes part of the "radical inquiry into the political construction and regulation of identity,"[67] as well as a representation of radical female identity.

There is no doubt that Emma Goldman did not write *Living My Life* alone. Before she even began she lined up ideas, money, a secretary, and Berkman's opinions. As the project progressed, many of the same people gave their opinions about the project, and so by the end what is constructed is a multi-faceted Emma Goldman, created by groups of people with similar opinions.

One Emma Goldman is loyal, grateful, and finds inspiration in Alexander Berkman. In her biography *Emma Goldman in Exile*, Alice Wexler goes so far as to state that *Living My Life* is "an extended love letter to Berkman"[68] and at the same time "an act of revenge against those who had slighted or hurt Goldman."[69] In fact, this can be extended to those who "had slighted or hurt Goldman" and Berkman. Two people in particular who felt the result of this were Johann Most and Ben Reitman.

In 1931, when *Living My Life* was finally published, Reitman declared, "Never in my whole life was I [so] outraged, humiliated, bitter, disappointed and crushed."[70] Years later his daughter, Mecca Reitman Carpenter, wrote a biographer of her father called *No Regrets: Dr Ben Reitman and the Women Who Loved Him*, and even in 1999, the family was still noticeably unhappy with the description of Reitman that had appeared in Goldman's autobiography:

> Emma Goldman's version of her relationship with my father is
> the most exciting, the most passionate, the most widely
> known, and by far the most damning to his character of any
> of my father's love stories.[71]

Goldman describes herself when she met Reitman as "a school girl in love for the first time."[72] He was not a person who could ever be interested in her as an intelligent individual, as she knew "her reason repudiated the man."[73] She describes him as having an almost devil-like control over her; she decided to get involved with him after "a strange dream" involving "flames" and "fire." In the end, she surrendered to him and his demands, as he asked her to believe in him, and she also comments, "Whatever might have been at stake, I had to believe in him with an all-embracing faith."[74] Nevertheless, Goldman insists that she eventually realized that Reitman was "primitive,"[75] "emotional,"[76] and that, "like nature unleashed, he would destroy with one hand the lavish gifts of the other."[77]

Goldman also admits that, while none of her friends ever were "unkind" to Reitman, the strain of trying to behave became unbearable for him, as "he began to show off and brag, boast of his exploits, and talk nonsense, which made matters worse."[78] Goldman explains that it was Berkman who pointed out to her that Reitman "lacked social feeling, he had no rebel spirit, and he did not belong in our movement." Goldman complained to Berkman at that time, calling him a "zealot,"[79] and declaring that Berkman's problem was that he judged everyone in terms of value to "the Cause."[80] Yet Goldman also admits:

> I was sick from the scene with Sasha [Berkman], the harsh
> words I had hurled in his face; and I was tortured by my own
> doubts. I had to admit to myself that much that Sasha had
> said about Ben [Reitman] was true.[81]

Berkman is the one who sees, knows, and says what needs to be said first; Goldman is, once again, the one who has to catch up with Berkman's insights and superior knowledge of people and their worth to the cause.

Despite what was written in *Living My Life*, in letters written to Berkman around this time (1927–1931), Goldman, while admitting Reitman's faults (she called him "spiritually colorblind"[82] at one point), later defended him: "he had much in him which might have been developed had not my friends knocked him on the head from the first moment he came to us."[83] Goldman accused Berkman of being "a prig that constantly worries what the comrades will say and how it will affect the movement when you yourself lived your life to suit yourself."[84] In the same letter Goldman chastised Berkman for his lack of faith in Reitman (Berkman wrote to Reitman to make sure he did indeed graduate with a medical degree), which ultimately drove "him back to the depths he sprang from." Goldman went on:

> The trouble with you dear was, as with all our comrades, you
> are a puritan at heart, you all talk about how one must help

the outcast and the criminal, but when you are confronted with such a creature you turn your back on him in disgust.[85]

Why such a contrast in Goldman's reaction to Reitman? How could Goldman defend Reitman so vigorously in private, and ridicule him in public? How could she give Berkman so much credit in public, and yet in private deride him for his small-mindedness? One of the issues seems to have been that, when Reitman heard that Goldman was writing an autobiography, he wrote to her and explained that he too was writing a book in which he was going to be completely explicit about their relationship. Goldman was very nervous about that possibility, especially as one of the main reasons for writing the book was to show that she was not the infamous sex-crazed Emma Goldman, so well-known in the United States prior to 1919. Image and public opinion were vital here. Goldman wrote to him, asking him not to publish any of their private letters, insisting:

> Letters should only be published as letters after the death of the writer – not that I am ashamed of anything I might have written. But love letters are written to a lover, not for every Tom, Dick, and Harry. I feel you will comply with my request and never to use my letters in your story.[86]

Reitman agreed, but insisted that he would never have embarrassed her in any way and he wished her well for her book:

> I wish you well. I want you to write a great book. I feel certain that in spite of all my neglect and weakness and brutality, your love and justice, your sense of honesty, your willingness to give the other fellow fair play will entitle me to a page in your book. I hope you can say of me what I will say of you in my book, "that the ten years with you were not only the best ten years of my life."[87]

Yet she does not. Reitman instead is seen as small-minded, frivolous, and someone with devilish powers over her. Berkman is her saviour.

The "Emma Goldman" seen in *Living My Life* is very much a creation, a political production of a woman; as Jane Tompkins points out, an "extension," "a mirror," "a device" with the sole purpose of "showing off" for men. Or, in this case, one particular man: Alexander Berkman. All other men, especially Ben Reitman and Johann Most, are cast in this theatre as thugs and devils, while Berkman is constantly described in angelic, heavenly language. When Berkman and Goldman decided to go to Homestead, she describes their reaction as "an awakening," and the "resurrection of the American worker."[88] When Berkman was in jail, Goldman describes him as "consecrated,"[89] her "tower of strength," and a "white light that purged one's soul." Even visiting Pittsburgh, which she associates with Berkman, is described as the place of "Sasha's martyrdom and pilgrimages."

When Goldman finally agrees that "Berkman was right"[90] (this time about the need for few luxuries in the life of an anarchist), she agrees to grow "more spiritually"[91] to convince him of her ability to "serve [the cause] completely,"[92] and thus is ready to prove her worth.[93] When Goldman compares Berkman and Most, she notes "that of the two, Most was more of this earth." Berkman, by implication, was spiritual; he carried the "message" and was the "messenger."[94] So how does Goldman (and Berkman) explain her initial attraction and relation to Most? Simply: "Most became my idol. I worshipped him,"[95] she explains. Most is the one for whom harshest criticism is reserved. Not only is he an idol, but he is described as being anti-Semitic[96] – "Here's my pound of flesh, you Shylocks"[97] – and ultimately as "Judas."[98]

By the time Goldman wrote her autobiography, Most had been dead for twenty years. Goldman had long since softened in her approach to him in public, having written an article about him for the American Mercury at the same time as she was preparing to write her autobiography. In the American Mercury, she writes, "Johann Most was essentially a leader of masses. He hardly any personal life; his whole being was consumed by his work for humanity."[99]

Later in the same article, she explains:

The pathos of Most's last years is the tragedy of all leaders who are carried away from numbers and intoxicated by applause. He joined the labor movement at the period of its idealistic beginning. Owing to his extraordinary oratorical gifts, his powerful and unique pen, his passion faith and personal magnetism, he was able to rouse the masses as few before him, but in his onrush towards the heights he took no time to look behind to see whether the masses could or would keep pace with him.[100]

She explains Most's problem with the masses as:

The earlier German immigrants became weary of the struggle and their children were Americanized. They had nothing of the independent quality of their parents and were quickly absorbed by what is coarse and common in a new land. Gradually Most found himself a general without an army, a prophet without disciples, an alien in his environment. Yet the man's spirit could not be broken. He died a fighter to the end.[101]

The comparison of Goldman's language about Most is worth noting because, in a two-article span, he changes from being "a prophet" to "a snake." Had Goldman's opinion really changed that much, or was this a repercussion of the construction of a particular "Emma Goldman" in *Living My Life*? The letters she wrote at the time seem to indicate that her new representation of herself was more important than her previous opinion. In a letter to Berkman discussing violence as a means to revolution, she pointed out to Berkman that his failure to support or at least sympathize with Leon Czolgosz's assassination of President McKinley was:

A greater blow to me than anything that happened during that terrible period. It affected me more than Most's stand on your act. After all Most had only talked about violence. You had used it and went to prison for it.[102]

Once again Berkman, not Most (or Reitman), is deemed, at least in private, to be found wanting in Emma Goldman's opinion, but in her autobiography, he can do no wrong. This is what can only be described as a deliberate misrepresentation of Most in the autobiography. According to Wexler, this is Goldman "avenging Berkman against Most,"[103] knowing this book would reach a much wider audience than any article in *The American Mercury*.

The influence of Berkman in this chapter and in creating this "Emma Goldman" is astounding. Here Goldman is a follower, a woman who needs to follow, because when she decides on her own the outcome seems to be disastrous for her and for the anarchist cause. Also, note the number of sexual encounters which seem in the autobiography to have lead Goldman to a lonely life, alone without companionship. So where is Goldman's sexual radicalism? In *Living My Life* it is tame, an addiction rather than a choice, a struggle with rationale rather than a freedom. The "sexual Emma Goldman" needs to be sought out elsewhere.

CHAPTER EIGHT

Sex and Sexuality: The Silenced Skein

For nearly thirty years, Goldman taunted mainstream America with her outspoken attacks on government, big business and war. Goldman condemned capitalism, denounced marriage, and crusaded for birth control. The newspapers called her a "modern Joan of Arc." A heretic. A woman possessed of an uncompromising single-mindedness.
–PBS documentary, "Emma Goldman"

After that I always felt two fires in the presence of me. Their lure remained strong, but it was always mingled with violent revulsion. I could not bear to have them touch me.[1]

Sex and sexuality were vital and revolutionary aspects of Goldman's anarchism. She was perceived by the public as one of the sexually radical persons of her day. Yet many of her biographers have pointed to some ambiguities in her lifestyle. For some biographers, her actual life was a dichotomy between her theory of women enjoying many open sexual relationships and the reality that she longed for a family of her own. Bonnie Haaland, in her book *Emma Goldman: Sexuality and the Impurity of the State,* suggests that Goldman's radicalism is found more in her cult status than in a close study of her sexual life. Janet Burstein, in her book *Writing Mothers, Writing Daughters*, points to the irony that Goldman knowingly lived an almost double life of trying to be mother and lover to her partners, while at the same making herself part male as she attempted to become a sexual being.[2] Those who knew Goldman, when interviewed by Paul Avrich many years later, all had a view of her vivacious sexual appetite.[3] All insisted that, despite her well-known appetite, either they or their husbands had resisted her persistent advances. Alice Wexler points out that Goldman's "outspokenness on sexual issues and her unconventional love life shocked many of her own comrades as well as those outside the movement."[4]

When Goldman's life went from the private to public domain after Berkman's attempted assassination of Henry Clay Frick, all the newspaper interviews questioned her views of marriage. The country seemed to be shocked but intrigued by the fact that she and Berkman openly lived together, but were not married. During Goldman's first interview with *The New York World* in 1892, she was asked:

> "But are you his [Berkman's] wife?"
> "Ha! Ha! Yes, I am his wife, but in the anarchistic way, you don't know what that is! The anarchists don't believe in marriages by law. We want no law and when we agree to marry, why ha! Ha! There you are!"
> "The anarchist wife then does not expect the confidences of her husband?'
> "Why should we? But that is a matter I don't propose to discuss."[5]

A year later, in another interview for *The New York World*, Goldman was once again asked about her attitudes toward marriage by reporter Nelly Bly:

> "There is something else I must ask you. We look upon marriage as the foundation of everything good. We base everything upon it. You do not believe in marriage. What do you propose shall take its place?"
> "I was married," she said with a little sigh,"'when I was scarcely seventeen. I suffered – let me say no more about that. I believe in the marriage of affection. That is the only true marriage."[6]

Goldman had come in contact with the free-love sex radicals of late nineteenth-century Britain, and had been highly impressed by their attitudes and practice of open relationships. The idea behind this movement was that adults have the rights to unions based on pleasure and freedom of choice, outside of any rules and regulations instituted by church and state. One of the most important notions for this group was that women had the right to expect pleasure from intimate sexual relationships.

One of the early proponents of free love was Mary Wollstonecraft. Wollstonecraft did not marry her partner, Gilbert Imlay, even though the two had a child together. When the relationship ended, Wollstonecraft began a relationship with the early English anarchist William Godwin. Later supporters of free love with whom Goldman came in contact were Olive Schreiner, Havelock Ellis, and Edward Carpenter, as well as the Fellowship of the New Life, a community based on the ideal of free love that also supported the notions of pacifism and vegetarianism. Many of this group later decided that political action was needed to push their ideas, and so many of them formed the Fabian Society.

In fact, just before she began writing her autobiography, Goldman contacted Frank Harris, who had earlier detailed his many sexual exploits in his autobiography *My Life and Loves*. Harris encouraged her to write a female version of his:

> Furthermore we want a woman's view of life and freedom in sex matters, want it badly: you life and mine will be the first chapters in the Bible of Humanity.[7]

Frank Harris was born James Thomas Harris in Galway, Ireland, on February 14, 1856. He immigrated to the United States in 1869 and settled in Kansas, where he married Florence Ruth Adams, who died within a year of their marriage. Harris then returned to London, where he became known for editing such newspapers as *The Evening News*, *The Fortnightly Review* and *The Saturday Review*. This editing put him in contact with George Bernard Shaw, among others. After more time spent in the United States he moved to Berlin, Germany, where he published his book *My Life and Loves*. This was a four-volume autobiographical account of his life and sexual encounters.

While Goldman appreciated Harris' opinion, she was not so sure that such a book would benefit her. In another letter to Hutchins Hapgood, another member of the free love associations, Goldman was very clear about the memoirs: "I certainly don't intend to make it a sensational sex story."[8]

When it came time to write her autobiography, Goldman had to persuade an American audience that her values were as American as theirs. As Alice Wexler points out, Goldman needed to separate herself from "the demonic legend that surrounded her years in America."[9] This image, Wexler notes, was in part created through the government and media, but in great part by Goldman herself as she exploited situations to get attention.[10] But who created the myth did not matter at this point; what mattered was that Goldman had to tone it down.

The irony of the Goldman-Berkman relationship was that, while Goldman and Berkman were seen as sexual partners by the American public, the truth was that since Berkman's release from prison in 1906, they had not been together sexually, and politically had disagreed on a number of issues. Nevertheless, the fact remained that what the American public saw was: they were deported *together*, left Russia *together*, and were now living in Europe *together*. Berkman, since his release from prison, had been involved in a series of long-term relationships with different women, while Goldman had had a series of short-term relationships, none of which seemed to mean a great deal to her, and two long-term relationships, one with Ed Brady and the other with Ben Reitman. Their lives had actually grown apart in so many ways, but this book was about to join them back together, politically and sexually, all over again.

So looking at *Living My Life*, how was a milder and even more understandable sexual Goldman created, and how has this aspect of her life been reported ever since? What of her sexual life has been included, and much more importantly, what has been omitted, and why? How has the silence contributed to the creation of her identity, and why do her biographers continue the silence, raising their voices only to the level of whispers at best?

In *Living My Life* Goldman describes her earliest sexual experiences at the age of six, when she used to spend time with a young peasant, Petrushka:

> In the evening he would carry me back on his shoulders, I was sitting astride. He would play horse – run as fast as his legs could carry him, then suddenly throw me up in the air, catch me in his arms, and press me to him. It used to give me a peculiar sensation, fill me with exultation, followed by blissful release.[11]

As her infatuation with Petrushka increased, she would steal cake and fruit and bring them to him. Goldman writes that she became "obsessed" with him, thinking of him day and night, and he became part of her erotic dreams:

> One morning I felt myself torn out of sleep. Mother was bending over me, tightly holding my right hand. In an angry voice she cried: "If ever I find your hand like again like that, I'll whip you, you naughty child!"

After Petrushka, she dreamt about the *Feldscher* (Assistant Doctor) who had come to examine her when she had begun to menstruate. However, it is her account of her first sexual intercourse that is worth commenting on. She writes of it:

> After that I always felt between two fires in the presence of men. Their lure remained strong, but it was always mingled with violent revulsion. I could not bear to have them touch me.[12]

At the age of fifteen, Goldman was working in a clothing factory in St. Petersburg. On her way home each day she passed a hotel and soon she and one of the clerks began to meet. One day he asked her if she would like to see the hotel and the rooms. She agreed, explaining that she had never been inside a hotel before. Once inside and in one of the rooms, her friend gave her wine:

> Suddenly I found myself in his arms, my waist torn open – his passionate kisses covered my face, neck and breasts. Not until after the violent contact of our bodies and the excruciating pain he caused me did I come to my senses. I screamed, savagely beating against the man's chest with my fists.[13]

Initially she notes she was not ashamed, only shocked that "contact between man and woman could be so brutal and so painful."[14] Later, she notes, "the shame I did not feel in the arms of the man now overwhelmed me."[15]

Recalling her mother's threats and the pain of her first sexual encounter was designed to show specifically to the still-puritanical American audience that she had a somewhat damaged, unsafe childhood. Hers was not the shared childhood of the average American child; hers was about survival.

By the time Goldman was writing her autobiography, she had

come into contact with the writings and ideas of Sigmund Freud. She attended Freud's lectures in Vienna in 1895, and later at Clark University in Massachusetts, in 1909. Goldman, and many of her generation, liked Freud's theories, which confirmed and explained her belief that childhood formed the basic influence behind all actions, and that sexuality was a social force, made more difficult for women through their repressed sexuality. Goldman's autobiography reflects this belief in Freudian theory: her sexuality was repressed, and recounting the fact that her first sexual encounter was possible a rape explained to her audience her attitude toward marriage.

By the 1890s, she was also involved in many of the American free love groups around Greenwich Village in New York City. These middle- and upper-class groups enjoyed the company of Goldman, and she gave lectures in the living rooms of the rich.[16] "Sex slavery" and "wage slavery" were discussed, as these groups wished to get away from the legal entanglement attached to marriage and instead introduce a new morality in which marriage would be an agreement between the parties, and female sexual desires and needs would be celebrated.

Goldman's involvement with these various groups coincided with two other political factors: the rise of the birth control movement and the Comstock Laws. Sex and sexuality moved at this time from the personal into the realm of practical politics.

The Comstock Laws were passed in 1873 in response to pressure from Anthony Comstock, Head of the New York Society for the Suppression of Vice, an organization he founded with the purpose of supervising public morality. Comstock was a Civil War veteran who, through his political connections, had himself named a Special Agent of the Post Office, which gave him extraordinary powers to prosecute people suspected of sending any immoral material through the mail. George Bernard Shaw coined the phrase "Comstockery" after Comstock alerted the New York Police to the immoral and lewd nature of his play *Mrs. Warren's Profession.*

The Comstock Laws outlawed the delivery or transportation of material deemed "obscene, lewd, or lascivious," including anything to do with birth control. The ironic practical result of these laws was that even many medical textbooks could not be mailed. Ultimately more than three thousand people were arrested; fifteen tons of books and four million pictures were destroyed.

Emma Goldman and Anthony Comstock clashed when Goldman, working as a nurse in the East Side Tenements, was faced with the reality of the choices the women living there had in their lives. Women were forced to have any number of pregnancies, regardless of economic condition or health. They had no education on sexual matters, and certainly no access to medical information.

By the time the birth control movement, led by Margaret Sanger, began in the United States in 1914, Goldman was back in the U.S. from one of her trips to Europe, and was anxious both to help the women in a practical way and ready to test the Comstock Laws. When Sanger decided to flee to Europe, rather than be arrested and face a probable long period in prison, Goldman advised her legally, spoke at rallies on her behalf, and distributed literature in Yiddish and English around New York.

Upon Sanger's return, she decided it was necessary that, in order to get the necessary legal changes which would give her organization sure footing, she would have to purge the birth control movement of some of its more radical members, and this included Emma Goldman. In her autobiography, Goldman notes that while she continued to distribute literature and support those jailed because of the Comstock Laws, it was Sanger who turned her back on the original organization. Goldman insists that she continued to help educate the poor women, but at the same time, she realized that there were bigger issues involved if she was to successfully help the workers.

Goldman's understanding of the importance of Sanger in American history results in Sanger being described as "the only woman in America in recent years to give information to women on birth-control."[17] Goldman was aware of this issue and the specific need for massive change which did not mean a political revolution. Also, by stating that she (and Berkman) continued to struggle against the Comstock Laws, placed her, by 1930, on the same political plane as many in the U.S. who saw these as nothing but the antithesis to the First Amendment. Goldman's position on the birth control movement, or at least her part in it, was an American fighting for Americans and the American constitution. It had nothing to do with sex, sexuality, vice, or pornography. It was about the First Amendment and women's health issues. Goldman's Americanness was shining through!

However, if birth control as a political issue allowed Goldman to appear mainstream, her series of lovers did not. Berkman had some very clear ideas about what should not be mentioned or even hinted at by Goldman: the mention of most of her lovers, he insisted, would be a major mistake. He was aware that, although Goldman would enjoy the shock value it would create, she would have to spend a great deal of time explaining these relationships, which Berkman felt was impossible, at least in the context of memoirs. Goldman, for once, agreed.

So while Goldman did not attempt to ignore her relationships with Johann Most, Alexander Berkman, and Ben Reitman, most other relationships were omitted from the autobiography. She did not, for example, mention her relationships with Arthur Swenson, a much younger Swedish man; Frank Heiner, an anarchist; or Frank Oerter, as well as many other short-term lovers.[18] These omissions were suggested by Berkman, "if they represent only a *repetition* [italics his] of former experiences, even if different in form,"[19] which she agreed to, assuring him, "Of course dear heart, I do mean to cut out only casual affairs."[20] It would be impossible, Goldman realized, to write acceptable memoirs that were inter-woven with brief sexual affairs.

There is another particular aspect of Goldman's life that remained hidden at the time, and since then has been a matter with which many of her biographers refuse to deal with, or even deny: Goldman's physical relationships with women.

In *Living My Life,* Goldman writes:

> Ever since I had come into the anarchist movement I had longed for a friend of my own sex, a kindred spirit with whom I could share the inner most thoughts and feelings I could not express to men, not even to Ed. [Brady] Instead of friendships from women I had met with much antagonism, petty envy and jealously because men liked me.

This statement has been considered a summary of all of Goldman's relationships with women. Goldman wanted a female friend, and she blames women such as Voltairine DeCleyre and Louise Michel, two other well-known anarchists of the time, for their inabilities to appreciate her. Most people have chosen to understand that Goldman's own fiery, quick-tempered nature made any friendships difficult. So it was no surprise that Goldman did not have any female friends.

However, Goldman, along with such people as Havelock Ellis and Edward Carpenter, were some of the first people to speak in public about homosexuality. This despite the fact that many of her fellow anarchists thought it ill-advised, saying, "Anarchism was already enough misunderstood, and anarchists considered depraved; it was ill-advisable to add to the misconceptions by taking up perverted sex-forms, they argued."[21] Goldman decided to ignore her comrades, saying, "I minded censors in my own ranks as little as I did those in the enemy camp." Besides, she argues, "The men and women who used to come to see me after my lectures on homosexuality, and who confided to me their anguish and their isolation were often of finer grain than those who had cast them."[22]

Goldman in *Living My Life* is clear that the shame placed on people because of their sexual preference is wrong, and that anarchy should allow people to live freely:

> Pitiful stories made the social ostracism of the invert seem more dreadful than I had ever realized before. To me anarchism was not a mere theory for a distant future; it was a living influence to free us from inhibitions, internal no less than external, and from destructive barriers that separate man from man.[23]

Yet despite this obvious understanding of the gay issue, before actually beginning her autobiography, in a November 1927 letter to Evelyn Scott, Goldman wrote a very long and complex account of Walt Whitman. Goldman recounted that she:

> Found this extraordinary disparity between his brutal frankness in treating the question of sex, for instance, and his absolute reticence regarding his own sex experiences.[24]

She went on to explain that while she and everyone else knew about his relationships with men, "He absolutely denied it, and even advances the story, whether true of not has never been proven, that he was the father of six children." While she wondered why Whitman denied his homosexuality, she wrote:

I am inclined to think that even his most devoted friends, with the exception of Horace Traubel, would have dropped him like a shot if he had owned up to his leanings.

She then explained to Scott:

I dwelt on Walt Whitman largely because I feel it will be extremely difficult to write a frank autobiography, not so much because I do not believe in frankness, but because one's life is too much interwoven with the lives of others, and while I am glad to say that very few people in my life were purists, still *there are certain intimacies which they may not want to give to the public.*[25] [italics mine]

She went on to explain that her reticence was not based on a fear of how she would appear but what right she had to throw other people's personal lives into the public:

I am not pathologically modest. I am quite willing to openly discuss anything that pertains to my own self, but it is another thing to take liberties with the motives and actions of people who have been in your life.[26]

Silence surrounding sexuality is so much the norm in women's autobiographies and biographies that Wagner-Martin describes it as "tradition."[27] Wagner-Martin notes that Goldman and Margaret Sanger, for example, omit certain heterosexual relationships.[28] Blanche Wiesen Cook notes that there are extra problems surrounding questions of sexuality for women who love women, and women who love younger men have understood for generations that it was necessary to hide their love, lest they be the target of slander and cruelty.[29]

Goldman had decided that she was not going to write about all her relationships. She and Berkman had agreed that short-term lovers did not have a place in *Living My Life*, but she obviously had also decided that this definition of short-term lovers would include her sexual relationships with women, in particular her relationship with Almeda Sperry.

Goldman met Sperry in 1912, in Pittsburgh, when Sperry was working as a radical-activist union organizer. Sperry wrote for one of the radical periodicals and was interested in getting Goldman to speak, not just on political issues, but specifically to groups of working women on issues such as birth control. Almeda Sperry was born in Pennsylvania in 1871 to German immigrant parents. In 1903 she married Fred Sperry, originally from Andover, Ohio, who had moved to Pittsburgh some time previously. Sperry had grown up in a physically abusive home and her marriage was equally abusive. In a letter to Goldman, Sperry describes her husband as a "hunk of humanity" who, like herself, "had started out wrong in life."[30] Sperry seems to have been deeply impacted by Goldman's lecture "White Slave Trade." In this lecture, later published by *Mother Earth* in 1910, Goldman demands that the moral authorities of the state stop pretending they are shocked to know that prostitution exists, and instead devote time to understanding and curing its causes:

> Nowhere is woman treated according to the merit of her work, but rather as a sex. It is therefore almost inevitable that she should pay for her right to exist, to keep a position in whatever line, with sex favors ... Whether our reformers admit it or not, the economic and social inferiority of woman is responsible for prostitution.[31]

Sperry's admiration for Goldman developed into an infatuation soon after they met. They began writing to each other, though it is necessary to point out that, while Sperry's letters to Goldman have survived, none of Goldman's letters to Sperry seem to exist today.

Sperry worked as a prostitute, and her early letters to Goldman reflected her hatred and contempt for men, discussing why she was forced into prostitution and why prostitution was really nothing more than another role assigned to women by men. "Nearly all men try to buy love, if they don't do it by marrying they do it otherwise, and that is why I have such contempt for men," Sperry wrote in August 1912. In another letter, she explained to Goldman, "No I have never deeply loved any man. I seem to act too much. The men are lying pimps and all they are after is sex."[32] In the same letter she also wrote of her passion for Goldman:

> And it is the wild part of me that would be unabashed in showing its love for you in front of a multitude or in a

crowded room. My eyes would sparkle with love – they would
follow you about and love to gaze upon you always and every
part of my body would be replete with satisfaction of its
expression of love. God! God! God! God![33]

In the next few letters, Sperry expressed her feelings for Goldman by referring to her as her "lovely bruised purple grape – you
crushed pineapple, you smothered crab apple- blossom – you beautiful odor of rotten apples." They continued to write to each other,
even as Goldman continued her lecture tours. After a while,
Sperry's letters began to suggest the two women had begun a physical relationship:

Dearest: It is a good thing that I came away when I did – in
fact I would have had to come away anyway. If I had only had
the courage to kill myself when you reached the climax then –
I would have known happiness, for then at that moment I had
complete possession of you. Now you see the yearning I am
possessed with – the yearning to possess you at all times and it
is impossible. What greater suffering can there be – what
greater heaven – what greater hell?[34]

Sperry and Goldman seemed to have had at least a two-year
relationship, one that Ben Reitman was jealous of and unable to
stop. Reitman had been involved with other women along with
Goldman, and though Goldman had not liked Reitman's actions,
her belief in free love meant she felt she could not say anything.
Reitman, though, was worried about the intensity of the Goldman-
Sperry relationship, as not only were the women involved sexually,
but also intellectually. Sperry and Goldman were discussing politics
and books – something Reitman never felt comfortable doing.
   Both women discussed the lives of women of previous generations and the fact that those women had to suffer from the ignorance of others, in particular men. After reading Wollstonecraft,
Sperry wrote to Goldman:

I have read Mary Wollstonecraft twice since I have the book.
Poor soul! The human soul is like a plant; the beauty of its
maturity is wholly governed by the quality of its seed and its
environment while growing ... Poor soul. She had a vision for

the future and was strained to the uttermost by the war between her intellect and her emotions – the fate common to all genius.[35]

Sperry's enthusiasm and intellectual understanding of Wollstonecraft was important to Goldman. In 1911, Goldman published an article on Mary Wollstonecraft in *Mother Earth* entitled, "Mary Wollstonecraft, Her Tragic Life and Her Passionate Struggle For Freedom." In the article, described by Alice Wexler as "the most revealing self-portrait she [Goldman] ever wrote," Goldman "also described her vision of herself."[36] Goldman sees Wollstonecraft as "a genius," "born but not made through this or that individual incident in her surroundings." Goldman writes about "her fate and tragedy," her "bruised and scarred soul," and her "indomitable courage" which got her through "infidelity" and "alienation," and "terror." Sperry and Goldman's common heroine had to have brought them closer.

Reitman's issues, at the same time, were much more practical. "Baby I love you and I am completely yours. I hope you enjoy your visit with Sperry and I trust you will not develop any TECHNIQUE [capitals his] where by you can displace me."[37] Sperry and Reitman had met on a visit to New York. The jealousy between the two must have been obvious, and Sperry wrote to Goldman to explain her harsh language toward Reitman:

> I don't think I used any worse language to Reitman than he has used to me; he asked Hutch Hapgood to suck one of my breasts while he sucked the other so I could have two orgasms at the same time, and that was just after I had had the most divine conversation with Hutch. He also asked me how many men there are in this town that I had not fucked yet.[38]

The two relationships faded around the same time. Goldman began to campaign against the First World War, while Reitman, who was being pushed out of the anarchist movement by Berkman and others, wanted Goldman to be his wife.

With Goldman's memoirs already published, she was allowed to return to the United States in 1934 for a brief (eight-week) lecture tour. When Goldman was in the U.S. Reitman contacted her and explained that he was thinking of writing another book, this one about "wandering women," mostly women hobos. But he also explained to her that he intended to write a chapter on homosexual women as "they make up a large proportion of the hitch-hiking women of the day." He insisted to Goldman that her intense relationships with Sperry, Margaret Anderson, and others meant that she was bisexual, and whether she recognized it or not he was going to be the first to write about this unknown side of Emma Goldman.[39] When Goldman was in Chicago, she met with Reitman and they seemed to have discussed a number of issues, even restarting their almost-daily letter writing. Reitman never wrote the book. Goldman was never outed.

Goldman's relationship with Sperry[40] has been ignored not only by Goldman in her autobiography (there no mention of Sperry at all), but by most of her biographers as well. Some biographers find it necessary to even "defend" Goldman in some way. Richard Drinnon does not mention Almeda Sperry at all; neither do Marian J. Morton, Alix Shulman, or Martha Solomon. John Chalberg mentions Sperry but insists that Goldman was "an avowed heterosexual,"[41] while Sperry was "a lesbian who made overtures to her to be her lover" while Ben Reitman was away. Chalberg then notes Sperry was "a reformed prostitute" who had listened to Goldman's lecture about "White Slave Traffic" and agreed with Goldman's comments and views on men. But Chalberg insists "it is doubtful that Goldman reciprocated in any physical sense." He continues: "The two women shared their distrust of men, but they did not have similar sexual agendas or inclinations."[42] Chalberg comments that in Goldman's letter writing "to Sperry she wrote civilly; to Reitman she wrote passionately." He makes this comment despite the fact that none of Goldman's letters to Sperry have survived.

Even Candace Falk's biography struggles with this topic. While Falk does admit that "Emma did in fact consummate her attraction for Almeda,"[43] she refers to their relationship as "Emma's unusual friendship."[44] Falk's explanation for the sexual relationship between the two women is that it happened "when Emma's infatuation for Ben[45] was waning"[46] and Falk also seems to suggest that Sperry was emotionally unstable, trapping people into abusive relationships:

> Her [Sperry's] letters also suggest Almeda's tendencies to seek out, even create, situations that evoked the experience of guilt

and the inflicting of pain on her loved one and on herself – she had been a battered child – which emerged in her relationship with her husband and later with Emma.[47]

Alice Wexler doubts that any sexual relationship between Goldman and Sperry ever existed: "that Sperry's sexual feelings toward Goldman were ever reciprocated seems unlikely."[48] Wexler sees Sperry as an example of "a young, literate, working class radical from an industrial suburb of Pittsburgh" who met and fell in love with Goldman, seeing her as a mother figure: "Sperry quite openly admitted her wish that she had a mother like Emma – 'you are my mother,' she once told Goldman."[49] Wexler continues that Sperry's letters are "filled with erotic fantasies that sometimes became quite bizarre."[50]

All these biographers refuse to deal even remotely with Goldman's bisexuality. Goldman's complicated views on violence – she would not denounce individuals who partook, but did not recommend it for herself – are all discussed by all biographers and indeed by Goldman herself. But her lesbian relations are mostly ignored and always avoided. It seems as if her biographers see a need to continue Goldman's definite heterosexual reputation by either ignoring her lesbian relationships completely (as in Drinnon), denying thrm (as in Chalberg), or downplaying them (as in Falk or Wexler). Goldman's biographers seem to be determined to avoid her being "suspected of perversion,"[51] sending relations back into the world of "repression and conformity,"[52] resulting in "the romance of the closet."[53]

Goldman's autobiography is an example of a bizarre but careful construction, one in which even a radical, because of political ideas and private demands, agrees to be silenced and to silence herself in order to fabricate a simple story of a misunderstood, adventurous American who sought to promote American ideals and to improve the working and living conditions of the poor. Who continues this image? Why? And do the writers have their own agendas?

CHAPTER NINE

Posthumous Reputations – Scholarly Biographies

> I was returning to France, to lovely Saint-Tropez and my enchanted little
> cottage to write my life. My life – I had lived in its heights and its depths,
> in bitter sorrow and ecstatic joy, in black despair and fervent hope. I had
> drunk the cup to the last drop. I had lived my life. Would I had the gift to
> paint the life I had lived!
> –Emma Goldman, *Living My Life*, 993

> It is inevitable that the advance guards should become aliens to the very
> ones they wish to serve; that they should be isolated, shunned, and repu-
> diated by the nearest and dearest of kin. Yet the tragedy every pioneer
> must experience is not the lack of understanding – it arises from the fact
> that having seen new possibilities for human advancement, the pioneers
> can not take root in the old, and with the new still far off they become
> outcast roamers of the earth, restless seekers for the things they will
> never find.[1]

In *The Politics of Literary Reputation: The Making and Claiming
of 'St. George' Orwell*, John Rodden notes, "Reputations are
made, not born."[2] Later, he asks perhaps a more important question: "reputations get made but how?"[3] Rodden later attempts to
answer his own question by pointing to the role biography plays in
the creation of reputations. The danger of biographies, Rodden
warns, is that they are capable of "blurring" and "muddling,"
resulting in the "proliferation of images."[4] Ultimately, Rodden
notes, "the biographical act not only strips and dismantles a self-
portrait; it also puts another portrait in its place."[5] Rodden continues to explain: "These 'metaphors' or 'images' or 'portraits' are
neither 'true' nor 'false';" instead "only the factual claims made via
them possess or lack validity."[6]

Between 1940, when Goldman died, and now, most of
Goldman's reputations have been created by scholars and academ-
ics, in particular by her biographers. Such are the varied descrip-

tions of her that Karen Rosenberg and Bonnie Haaland both refer to Goldman as a "cult figure." Oz Frankel also sees the variations of descriptions, noting that Goldman's legacy is "fractured," and offers different versions to various constituencies:

> [Goldman was] a fighter for free speech, a communitarian, a libertarian, and anticommunist, an extreme individualist, a precursor of modern feminism, a true subversive, a harmless visionary expelled for voicing innocent ideas, a suffering victim, a cheerful, life affirming woman, or an amusing sharp-tongued, Jewish grandmother. There is the tough politico Goldman and the nurturing, gentle spirit *Emma*.[7] [Italics his]

These more recent, contradictory images of Goldman are not, however, new concepts in themselves. In 1910, Hippolyte Havel, Goldman's friend, onetime lover, and first biographer, noted that "the real Emma Goldman is almost quite unknown."[8] Havel went on to explain,

> The sensationalist press has surrounded her name with so much representation and slander, it would seem almost a miracle that, in spite of this calumny, the truth breaks through and a better appreciation of that much maligned idealist begins to manifest itself."

Yet if press representation during her lifetime had political motives, it should also be noted that even her academic biographers seem to have come to their respective projects with particular missions in mind. Most biographers admit a combination of political and personal reasons when choosing Goldman as their research topic, which, according to Blanche Weisen Cook is not at all unusual: "For biographers, I think, all choices are autobiographical." Bell Gale Chevigny backs up this point when she points to the ever-present tension between the author's identification with the subject and the writer's need for "integrity."

Oz Frankel's 1996 article "Whatever Happened to 'Red Emma'? Emma Goldman, from Alien Rebel to American Icon" in *The Journal of American History* summarizes the popular and academic changes toward Goldman. He notes that there are two pivotal times in Goldman's life when perception was everything: the first was 1934 as she began her short literary tour of the U.S., and

then from the 1960s to the present day, when Goldman was redis-
covered mainly by what Frankel refers to as "radical feminists."[9]

He summarizes various biographies and articles, noting
Goldman has become an "iconic presence";[10] no longer just
woman; yes, importantly Jewish; no longer just political, but social
as well. She is "a martyr for rights,"[11] a "rugged individualist."[12]
She is now compared to Malcolm X,[13] and Andrew Carnegie,[14] she
is packaged, constructed,[15] and institutionalized.[16] Ultimately,
Frankel notes, "Today the radical and tamed Goldman cohabit in
virtual space."[17] The biographers have all played a part in this myr-
iad of images.

The first academic work published on Goldman was Richard
Drinnon's *Rebel in Paradise* in 1961. Drinnon's decision to write
this biography was his personal reaction to a post-McCarthy era
America.[18] He admits his own agenda when, in the opening line of
the preface, he states:

> "To write," observed the late Albert Camus, "is already to
> choose." To choose Emma Goldman as a subject is already to
> say something forcibly, one way or another, about the writer's
> values. Even a simulated indifference to the thrust of her per-
> sonality is scarcely conceivable. I may as well record here at
> the outset, then, that I like her and trust her. No doubt my
> basic sympathy for the radical style in politics helped shape
> this empathy and understanding.[19]

Drinnon concentrates on a chronological account of her public
life. He sees her as part of cultural and historical events and refers
to her as "remarkable."[20] Drinnon also insists on referring to
Goldman throughout the book as "Emma." Only on the last page
of the book does he admit "one serious lapse"[21] in Goldman's life
– the issue of violence. But this one moment of doubt is soon covered by his last two lines: "Emma died triumphant. She had lived
to the end a life of unique integrity."[22]

It was another ten years, 1971, before a second biography of
Goldman was added to the academic world: Alix Shulman's *To the
Barricades*. Shulman, like Drinnon, uses "Emma" rather than the
more academic "Goldman" through the book. Later Shulman
admits she wrote as a "novelist," "totally ignorant of history."[23]
Goldman at the time represented Shulman's own political thoughts

in a sixties anti-war student America. Perhaps the prime example of personal and political exaggeration is found in the story behind the often-misquoted Goldman phrase: "If I can't dance I don't want to be part of your revolution." Goldman never said this. But this does not seem to matter. Alix Shulman was asked for a photo and a phrase of Goldman's that could be reproduced on t-shirts as part of an anti-Vietnam rally. She supplied the photo along with the quotation, "Freedom, the right to self-expression." However, when Shulman went to buy a shirt, there was Goldman with a floppy hat and the "If I can't dance I don't want to be part of your revolution" slogan. Shulman never worried about either the misquote or change of image as she was "delighted by the opportunity to publicize Emma's feminist side,"[24] though she also realized that Goldman had then "soared up into the realms of myth."

José Peritas's book, *Emma Goldman Anarquista de Ambos Mundos,* published in 1978, has not as yet been translated into English and is also the only book on Goldman's life which deals primarily with her time in Spain. The following year, 1979, B.N. Ganguli published *Emma Goldman: Portrait of a Rebel Woman,* Ganguli's brief work has a political, though still deeply personal, motive and is written to be supportive of "anarchist ideas for a modern audience."[25] Ganguli does not criticize Goldman or her ideas; instead she promotes Goldman as a hero for all ages.

One of the more important biographies written was Candace Falk's *Love, Anarchy, and Emma Goldman.* Falk would later establish the Emma Goldman Papers Project in Berkeley, California, and begin a time of intense renewed interest in Goldman. Falk's biography about Goldman was written after she was literally handed a series of letters written between Goldman and Ben Reitman, in a store in Chicago. Her own beliefs and interest in Goldman can be seen by the fact that she had previously named her dog "Red Emma."[26] Falk notes that the reason for naming the dog Red Emma was a combination of the t-shirts with her face, the phrase "If I can't dance ..." and the fact that:

> ...at a time when the resurgent feminist movement was beginning to assert women's right to untraditional career and family choices, we looked for models, for women who dared to defy convention. Emma Goldman's autobiography became required reading.[27]

Falk continues:

> Emma became a symbol of courage and passion; her example
> evoked feelings of hope and expectation in people taking their
> first steps into political activism.[28]

That Falk also has a non-academic, personal interest and relationship with the subject is again clear through her use of "Emma."
Falk also admits she was hesitant to write a biography of Goldman
using these "love letters" as she "did not want to expose Emma to
public scrutiny."[29] Eventually she decided that "respect for Emma
Goldman would enable me to tell the story of her private life in a
sensitive manner that might cast new light on her inspiring political vision."[30]

One of the more prolific and important biographers of Goldman has been Alice Wexler. Wexler published two biographies: *Emma
Goldman: An Intimate Life* (1984) and *Emma Goldman in Exile*
(1989). She also published a number of articles on Goldman's politics and on issues relating to writing biography. Like so many biographers before her, Wexler's initial interest in Goldman grew out of
her own political beliefs and some shared cultural history. In a
1992 article, Wexler explains:

> A few years later Emma Goldman captured my imagination.
> The militance of the 1960s, and especially the movement
> against the war in Vietnam, had heightened the appeal of the
> historical anarchists. With the antiwar legacy, their tactics of
> direct action, and their critique of hierarchy, domination, and
> power, they spoke to us as our contemporaries. With the flow-
> ering of feminism in the early 1970s, Emma Goldman in par-
> ticular became a new heroine. Her outspoken sexual radical-
> ism and her brief brush with Freud in Vienna (echoes of my
> own family's involvement with psychoanalysis) further
> enhanced her appeal for me. Moreover, I could identify with
> her background as an East European Jewish immigrant, since
> my parents were also Russian Jews who had come to
> American in the late nineteenth century.[31]

Martha Solomon (1987), John Chalberg (1991), and Marian
Morton (1992) also wrote biographies. Like Wexler these three

biographers move away from the personal "Emma" to the more academic "Goldman," but all three admit what they are not doing as much as what they are trying to achieve. None are attempting any new ideas about Goldman. In 1987, Martha Solomon published *Emma Goldman*, a brief account of "Goldman as a writer and rhetorician."[32] Solomon's account is a history of Goldman's publications rather than an in-depth theoretical look at her writings, or indeed another story of Goldman's life. Indeed, the lack of detail in Solomon's work extends to the fact that she does not really even look at the influences on Goldman's writings. Instead, the focus is the so-called finished product. Marian Morton's 1992 account, *Emma Goldman and the American Left: Nowhere at Home*, focuses on the "unhappy evolution of her political philosophy,"[33] while she connects "her personal story to her politics."[34] Morton's summary of the reason for this biography is almost dull:

> Emma Goldman is interesting and important today because of the political life she led and the political times in which she lived it.[35]

In John Chalberg's 1991 *Emma Goldman: American Individualist*, he is intent on making Goldman a quintessential American figure:

> The American dream was Goldman's dream just as much as it was that of Andrew Carnegie or Woodrow Wilson or anyone else who felt that sting of her wrath. In fact the American dream has always been many dreams. Some people dream of acquiring great wealth; others dream of little more than a home to call their own. Some seek to wield great power and achieve great notoriety; others seek to lead peaceful and anonymous lives. Goldman's American dream focused on achieving equality and individuality for all – and on possessing power and fame for herself.[36]

Only two biographies published in the 1990s admit to any kind of critical analysis of Goldman's person, politics, or philosophy, though their criticism comes from very different perspectives. They are Bonnie Haaland's *Emma Goldman: Sexuality and the Impurity of the State* (1993) and Kenneth C. Wenzer's *Anarchists Adrift* (1996).

Haaland steps away from criticism of Goldman and instead admits to a "discomfort"[37] with Goldman's political and so-called feminist stance that stems from what Haaland sees as Goldman's "endorsing the private over the public."[38] Her focus is on "Goldman's *ideas*" (italics hers) on "sexuality and reproduction within feminist debates."[39] She notes her own "caution"[40] at Goldman's political ideas and their practicality.

Kenneth C. Wenzer's own political views toward anarchism are clear when he points to the position taken by Goldman relating to the USSR. His objection to Goldman (and to Berkman) is that they both failed the modern anarchist movement by leaving the Soviet Union, and a possible revolution never occurred; instead, the anarchist movement in the USSR was obliterated.

The final four biographies – Martin and Kathleen Gay's biography *The Importance of Emma Goldman* (1997), Leslie A. Howe's *On Goldman* (2000), Theresa Moritzs *The World's Most Dangerous Woman: A New Biography of Emma Goldman* (2001), and Sharon Rudahl's *Dangerous Woman: The Graphic Biography of Emma Goldman* – are all sympathetic to both Goldman and the anarchist cause in America. The Gay biography has a self-explanatory title: *The Importance of Emma Goldman*. They have also edited an encyclopedia of anarchy in America and see Goldman as a vital political and inspirational figure.

Howe concentrates on Goldman's ideas, but does not criticize at all, preferring to state that "many of her ideas were not developed much past a very preliminary stage."[41] Instead, "her significance as a feminist is seen primarily in terms of her activism,"[42] and her "insistence on individualism,"[43] which separates her out from other revolutionaries.

Moritz's book is a chronological account of Goldman's life and her Canadian anarchistic connections. It is an attempt to find new facts and new figures to interview, but is noticeably devoid of criticism. Indeed, the book was the inspiration behind the production of a documentary simply titled *Emma Goldman in Canada*.

In September 2007, New Press published *Dangerous Woman: The Graphic Biography of Emma Goldman* by Sharon Rudahl. Rudahl combines her art with Goldman's life and turns out what has been described as a graphic novel-type account of her life. The result is a very twenty-first-century Goldman, but a biography that remains on the level of straightforward story-telling.

Who is the "Emma Goldman" created by these biographers? Have they really "blurred" her image, as Rodden fears for all biographies, or have they instead added to our insights on Goldman? What is interesting and unusual to note is that many of her biographers (Drinnon, Shulman, and Falk in particular) seem to claim a personal relationship with Goldman, referring to her as "Emma" throughout their books. This personal Goldman – Emma – makes her a gentle soul, misunderstood by authorities, searching for love and adventure. There is also a certain reverence in these biographies – an unwillingness to question Goldman and her motives. Finally, these biographies, by using this familiar "Emma," do succeed in creating a much gentler Goldman, and much more misunderstood, far from the most dangerous woman in America of J. Edgar Hoover!

Despite this use of "Emma," there are a series of different images also created by each biographer. Drinnon, who sets the standard for any Goldman biography by being the first, also creates "Emma Goldman" the political being. Drinnon's Goldman is representative of the political and cultural changes of the late nineteenth and early twentieth centuries. His book combines the changes in American society, immigration, politics, and even technological inventions around Goldman. For Drinnon, Goldman is neither a female in politics, nor a feminist activist; instead, she is a creation of her time, representative of a rapidly changing American society.

Shulman's approach is a clear contrast. Her Goldman is a romantic heroine – avenging the wrongs on behalf of the poor, pointing out the faults in the democratic system, all the time maintaining her joy of life, her insistence on dance, music, and fun. This theatrical Goldman is a woman of few problems; she is one who has chosen a lifestyle of change, a woman who neither needed nor wanted security. Candice Falk's biography begins the creation of a more complex Goldman. While Falk does spend a great deal of time in her book detailing the complex relationship between Emma Goldman and Ben Reitman, she also shows us the complexity of Goldman's life, in which sex, politics, relationships, financial insecurity, and political complications were all a part of her days. Falk also is clear that Goldman was a person, both politically and personally, who was comfortable with the role of opposition. She opposed very well – marriage, prostitution, the vote, banks, war, communities, socialism – but Goldman was never as sure of her role as a proponent.

Wexler, when she begins to write about Goldman, initially uses a fashion similar to Drinnon – portraying Goldman as an idealistic figure, naïve to the complex ways of American democracy, ultimately left expelled and misunderstood. However, Wexler's second biography of Goldman shows a change in Wexler's approach to the whole subject of how to write about and portray Goldman. In *Emma Goldman in Exile* (1989), Wexler approaches Goldman as a person and character, a historical figure and political icon. This multi-faceted approach succeeds in recognizing that "Goldman's significance and interest extends beyond the causes to which she devoted her life."[44] In this book, Wexler wants to show the "crosscurrents of her character"[45] so that a more complex "Emma Goldman" can emerge. What Wexler has perhaps succeeded in doing in both this biography and in her 1992 article "The Anxiety of Biography," is making clear that there is not one Emma Goldman, that she is instead a multi-dimensional person with "her fictions and her truths, her limitations and her legacy."[46]

Wexler's urging of reviewing Goldman and recognizing the complexity of the character and events that surrounded her allows Haaland's "discomfort"[47] toward Goldman to be more clearly understood. As stated previously, Haaland is one of the very few biographers who admits any sort of even mild criticism of Goldman. Haaland admits her attraction "to Goldman's message of liberation for women, yet [is] cautious of the implementation of the message"[48] as the power difference between the sexes "would not disappear should Goldman's anarchist vision come to mind."[49] Nevertheless, Haaland recognizes that Goldman successfully integrated the public and private sphere into one life choice, which for Goldman meant equating sexual freedom with individual freedom and freedom from the state.[50] Haaland considers Goldman's concept of "power" too simple. She insists that the idea that the state has all the power and that freedom from the state will give power to the individual is not a real possibility. Haaland's political and theoretical account of Goldman's ideas is the first study in which we seriously view the theoretical and practical notions of Goldman's anarchy. For the first time Goldman moves from activism to philosophical thought, with the result that Goldman's intellectual plans can be discussed and evaluated.

Goldman at this stage is a nexus of multiple stories, each valid, each with merit, and each exploring Emma Goldman a little differently. What is common throughout each biography is the use made of Goldman's autobiography, *Living My Life*. Oz Frankel makes it clear that *Living My Life* is a complex mixture of fact and fiction, and at the time offered a simplistic and safe view of Goldman.

> Goldman's autobiography, *Living My Life* (1931), has assumed a pivotal role in rediscoveries of her. Providing an enormous wealth of detail besides profound ambiguities, it has enticed rereading and reinterpretation. Historically, the autobiography functioned in contradictory ways: it presented Goldman as an uncompromising radical role model but suggested an opening for making peace between the anarchist rebel and the American mainstream. Moreover it offered itself and Goldman's private self as alternative subjects for scrutiny and identification, separable from Goldman's rich political writings and public career.[51]

For many of her autobiographers, however, *Living My Life* provided a constant source of facts and insights about and into Goldman. The autobiography is used by most of her biographers as a valid historical source. For Drinnon *Living My Life* is a great book, insightful and meaningful in its explanation of Goldman's life and the anarchist movement at the beginning of the twentieth century. Shulman uses it as her basic history book, while Falk does likewise, though she does use other sources, especially correspondence between Goldman and Reitman, to explain the complexity of her life. Wexler's first biography, *Emma Goldman: An Intimate Life,* uses *Living My Life* as a useful source, though her second biography is where she expresses some doubts about the value of the autobiography, explaining that it needs to be seen in more subjective terms.

Richard Drinnon describes herself as, "like Thomas Wolfe, a great exponent of putting in even more than the full story."[52] According to Falk, the autobiography, while initially a consultation with other radicals, ultimately became a means of revenge on Ben Reitman. Reitman is portrayed as uncaring, politically stupid, and most important of all, not capable of loyalty.

For her other biographers, such as Chalberg and Morton, the autobiography depicts her battles with herself, her cultural and

personal background: "a woman who had warred with her oppres-
sors," "a victim,"[53] "with the loneliness of her self-portrait."[54] Ultimately, however, it is these biographers who accept what is presented in *Living My Life* as historically factual, although sometimes
personally emotional. However, few biographers dare to criticize
Goldman or to ask more questions about the details of her political ambitions.

Bonnie Haaland looks to Goldman's writings from all sources:
essays, lectures, articles, and other books, while Alice Wexler notes
that the timing of her writing both for personal, financial, and
political reasons meant she began to write with a series of objec-
tives in mind that meant a curtailing of voice and the self.

Thus, the result is that the "Emma Goldman" created in and by
Living My Life, and then her series of biographers, becomes the
most well-known and highly popular version. As Oz Frankel points
out, there is little to distinguish Emma Goldman in *Living My Life*
and the Emma Goldman in American consciousness. The writing of
her autobiography worked. Emma Goldman has become an
American icon, but remains dangerous.

Goldman – Unearthed

Later Robert Henri asked me to sit for my Portrait. I was very busy at the time; besides several people had already tried to paint me, with little success. Henri said he wanted to depict the "real Emma Goldman." "But which is the real one?" I asked; "I have never been able to unearth her."[1]

When in the course of human development, existing institutions prove inadequate to the needs of man, when they serve merely to enslave, rob and oppress mankind, the people have the eternal right to rebel against, and overthrow, these institutions.[2]

Emma Goldman's autobiography, *Living My Life,* may be a sexual, political, and somewhat compromised publication, but all her writings show her to be highly opinionated, someone who believed in the need for revolution, and a complete change in society. Some speeches show her to be fiery and demanding change, while some of her actions display her as being physically tired, emotionally exhausted, and at times even spiritually in doubt. Trying to find the one real Emma Goldman is not possible, as there is no one such Goldman to unearth. Instead Emma Goldman is a complex web of skeins, all of which combine to produce a person, character, and caricature. All are Emma Goldman.

In "What I Believe," which Goldman wrote for the *New York World* in 1908, she commented:

"What I believe" is a process rather than a finality. Finalities are for gods and governments, not for the human intellect. While it may be true that Herbert Spencer's formulation of liberty is the most important on the subject, as a political basis of society, yet life is something more than formulas. In the battle for freedom, as Ibsen has so well pointed out, it is the

struggle for, not so much the attainment of, liberty that
develops all that is strongest, sturdiest and finest in human
character.[3]

This constant search is what is perhaps different about
Goldman, especially when comparing her to Berkman. Goldman's
ideas changed, and evolved. She did respond differently to various
situations at various times in her life. After her death, the American
mainstream press commented on the differences they perceived in
her life and opinions: "She had a quality rare among the devotees
of economic dogma, she was honest."[4] And while *The New York
Times* editorial may be described as over-simplistic, the difficulty of
placing Goldman within a system is typical of the complexity of
studying women, particularly radical women, and understanding
their ideas and deeds within the conventional bounds of history.

This issue of finding and understanding women's political
ideals, seeing how, where, and when they were influenced, how
they changed, and if they changed, has been a difficult task for historians, not just when dealing with Emma Goldman but with all
politically active women. Linda Kerber notes that studying the
ideas of women has for so long been deemed difficult, if not impossible, by academia, as the usual places to find ideas were not contexts that were open to nineteenth- and early twentieth-century
women. Formal university debates and discussions, sermons, lectures, and pamphlets were indeed woman-less for the most part;
but Kerber insists that what is needed is a new method of research,
one in which historians look at diaries and letters in particular.
There, according to Kerber, any historian can find the necessary
serious and complex discussions of ideas within various female
communities.[5] In addition to the diaries, minutes of book clubs and
nineteenth-century literary societies show a clear understanding of
the depth of women's knowledge on the particular subjects and
ideas of the society in which they lived.

A final factor that needs to be considered is the ease with which
pamphlets could be published. Pamphlets were not books; they
were unedited streams of thought. Written for a specific audience,
published usually privately by friends with similar ideas and political views, they allowed for issues to be read, discussed, and debated in a public arena. As well as publishing pamphlets, albeit for a
small select audience, new forms of communication allowed women

to discuss their ideas in different structures. Margaret McFadden outlines six avenues of communication that opened up for women at the end of the nineteenth century that made it possible for a whole new complexity of thought to be discussed. These are: (1) "New communication systems," including the possibility of travel for women. Their journals and published accounts gave women new possibilities in their lives. (2) Newly organized evangelical women, who set up systems of communication and dialogue for women all over the world. (3) The interaction between women in a variety of political movements, ranging from the temperance movement, to birth control, to peace. (4) The utopian movement that developed in the U.S. with its European links. (5) The European and U.S. political revolutionary links. (6) The rise of the number of successful female authors. What McFadden succeeds in doing in her study is to show that women did not just cross the Atlantic successfully in terms of communication and complex ideas, but also that women were involved in a variety of political issues.[6] By looking at these newer methods of studying women's thought, it becomes possible to find the more radicalized and politicized Emma Goldman, one not represented in *Living My Life*.

Emma Goldman's "conversion" to anarchy was a more spiritual then intellectual experience. Her reaction to hearing about the Haymarket protests, the trial, and their death, resulted in her walking home "in a dream."[7] The result of such a emotional response was that, when Goldman was asked any questions about anarchy for years, she would repeat that she did not need to explain or elaborate, as she was an anarchist. However, during her initial time in jail in Blackwell's Island, in 1893, Goldman's attitude changed. First of all, Goldman learned English. This was vital. Upon her release she could now communicate directly to a much larger audience than she could previously, and she could speak English more than most other anarchists. Johann Most, for example, usually only lectured in German, while many of the Jewish anarchists would lecture and write only in Yiddish. Goldman could now communicate directly with the mainstream press and could in turn correspond with a variety of people from many different interest groups. Goldman's correspondence is astounding. The number of people to whom she wrote and who, in turn, wrote to her is amazing. She counted George Orwell, Merle Curti, Rose Pesotta, and Upton Sinclair among her correspondents.

Another important factor about her jail time was that it allowed her to read much more. This was particularly important in the "Americanization" of Goldman. Up to this point, she thought very little of the nativist anarchist movement that had existed in the United States. After her time in jail, because of her reading and the visits by prominent American individualists, she moved in the direction of understanding specific American needs for change. By the 1907 International Anarchist Congress in Amsterdam, Goldman's speeches showed a more polished understanding of anarchism, and also of the role of the movement in the United States:

> Emma Goldman, for the American movement, brought a long account of the situation in the United States ... She described how in her three journeys across the American Continent, visiting twenty-eight states. She found anarchists groups all over the country speaking every language from Dutch to Japanese. But the purely American movement is very young in spite of the strong foreign movement in its midst.[8]

The following day, in a session entitled "Anarchism and Organization," Goldman outlined the notion of anarchy, organization, and society:

> We are often accused of a desire to annihilate society, we are constantly called the enemies of organized society, and there have been some who, calling themselves Anarchists, have put forward an ideal of society without organization. But this merely destructive conception of Anarchism rests on the fallacy of considering present society as organized. That is not so ... for us organization is a natural organic growth, and the test of such organization must be that it shall increase and liberate our own individuality, the very contrary of all the so-called organization of to-day. Certainly we do not want such organization of non-entities, but an organization of self-conscious individualities.[9]

As McFadden points out, what has happened here is that Goldman availed herself of travel opportunities, and also found herself in communication with women from a variety of organizations – remember Goldman was not in favour of women's suffrage as she did not think it would solve any issues for women – and discussed ideas on revolution with Europeans and all sorts of American groups.

A lesser-known factor in Goldman's life was her involvement in various West Coast utopian movements. When Goldman's 1898 lecture tour in Seattle and Tacoma collapsed through a combination of a strong police presence and lack of financial support, Goldman instead visited Home, Washington, where for three evenings she lectured on "The Woman Question," "Authority vs. Liberty," and "Patriotism."[10] Two years previously, in 1896, an anarchist community had been established there that consisted mainly of people from earlier, failed utopian communities.[11] This group supported a wide variety of ideals: communal land owning, free love, sexual liberation, and nudity. Goldman visited several more times, staying in part to lecture and in part to rest and mix socially with the group.[12] While Goldman may have understood and believed in the individual as the primary aspect of society, it is clear through her involvement with a wide variety of groups, socially and politically, that specific communities, particularly the educational community, were *the* places where anarchy would be established.

Such was Goldman's belief in the power of education that in 1931, when noting the state of chaos in Weimar Germany and the rise of fascism, Goldman suggested education as a means of preventing the rise of "Prussian militarism"[13] and "a growing military spirit."[14] In two particular schools in Germany, in Dresden and Hellerau, Goldman noted the novel concepts of education that included "comfortable tables and chairs, the walls ornamented with warm color designs, lamps covered with lovely shades." She noted, "free initiative and self-reliance has proven an aid to self-discipline, and has developed a strong sense of responsibility within the different groups."

Earlier in her public career, while still in the United States, Goldman had been among the founding members of the Modern School Movement, based on the ideals of Francisco Ferrer. For Goldman, education as it was in the U.S. was a "veritable barrack, where the human mind is drilled and manipulated into submission to various social and modern spooks, and thus fitted to continue our system of exploitation and oppression."[15] The result of Goldman's belief in and hope for education as the basis for a revolution was that, as Paul Avrich notes, she "plunged into the day-to-day work of raising funds, publishing literature, starting schools, and securing pupils and teachers."[16]

This work in education brought Goldman into contact with various people from a variety of political sources. As McFadden has shown, communicating between the various European and American revolutionary groups was an everyday reality. Avrich points out that freethinkers, sex radicals, anarchists, socialists, syndicalists, and all kinds of progressives were part of the "Ferrer Association."[17] Revolution was not a once-off political moment but a progression of ideas possible through modern communication and influenced by a variety of political backgrounds. Goldman was not simply an anarchist but a modern thinker, very much part of the political and social dialogue made possible at the beginning of the twentieth century through travel, and the ease with which news was reported across the Atlantic.

GOLDMAN AND BERKMAN – POSTSCRIPT

Without a doubt, the cruelest event in Emma Goldman's life occurred on her sixty-seventh birthday, June 27, 1936, when Alexander Berkman committed suicide. They had previously planned to take a boat trip together, but Berkman's pain following his second operation for cancer was too severe and they postponed.

That day, Goldman had written to him, as usual:

My dear,

Whom else should I write on this day but you? Only there is nothing to tell. I keep thinking what a long time to live. For whom? For what? But there is no answer. Unless to rake one's brain.

I have asked Michael and his family to lunch today. One thing I can still find relief in is housework and cooking. Need I tell you that I miss you on this day? And Emmy, who would have enjoyed the chicken. But if you feel better and are gaining strength, I do not mind the disappointment. Indeed it would have been a grand surprise. And your room so nice and inviting. It looks sad today. Imagine, I had a wire yesterday, you'll never guess from whom. From Demie Coleman, to my birthday. Wonderful that she should remember. She is evidently in England. Cannot make out the name of the town.

Let me hear from you, how you are, Sasha dear. Greetings to Emmy.
Affectionately,
Emma.

The same day, Berkman sent her a card wishing her a happy birthday:

Dear,

This is your birthday. Sorry I can't be with you. Some other time I hope.

Nothing new here. Both feeling some better. Will call up later in the day – it's only 7 AM No autobuses yet. How is everything with you, and the visit of the Cohn family?

Got yours of the 25th. Will answer your points by and by.

I hope you have a nice day there (the weather uncertain here today) and enjoy the day.
Affectionately,
S.

Later Berkman had called her to wish her a happy birthday, and while he did not feel well enough to travel to be with her, he told her not to worry, that he was feeling somewhat better. However, that night, while in severe pain, he took a gun and shot himself in the chest. The bullet perforated his lungs, finally lodging in his spine. He died sixteen hours later. His note was brief:

I don't want to live a sick man, dependent. Forgive me Emmy darling, and you too Emma. Love to all. Help Emmy.
Sasha

In a letter to anarchists in Spain, Goldman explained her feelings: "It is only two weeks since our beloved comrade Alexander Berkman passed away, yet it seems an eternity to me. The blow his untimely death struck me has left me completely shattered. I find it difficult to collect my thoughts."[18]

Goldman then explained the events of that night: at 2 AM, on Sunday morning, Goldman was awoken by a phone call telling her what had happened and urging her to immediately to travel Nice if she wanted to see Berkman. Goldman took the first bus. There she found Emmy, who had been initially arrested for the attempted murder of Berkman. Berkman was in severe pain and Eckstein had gone to fetch the doctor. While she was out, Berkman had shot himself and had not told Eckstein. When medical help came, the gunshot wound was discovered, Berkman was brought to the hospital, and Eckstein was arrested.

When Goldman arrived at the hospital, Berkman was in severe pain, but did recognize her. He eventually lapsed into a coma and died at 10 PM Sunday, June 28.

In death, finally, for the first time probably since Berkman's release from jail, Goldman had a few moments alone with her long-time friend and partner:

> Death had robbed me of the chance to be with my lifelong friend until he breathed his lat. But it could not prevent me from a few precious moments with him alone in the Death House – moments of serene peace and silence in contemplation of our friendship that had never wavered, our struggles and work for the ideal for which Sasha had suffered so much, and to which he had dedicated his whole life.[19]

Goldman was shattered. Her sorrow was "all embracing,"[20] her pain and loss "beyond mere words."[21] But her devotion to Berkman was never in question, as she promised to continue his work, insisting, "the House of the Dead will spur me on to continue the work Sasha and I began on August 15, 1889."[22]

August 15, 1889 is the date she referred to throughout her life as the moment in time when she began her work. Her loyalty to Berkman, so obvious throughout her autobiography, was still apparent even in the letter to the Spanish anarchists, as she did not mention that his suicide was on her birthday. Instead, she explained:

> Comrade Berkman had always maintained that, if ever he would be stricken with suffering beyond his endurance, he would go out of life by his own hand ... Anyhow Sasha remained alone in his apartment and as he always had a revolver with him, in fact since he was released from the living tomb in 1906, Sasha found courage to make an end of his agony.[23]

Goldman's iconic devotion to Alexander Berkman is the foundation of her public and private life. Their complicated relationship, sexually, philosophically, and politically, framed each action and reaction in her life. Whatever she felt, whoever she was involved with, all centered on Berkman. In turn, when he edited her life story, he created just another Emma Goldman, and as long as Berkman was involved in the process, she trusted whatever was produced. Indeed, by 1939, when she was living in Canada, she referred to August 15 as her "birthday" and organized a series of dinners to raise money for the Emma Goldman Spanish Refugee Fund.[24]

Goldman did adhere to Berkman's final wish of helping Eckstein. She was initially angry at Berkman for burdening her with Eckstein, especially when Goldman began to organize Berkman's papers and she saw the ream of letters Eckstein had written complaining about her. As always, and even in death, Goldman remained loyal to Berkman and financially gave what she could to Eckstein.

Goldman left France for Canada in April 1939. There, she received another request from Eckstein looking for money for yet another operation on her stomach, which Eckstein insisted was needed. Though Goldman had long believed that Eckstein was a hypochondriac, she nevertheless sent her more money. Within a year Emmy Eckstein was dead. Goldman spent what little money she had on her funeral.

DEATH OF GOLDMAN

When Emma Goldman arrived in Canada for the last time in March 1939, she was initially disappointed by the lack of fuss on her arrival, but she soon perked up deciding on her "birthday," August 15, to create an Emma Goldman Spanish Refugee Rescue Fund to help rescue and support anarchists from the Spanish Civil War. She settled into her own apartment in the house of two Dutch anarchists and enjoyed "the freedom and independence"[25] of her life. All that winter Goldman was involved in politics, arguing about the obvious forthcoming war in Europe, the question of refugees, and getting personally involved in a few political cases.

On Saturday, February 17, 1940, as a group of her friends and comrades planned to meet at her house for their usual weekly meal and political discussion, Goldman suffered a massive stroke. She was completely paralyzed and speechless. In hospital, she made some progress after receiving physical therapy, and some of the symptoms eased.

She was allowed home in March, though got frustrated easily as communication was still difficult. In early May she suffered another stroke and died on May 14, 1940.

Having been refused entry into the United States for so long, finally in death she was allowed back to the United States, to be buried in Chicago, at Waldheim Cemetery, near the graves of the Haymarket martyrs. At her funeral on May 17, 1940, Harry Weinberger began:

> For more than thirty years I have known Emma Goldman, as her lawyer and her friend. Never in all those thirty years have I known her except as a battler for freedom and justice. She was tireless; she was fearless; she never compromised. Liberty was always her theme; liberty was always her dream; liberty was always her goal.
>
> In a machine age, Emma Goldman always seemed to me the glorification of individuality. She was symbolical of the greatness of mental freedom in an age of regimentation.[26]

He also realized that, though Emma Goldman was dead, she would never be forgotten, promising, "You will live forever in the hearts of your friends and the story of your life will live as long as the stories are told of women and men of courage and idealism."[27]
And he finished:

> Emma Goldman, we welcome you back to America, where you wanted to end your days with friends and comrades. We had hoped to welcome you back in life but we welcome you back in death. You will live forever in the hearts of your friends and the story of your life will live as long as the stories are told of women and men of courage and idealism.[28]

All of this would have thrilled Goldman, who was never sure of her place in history and how her actions would be judged. A few years before she died she wrote a short article entitled "Was My Life Worth Living?" in *Harper's Weekly*, in 1934. There, she explained:

Considered from this angle, I think my life and my work have been successful. What is generally regarded as success – acquisition of wealth, the capture of power or social prestige – I consider the most dismal failures. I hold when it is said of a man that he has arrived, it means that he is finished – his development has stopped at that point. I have always striven to remain in a state of flux and continued growth, and not to petrify in a niche of self-satisfaction. If I had my life to live over again, like anyone else, I should wish to alter minor details. But in any of my more important actions and attitudes I would repeat my life as I have lived it. Certainly I should work for Anarchism with the same devotion and confidence in its ultimate triumph.[29]

Today Emma Goldman can be found on eBay, on Broadway, and in movies. The image of Goldman continues to be an ever-changing picture, subject only to the mood of the designer, as Goldman is a woman of all time to all peoples. As one comrade put it at a memorial service: "She had many faults, but she was a mensch."[30]

EMMA GOLDMAN: STILL DANGEROUS

Yet even in the twenty-first century the name of Emma Goldman conjures up a variety of reactions. In December 2002, when Candace Falk, Project Director of the Emma Goldman Project Papers at the University of California at Berkeley, quoted Goldman in a letter requesting contributions to support the Goldman project, she received a strong and surprisingly dramatic response. As part of the letter, Falk chose a quotation from a speech in which Goldman describes her fear about governments curtailing free speech: Individuals would "be obliged to meet in cellars, or in darkened rooms with closed doors, and speak in whispers lest our next-door neighbors should hear that freeborn citizens dare not speak in the open." Later in the same letter Falk used a further Goldman quotation, pointing out the danger of war: "In the face of this approaching disaster, it behooves men and women not yet overcome by war madness to raise their voice of protest, to call the attention of the people to the crime and outrage which are about to be perpetrated on them."[31]

The result of Falk's use of these two quotations was a censuring of the Goldman Project Papers by the U.C. Berkeley authorities and a demand that the Project recognize the inappropriate use of these quotations, considering the political climate at the time. Eventually the university relented, but not before the story was reported in *The New York Times* and sfgate.com, as well as by other news outlets. *The New York Times* of January 14, 2003 noted the irony:

> In her own day, the Lithuanian-born anarchist Emma Goldman roused emotions including considerable fear with her advocacy of radical causes like organized labor, atheism, sexual freedom and opposition to military conscription.
>
> "Emma Goldman is a woman of great ability and personal magnetism, and her persuasive powers are such to make her an exceedingly dangerous woman," Francis Caffey, the United States attorney in New York, wrote in 1917.
>
> Goldman died in 1940, more than two decades after being deported to Russia with other anarchists in the United States who opposed World War I. Now her words are the source of deep consternation once again, this time at the University of California, which has housed Goldman's papers for the past 23 years.[32]

Sfgate.com reported:

> Emma Goldman, America's iconoclastic turn-of-the-century muckraking anti-war activist, is at it again – 63 years after her death.[33]

Emma Goldman – still dangerous, even in the twenty-first century!

Selected Bibliography

NEWSPAPERS AND MAGAZINES

Boston Globe
Boston Herald
Chicago Herald
Chicago Tribune
Free Society
Freiheit
Jewish Daily Forward
Liberator
Liberty
Masses
Mother Earth
New York Sun
New York Daily Tribune
New York Times
New York Tribune
New York World
Peaceful Revolutionist
Washington Herald
Washington Post

BOOKS AND ARTICLES

Ackerman, Kenneth D. *Young J. Edgar Hoover.* New York: Carroll &
  Graf Publishers, 2007.
Alpern, Sara, and Joyce Antler, eds. *The Challenge of Feminist
  Biography.* Urbana: University of Illinois Press, 1992.
Anderson, Carlotta. *All-American Anarchist: Joseph A. Labadie and the
  Labor Movement.* New Jersey: Wayne State University Press, 1968.
Anderson, Margaret. *My Thirty Years War.* New York: Horizon Press,
  1969.
–"The Immutable." The Little Review 1 (November 1914).

Asbaugh Carolyn. *Lucy Parson: American Revolutionary.* Charles H. Kerr Publishing, 1976.

Avrich, Paul. *Anarchist Portraits: An Oral History of Anarchism in America.* Princeton: Princeton University Press, 1990.

–*Anarchist Voices: An Oral History of Anarchism in America.* Princeton: Princeton University Press, 1996.

–*An American Anarchist: The Life of Voltaire de Cleyre.* Princeton: Princeton University Press, 1978.

–*The Haymarket Tragedy* Princeton: Princeton University Press, 1986.

–*The Modern School Movement: Anarchism and Education in the United States.* Princeton: Princeton University Press, 1980.

–*The Russian Anarchists.* Princeton: Princeton University Press, 1967.

Barrett, Michelle. *The Politics of Truth.* Stanford: Stanford University Press, 1991.

Baum, Charlotte, Paula Hyman and Sonya Michel. *The Jewish Woman in America.* New York: Dial Press, 1976.

Berkman, Alexander. *Prison Memoirs of an Anarchist.* New York: New York Review of Books Reprint, 1999.

–*The Blast 1916-1917.* Reprint California: AK Press, 2005.

–*The Bolshevik Myth.* New York: Boni & Liveright, 1925.

–*Now and After: The ABC of Communist Anarchism.* New York: Vanguard Press, 1929.

–Ed.,*Selected Works of Voltairine de Cleyre,* New York: Mother Earth Publishing, 1914.

Bose, Atindranath. *A History of Anarchism.* Calcutta: The World Press Private Limited, 1967.

Butler, Judith. *Gender Trouble: Feminism and the Subversion of Identity.* New York: Routledge, 1999.

Burstein, Janet. *Writing Mothers, Writing Daughters.* Chicago: University of Illinois Press, 1996.

Cadegan, Una. "Neither Tired nor Poor nor Huddled: Emma Goldman and the Limits of the American Dream." *University of Dayton Review.* Winter, 23:3 (1995-96): 47-53.

Calberg, John. *Emma Goldman: American Individualist.* New York: Harper Collins, 1991.

Cahm, Caroline. *Kropotkin and the Rise of Revolutionary Anarchism.* Cambridge: Cambridge University Press, 2002.

Carpenter, Mecca Reitman. *No Regrets: Dr. Ben Reitman and the Women Who Loved Him.* Boston: Southside Press, 1999.

Carr, E.H. *The Russian Revolution from Lenin to Stalin 1917-1929.* New York: Palgrave Macmillan, 2004.

–*A History of Soviet Russia*. New York: Palgrave MacMillan, 1953.

Channing, Walter. "The Mental Status of Czolgosz, the Assassin of President McKinley," *American Journal of Insanity* 59, (1902).

Cole, Stephen. *Emma Goldman: A Guide to Her Life and Documentary Sources*. Alexandria: Chadwyck-Healey, 1985.

Cott, Nancy F. and Elizabeth H. Pleck, eds. A *Heritage of Her Own: Towards a New Social History of Women*. New York: Simon and Schuster, 1979.

Crenshaw Martha, ed. *Terrorism in Context*. Pennsylvania: Pennsylvania State University Press, 1995.

Dawley, Alan. *Struggles for Justice: Social Responsibility and the Liberal State*. Belknap Press, 1993.

DeLeon, David. *The American as Anarchist*. Baltimore: John Hopkins University Press, 1978.

Dinnerstein, Leonard. *Anti-Semitism in America*. Oxford: Oxford University Press, 1995.

Drinnon, Richard. *Rebel in Paradise: A Biography of Emma Goldman*. Chicago: University of Chicago Press, 1961.

–ed. *Nowhere at Home: Letters from Exile of Emma Goldman and Alexander Berkman*. New York: Schoken Books, 1975.

–"Neither God nor Master." Anarchy. 109, Vol. 10 no. 3. (March 1970).

Duberman, Martin. *Mother Earth: An Epic Drama of Emma Goldman's Life*. New York: St. Martin's Press, 1985.

Eakin, Paul John, ed. *American Autobiography*. Wisconsin, University of Wisconsin Press, 1991.

Evans, Sara. *Born for Liberty: A History of Women in America*. New York: Simon and Schuster, 1989.

Ewen, Elizabeth. *Immigrant Women in the Land of Dollars: Life and Culture on the Lower East Side, 1890-1925*. New York: Monthly Press, 1975.

Falk, Candice. *Love, Anarchy, and Emma Goldman*. New York: Holt, Rineholt and Winston, 1984.

Fitzgerald, F. Scott. *The Great Gatsby*. New York: Scribner, 1925.

Fine, Sidney. "Anarchism and the Assassination of McKinley." *American Historical Review* 60 (1955): 777-799.

Foglesong, David S. *America's Secret War Against Bolshevism*. Chapel Hill: The University of North Carolina Press, 1995.

Fisher, Jack C. *Stolen Glory*. California: Alamar Books, 2001.

Frankel, Oz. "Whatever Happened to 'Red Emma'? Emma Goldman from Alien Rebel to American Icon." *The Journal of American History*. 83 (1996):903-942.

Fitzgerald, F. Scott. *The Great Gatsby*. New York: Scribner, 1925.

Gentry, Curt, *J. Edgar Hoover: The Man and the Secrets*. New York: Norton, 2001.

Gilbert, Sandra M., and Susan Gubar. *Madwoman in the Attic*. New Haven: Yale University Press, 1979.

Goldman, Emma. *Living My Life*. New York: Dover Publications, 1969.

–*Anarchism and Other Essays*. New York: Mother Earth Publishing, 1911.

–*My Disillusionment with Russia*. New York: Crowell, 1922.

–*My Further Disillusionment with Russia*. New York: Doubleday Books, 1924.

Graff, Henry F. *The Presidents* (New York: Charles Scribner's Sons, 2002.

Haaland, Bonnie. *Emma Goldman: Sexuality and the Impurity of the State*. Montreal: Black Rose Books, 1993.

Heilbrun, Carolyn G. *Writing a Woman's Life*. New York: Ballantine Books, 1988.

Heinze, Andrew R. *Adapting to Abundance: Jewish Immigrants, Mass Consumption and the Search for American Identity*. New York: Columbia University Press, 1970.

Herschel, Susannah, ed. *On Being a Jewish Feminist: A Reader*. New York: Schoken Books, 1983.

Hollinger, David. *In the American Province*. Baltimore: The John Hopkins University Press, 1985.

Hollinger, David, and Charles Caper, eds. The *American Intellectual Tradition*. Oxford: Oxford University Press, 1993.

Howe, Leslie A. *On Goldman*. California: Wadsworth Thompson Learning, 2000.

Ishill, J. *Emma Goldman: A Challenging Rebel*. Berkeley Heights, New Jersey: Oreole Press, 1957.

Jelinek, Estelle C., ed. *Women's Autobiography*. Bloomington: Indiana University Press, 1980.

Joll, James. *The Anarchists*. Cambridge: Harvard University Press, 1980.

Kerber, Linda. *Toward an Intellectual History of Women* Chapel Hill: The University of North Carolina Press, 1997.

Kloppenberg, James. *Uncertain Victory: Social Democracy and Progressivism in European and American Thought 1870-1920*. Oxford: Oxford University Press, 1988.

Lender, Mark Edward, and James Kirby Martin. *Drinking in America*. New York: The Free Press, 1982.

Lewarne, Charles Pierce. *Utopias on Puget Sound, 1885-1915.* Seattle: University of Washington Press, 1978.

Lootens, Tricia. *Lost Souls: Silence, Gender, and Victorian Literary Canonization.* Charlottesville, VA: University Press of Virginia, 1996.

Marsh, Margaret. *Anarchist Women.* Philadelphia: Temple Univeristy Press, 1981.

Marshall, Peter. *Demanding the Impossible: A History of Anarchism.* London: Harper-Collins Press, 1992.

Martin, James J. *Men Against the State.* Colorado: Ralph Myres Publishers, 1970.

Mehring, Franz. *Karl Marx: The Story of His Life.* New York: Allen and Unwin, 1996.

McFadden, Margaret. *Golden Cables of Sympathy.* Kentucky: University Press of Kentucky, 1999.

McKinley, Blaine. "Anarchist Jeremaids: American Anarchists and American History." *Journal of American Culture* 6(Summer, 1983):75-84.

–"'The Quagmires of Necessity': American Anarchists and Dilemmas of Vocation." *American Quarterly* 34 (Winter 1982): 503-523.

Morton, Mariasn. *Emma Goldman and the American Left.* New York: Twayne Publications, 1992.

Murray, Robert K. *Red Scare: A Study in National Hysteria.* New York: McGraw Hill Books, 1955.

Olsen, Tillie. *Silences.* New York: Delacorte Press, 1978.

Porter, David. *Vision on Fire: Emma Goldman and the Spanish Revolution.* New York: Commonground Press, 1983.

Peirats, Jose. *Emma Goldman: Anarquista de Ambos Mundos.* Madrid: Campo Abierto Ediciones, 1978.

Poirer, Suzanne. "Emma Goldman, Ben Reitman, and Reitman Wives: A Study in Relationships." *Women's Studies.* 14(1988):277-297.

Polenberg, Richard. *Fighting Faiths.* New York: Viking Press, 1987.

Puleo, Stephen. *Dark Tide.* Boston: Beacon Press, 2003.

Rauchway, Eric. *Murdering McKinley.* New York: Hill and Wang, 2004.

Reichert, William W. *Partisans of Freedom: A Study of American Anarchism.* Bowling Green, Ohio: Bowling Green University Press, 1976.

Rich, Adrienne. *On Lies, Secrets, and Silence.* New York: W.W. Norton and Company, 1979.

Rodden, John. *The Politics of Literary Reputation: The Making of St. George Orwell.* Oxford: Oxford University Press, 1989.

Rodgers, Daniel. *Atlantic Crossings: Social Politics in a Progressive Age.* New York: Bellnap Press, 1988.

Rosenberg, Karen. "An Autumnal Love of Emma Goldman." *Dissent,* Summer (1983).

Rosenstone, Robert A. *Romantic Revolutionary: A Biography of John Reed.* New York: Alfred A. Knopf, 1975.

Roth, Walter and Joe Krauss. *An Accidental Anarchist.* New York: Rudi Publishing, 1997.

Rosenberg, Karen. "The Autumnal Love of Red Emma." *Harvard Magazine* (January-February 1984). 52-56.

–"Emma's Ambiguous Legacy," *The Women's Review of Books.* 2:2 (1984):8-9.

Rudahl, Sharon. *Dangerous Woman: The Graphic Biography of Emma Goldman.* New York: New Press, 2007.

Sayre, Robert. *The Examined Self.* Princeton: Princeton University Press, 1964.

Schnantes, Carlos A. "Free Love on the Pacific Northwest Frontier," *Oregon Historical Quarterly,* 82 1982.

Scott, Joan Wallace. *Gender and the Politics of History.* New York: Columbia University Press, 1988.

Schuster, Eunice. *Native American Anarchism.* New York: DaCapo Press, 1970.

Shor, Francis Robert. *Utopianism and Radicalism in a Reforming America: 1888-1918.* New York: Greenwood Press, 1977.

Shuman, Alex Kates. *To the Barricades: The Anarchist Life of Emma Goldman.* New York: Crowell Press, 1971.

–"Dancing in the Revolution: Emma Goldman's Feminism." *Socialist Review.* March-April 1982, 31-44.

–"Dances with Feminists." *Women's Review of Books,* 9:3, 1991.

—,ed. *Red Emma Speaks: Selected Writings and Speeches by Emma Goldman.* New York: Random House, 1975.

—,ed. *The Traffic in Women and Other Essays.* New York: Times Change Press, 1970.

Smith, Margaret Jackson. "Charlotte Perkins Gilman and Emma Goldman, Reformer and Radical." *Arkansas Review: A Journal of Criticism.* 3:2 (1994):52-67.

Smith, Sidone. *A Poetics of Women's Autobiography.* Bloomington: Indiana University Press, 1987.

Solomon, Martha. *Emma Goldman.* Boston: Twayne Publishers, 1987.

–"Ideology as Rhetorical Constraint: The Anarchist Agitation of 'Red Emma' Goldman." *The Quarterly Journal of Speech.* 74 (1988):184-200.

Sorin, Gerald. *The Prophetic Minority: American Jewish Immigrant Radicals 1880-1920.* Indiana: Indiana University Press, 1985.

Stansell, Christine. *American Moderns: Bohemian New York and the Creation of a New Century.* New York: Metropolitan Books, 2000.

Stone, Albert E. ed. *The American Autobiography: A Collection of Critical Essays.* Englewood Cliffs: New Jersey, Prentice-Hall Inc., 1981.

Trautmann, Frederic. *The Voice of Terror: A Biography of Johann Most.* Connecticut: Greenwood Press, 1980.

Thoreau, Henry David. *Civil Disobedience.* New York: Quill Pen Classics. 2008.

Vesey, Laurence. *The Communal Experience: Anarchist and Mystical Counter-Cultures in America.* New York: Harper & Row, 1973.

Waldstreicher, David."Radicalism, Religion, Jewish: The Case of Emma Goldman." *American Jewish History.* 80 (1990): 74-92.

Weinberger, Harry. *Speech at Funeral of Emma Goldman.* Berkeley Heights, New Jersey: Oriole Press, 1940.

Weiss, Penny A. and Loreta Keninger, eds. *Feminist Interpretations of Emma Goldman.* Pennsylvania: The Pennsylvania State University Press, 2007.

Wexler, Alice. *Emma Goldman: An Intimate Life.* New York: Pantheon Press, 1984.

–*Emma Goldman in Exile: From the Russian Revolution to the Spanish Civil War.* Boston: Beacon Press, 1989.

–"The Early Life of Emma Goldman." *The Psychohistory Review.* 8:4(1979):7-21.

–"Emma Goldman on Mary Wollstonecraft." *Feminist Studies.* 7:1(1981):113-133.

–"Emma Goldman in Love." *Raritan.* 4 (1982):131-132.

Whitehead, Don. *FBI Story.* New York: Random House, 1956.

Wiesen Cook, Blanche. "The Historical Denial of Lesbianism," *Radical History Review* 20 (1979).

–*Eleanor Roosevelt, Vol.1* New York: Penguin Books, 1992.

Woodcock, George. *Anarchism: A History of Libertarian Ideas and Movements.* New York: World Publishing Co., 1962.

Yezierska, Anzia. *Bread Givers.* New York: Persea Books, 1999.

Notes

INTRODUCTION

1 Paul Avrich, *Anarchist Voices* (Princeton: Princeton University Press, 1995), 52-53.
2 Ibid. 38.
3 Ibid. 49.
4 Emma Goldman, *Living My Life* (New York: Dover Publications: 1970), 153.
5 George Woodstock, *Anarchism* (New York: Broadview Press, 2004), 68.
6 James Joll, *The Anarchists* (Cambridge: Harvard University Press, 1980), 12.
7 Ibid. 66
8 Atindranath Bose, *A History of Anarchism* (Calcutta: The World Press Private Limited, 1967), 134.
9 Ibid. 197.
10 Ibid. 209.
11 Ibid. 203.
12 E.H. Carr *A History of Soviet Russia.* (New York: Palgrave MacMillan, 1953), 379-80.
13 Joll, *The Anarchists*, 101.
14 Franz Mehring, *Karl Marx: The Story of His Life* (New York: Allen and Unwin, 1996), 424.
15 Avrich, *Anarchist Voices,* 59.
16 Caroline Cahm, *Kropotkin and the Rise of Revolutionary Anarchism* (Cambridge: Cambridge University Press, 2002), 76.
17 Ibid. 76.
18 Goldman, *Living My Life,* 529.

CHAPTER ONE

1 Goldman, *Living My Life*, 710.
2 Editorial, *New York Times,* December 23, 1919, 23.
3 Ibid. December 23, 1919, 8:4.
4 Goldman, *Living My Life*, 717.

5 *New York Times* Dec 22, 1919.

6 *New York Times* Dec 22, 1919.

7 *New York Times* Dec 22, 1919.

8 Mark Edward Lender and James Kirby Martin, *Drinking in America* (New York: The Free Press, 1982), 131.

9 Ibid. 130.

10 Stephen Puleo, *Dark Tide* (Boston: Beacon Press, 2003), 96.

11 Ibid. 97.

12 Claude McKay, "If We Must Die," *The Liberator*, 2(July 1919), 21.

13 F. Scott Fitzgerald, *The Great Gatsby*, (New York: Scribner, 1925), 72-73.

14 Leonard Dinnerstein, *Anti-Semitism in America* (Oxford: Oxford University Press, 1995), 75.

15 Kenneth D. Ackerman, *Young J. Edgar Hoover* (New York: Carroll & Graf Publishers, 2007), 18.

16 *Chicago Daily Tribune* June 3, 1919.

17 Robert K. Murray, *Red Scare: A Study in National Hysteria 1919–1920* (New York: McGraw Hill Books, 1955) 72.

18 *Washington Post*, June 4, 1919.

19 Kenneth Ackerman, *Young J. Edgar Hoover*, 27.

20 *Washington Post*, June 4, 1919.

CHAPTER TWO

1 Goldman, *Living My Life*, 297.

2 Curt Gentry, *J. Edgar Hoover: The Man and his Secrets* (New York: Norton, 1991), 186.

3 Ibid. 187.

4 Don Whitehead, *FBI Story* (New York: Random House, 1956), 48.

5 Goldman, *Living My Life*, 59.

6 Alice Wexler, *Emma Goldman: An Intimate Life* (New York: Pantheon Books, 1984) 23.

7 Ibid.

8 Goldman, *Living My Life*, 12.

9 Ibid., *Living My Life* 11.

10 Ibid., *Living My Life* 11.

11 Ibid., *Living My Life* 12.

12 Ibid., *Living My Life* 16.

13 Richard Drinnon, *Rebel in Paradise* (Chicago: University of Chicago Press, 1961), 14.

14 Goldman, *Living My Life,* 10.

15 Paul Avrich, *The Haymarket Tragedy* (Princeton: Princeton University Press, 1984), 209.

16 Ibid.

17 Ibid., 193.

18 *New York Times* May 6, 1886.

19 *New York Times* May 6, 1886.

20 Goldman, *Living My Life,* 9.

21 Ibid., 10.

22 Ibid., 26.

23 Ibid., 25.

24 Ibid., 3.

25 James J. Martin, *Men Against the State* (Colorado: Ralph Myres Publishers, 1970), 281.

26 *New York Times*, May 13 1886.

27 Frederic Trautmann, *The Voice of Terror: A Biography of Johann Most,* (Connecticut: Greenwood Press, 1980), xxi.

28 *New York Times* March 18 1906.

29 *New York Times* March 21 1906.

30 Avrich, *Anarchist Voices,* 13.

31 *Freiheit,* June 20,1896.

32 Emma Goldman, "Johann Most," *American Mercury,* VIII: 160-161.

33 Ibid.

34 *Freiheit,* June 20,1896.

35 *New York Times* December 14, 1882.

36 The original notion seems to have been that of the Italian revolutionary Carlo Piscan (1818–57).

37 Avrich, *The Haymarket Tragedy,* 201.

38 It was later discovered that "Uncle Maxim" was Mark Natanson, one of the leaders of the anarchist Chaikovsky circle.

39 Alexander Berkman, *Prison Memoirs of an Anarchist* (New York: New York Review Books, 1970), 16-17.

40 Elizabeth Ewen, *Immigrant Women in the Land of Dollars: Life and Culture on the Lower East Side, 1890-1925* (New York: Monthly Press, 1975), 54.

41 Avrich, *The Haymarket Tragedy,* 23.

42 Ibid., 88.

43 Goldman, *Living My Life,* 40.

44 Wexler, *Emma Goldman: An Intimate Life,* 38.

45 Ibid.

46 David DeLeon argues that the American Revolution was in fact an anarchist movement in *The American as Anarchist* (Maryland: John Hopkins University Press, 1978).

47 Josiah Warren, "Individuality," *The Peaceful Revolutionist*, 1 (April 5, 1883), 1.

48 Josiah Warren, "Of Our State Difficulties," *The Peaceful Revolutionist*, I (February 5, 1833), 6.

49 Eunice Schuster, *Native American Anarchism* (New York: DaCapo Press, 1970), 87.

50 Ibid., 92.

51 Avrich, *The Haymarket Tragedy*, 22.

52 It should be noted that there were twenty-eight German language newspapers published each day in fifteen cities, while the *Jewish Daily Forward*, published in Yiddish, had a circulation of a quarter of a million.

CHAPTER THREE

1 Goldman, *Living My Life*, 36.

2 Ibid., 34.

3 Ibid., 36.

4 Ibid., 6.

5 Ibid., 6.

6 Ibid., 51.

7 Ibid., 53.

8 Ibid., 53.

9 Ibid., 54.

10 Ibid., 29.

11 Goldman referred to Stein as "Fedya" in her autobiography in an attempt to protect him from the authorities.

12 Perter was another member of the anarchist movement who is mentioned in notes Goldman made for her autobiography but was omitted from the published version.

13 Wexler, *An Intimate Life*, 63.

14 Goldman, *Living My Life*, 85.

15 Berkman, *Prison Memoirs of an Anarchist*, 5.

16 Goldman, *Living My Life* 87.

17 Wexler, *An Intimate Life*, 64.

18 Berkman, *Prison Memoirs of an Anarchist*, 10.

19 Ibid., 14.

20 Goldman, *Living My Life*, 93.

21 Samuel Schreiner, *Anarchism in Germany,* 102.

22 Emma Goldman, Letter to Max Nettlau January 24, 1932.

23 Emma Goldman, letter to Alexander Berkman, June 29, 1928.

24 Emma Goldman, letter to Alexander Berkman, July 3 1928.

25 *New York World,* July 28, 1892.

26 *New York World,* July 28, 1892.

27 *New York World,* July 28, 1892.

28 *New York World,* July 28, 1892.

29 *New York Times,* August 6, 1892.

30 *New York Times,* October 17, 1893.

31 Avrich, *Anarchist Portraits,* (Princeton: Princeton University Press, 1988), 14.

32 Goldman, *Living My Life,* 106.

33 Emma Goldman, letter to Max Nettlau January 24, 1932.

34 Emma Goldman, letter to Max Nettlau January 24, 1932.

CHAPTER FOUR

1 Emma Goldman, letter to Alexander Berkman, June 29, 1928.

2 *New York Daily Tribune,* October 7, 1893.

3 Hippolye Havel, "Emma Goldman," in *Emma Goldman, Anarchism and Other Essays,* (New York: Dover Publications, 1969) 2.

4 Berkman, *Prison Memoirs of an Anarchist,* 134.

5 Goldman, *Living My Life,* 101.

6 Emma Goldman, letter to Theodore Dreiser, December 15,1929.

7 Eric Rauchway, *Murdering McKinley* (New York: Hill and Wang, 2004), 17-19.

8 There is little doubt that such wounds would not have caused the president to die today. For a detailed discussion please see Jack C. Fisher, *Stolen Glory.* (California: Alamar Books, 2001).

9 Rauchway, *Murdering McKinley,* 45.

10 Goldman, *Living My Life,* 296.

11 Ibid., 301.

12 Richard Drinnon, *Rebel in Paradise:A Biography of Emma Goldman,*(Chicago, University of Chicago Press, 1961), 71.

13 Ibid., 72, Goldman, *Living My Life,* 310-311.

14 Berkman, *Prison Memoirs of an Anarchist,* 419.

15 *New York Times,* September 11, 1901.

16 Henry F. Graff, *The Presidents* (New York: Charles Scribner's Sons, 2002), 336.

17 Theodore Roosevelt, First Annual Message as President, *State Papers*, National Editing, 15:84-85.

18 *New York Times* Sep. 7, 1901.

19 *New York Times* Sep. 8, 1901.

20 *New York Times*, Letter from W.H. Allen, Brooklyn September 12, 1901 printed Sep. 16, 1901.

21 *New York Times*, December 5, 1903.

22 Goldman, *Living My Life*, 290.

23 Ibid.

24 *Free Society*, September 1, 1901.

25 Eric Rauchway in his book *Murdering McKinley* again insists that no proof ever existed for this, that it was a rumor that circulated at the time.

26 F.L. Oswald, "The Assassination Mania," *North American Review* 171:526, September 1900, 314.

27 Rauchway, *Murdering McKinley*, 27.

28 Walter Channing, "The Mental Status of Czolgosz, the Assassin of President McKinley," *American Journal of Insanity* 59 (1902), 268.

29 Goldman, "The Tragedy at Buffalo," *Free Society*, October 1901.

30 Michele Angiolillo assassinated the Spanish Prime Minister in 1897, while Gaetano Bresci shot the King of Italy in 1900.

31 Emma Goldman, "The Psychology of Political Violence," *Anarchism and Other Essays* (New York: Mother Earth Publishing Association, 1917).

32 Alexander Berkman, letter to Emma Goldman, November 1928.

33 Ibid.

34 Berkman, *Prison Memoirs of an Anarchist*, 423.

CHAPTER FIVE

1 Goldman, *Anarchism and Other Essays*, 165.

2 *New York World*, August 18, 1894.

3 Alexander Berkman.

4 Johann Most.

5 Edward Brady, her then lover.

6 Goldman, *Living My Life*, 148.

7 In 1911, in her article "Anarchism: What it Really Stands For," she refers to Thoreau as "the greatest American Anarchist."

8 Goldman, *Living My Life*, 155.

9 Emma Goldman, "Declaration of Independence," *Mother Earth*, 4:5, July 1909.

10 Ibid.

11 Goldman, *Living My Life*, 137-138.

12 Ibid., 141.

13 Ibid., 157.

14 Margaret H. McFadden, *Golden Cables of Sympathy*, (Kentucky: University Press of Kentucky, 1999).

15 Daniel Rogers, *Atlantic Crossings – Social Politics in a Progressive Age* (New York: The Belknap Press of Harvard University Press, 1998).

16 James T. Kloppenberg, *Uncertain Victory – Social Democracy and Progressivism in European and American Thought, 1870-1920* (Oxford: Oxford University Press 1986)

17 Kloppenberg, *Uncertain Victory*, 3.

18 Goldman, *Living My Life*, 169.

19 She used a combination of her own name and Edward Brady's name, realizing that she might not be allowed to travel freely if it were known that she was Emma Goldman.

20 Goldman, *Living My Life*, 268.

21 Ibid.

22 Henry David Thoreau, *Civil Disobedience*. New York: Quill Pen Classics. 2008.

23 Emma Goldman, "Anarchism: What It Really Stands For," *Anarchism and Other Essays*.

24 Ibid.

25 Emma Goldman, letter to Alexander Berkman, June 29, 1928.

26 Ibid.

27 Emma Goldman, letter to Tom Bell, July 13, 1937.

28 Emma Goldman, letter to Comrade Hall, May 27, 1938.

29 Emma Goldman, letter to Havelock Ellis, February 16, 1927.

30 Emma Goldman, "Minorities versus Majorities," *Anarchism and Other Essays*.

31 Ibid.

32 Emma Goldman, letter to C.V. Cook, September 29, 1935.

33 Wexler, *Emma Goldman, An Intimate Life*, 97.

34 Goldman, "Minorities versus Majorities," *Anarchism and Other Essays*, 78.

35 Emma Goldman, "Francisco Ferrer and the Modern School," *Anarchism and Other Essays*.

36 Avrich, *The Modern School Movement: Anarchism and Education in the United States*, (Princeton: Princeton University Press, 1980) 38.

37 Ibid., 38.

38 Goldman, *Living My Life*, 409.

39 Emma Goldman, "Francisco Ferrer and the Modern School,"
   Anarchism and Other Essays, 149.

40 Goldman, *Living My Life*, 408.

41 Emma Goldman, "Francisco Ferrer and the Modern School,"
   Anarchism and Other Essays, 152-153.

42 The name of Faure's school.

43 Goldman, *Living My Life*, 409.

44 Emma Goldman, "The Child and Its Enemies," *Mother Earth*, v 1:2,
   April 1906, 109.

45 Emma Goldman, "The Child and Its Enemies," *Mother Earth*, v 1:2,
   April 1906, 109.

46 Emma Goldman, "The Child and Its Enemies," *Mother Earth*, v 1:2,
   April 1906, 115.

47 Emma Goldman, "The Social Importance of the Modern School,"
   Mother Earth, v 1:1, March 1906.

48 Emma Goldman, "The Social Importance of the Modern School,"
   Mother Earth, v 1:1, March 1906.

49 Emma Goldman, "Francisco Ferrer and the Modern School," in
   Anarchism and Other Essays, 146.

50 Murray Bookchin, *The Spanish Anarchists*, (New York: AK Press,
   2001), Chapter 7.

51 Bookchin, Ibid.

52 Voltairine de Cleyre, "Francisco Ferrer", *Selected Works of Voltairine de
   Cleyre*, ed. Alexander Berkman (New York: Mother Earth Publishing
   1914), 300.

53 Goldman, "Anarchism: What it Really Stands For," *Anarchism and
   Other Essays*, 47-68.

54 Ibid.

55 Goldman, quoted in Havel's introduction to *Anarchism and Other
   Essays*, 35.

56 "I am broken in spirit and body, I feel weary. My struggle never seemed
   more useless, a lone voice against the multitude." Emma Goldman,
   letter to Ben Reitman, October 13, 1909.

57 Avrich, *Modern School Movement*, 359.

58 Ibid., 39.

59 Ibid., 37.

60 Ibid., vi.

61 Ibid., 9.

62 Ibid., 12.

63 Ibid., 37.

64 Ibid., 76.

65 Ibid., 34.

66 Wexler, *Emma Goldman: An Intimate Life*, 90.

67 Ibid.

68 Ibid., 91.

69 Drinnon, *Rebel in Paradise*, 104.

70 Wexler, *Emma Goldman: An Intimate Life*, 91.

71 Ibid.

72 Goldman, "The Hypocrisy of Puritanism," *Anarchism and Other Essays*.

73 Berkman, letter to Emma Goldman, December 7, 1927.

74 Berkman, letter to Emma Goldman, June 25, 1928.

75 Ibid.

76 Emma Goldman, letter to Alexander Berkman, June 29, 1925.

77 Christine Stansell, *American Moderns* (New York: Metropolitan Books, 2000), 124.

78 Goldman, *Living My Life*, 392-393.

79 Margaret Anderson, *My Thirty Years War* (New York: Horizon Press, 1969), 70.

80 *Mother Earth*, July 1914.

81 Wexler, *Emma Goldman, An Intimate Life*, 220.

82 Avrich, *The Modern School Movement*, 199-200.

83 Emma Goldman, letter to Ben Reitman, September 25, 1914.

84 Curt Gentry, *J. Edgar Hoover: The Man and the Secrets*, (New York: Norton, 2001), 85-86.

85 Ackerman, *Young J. Edgar Hoover*, 111.

86 Emma Goldman, letter to Leon Malmed, December 12, 1919.

CHAPTER SIX

1 Emma Goldman, letter to Evelyn Scott, June 26, 1928.

2 Alice Wexler, *Emma Goldman in Exile* (Boston: Beacon Press, 1989), 20.

3 Drinnon, *Rebel in Paradise*, 237.

4 Emma Goldman, *My Disillusionment with Russia*, (New York: Doubleday, 1923), v-vi.

5 Goldman, *Living My Life*, v.

6 Ibid.

7 Emma Goldman, letter to Arthur Ross, June 25, 1928.

8 Goldman, *Living My Life*, vi-vii.

9 Founder and long-time director of the ACLU.

10 Well-known civil libertarian.

11 Alexander Berkman, letter to Roger Baldwin and Robert Reinhart of the International Committee for Political Prisoners, October 1, 1931.

12 Wexler, *Emma Goldman in Exile*, 138.

13 Robert F. Sayre, *The Examined Self* (Madison, Wisconsin: The University of Wisconsin Press, 1988), x.

14 Ibid., xi.

15 Thomas P. Doherty, "American Autobiography and Ideology," *The American Autobiography: A Collection of Critical Essays*, ed. Albert E. Stone (Englewood Cliffs: New Jersey, Prentice-Hall Inc., 1981), 95.

16 Ibid.

17 Sayre, *The Examined Self*, xi.

18 Albert E. Stone, ed., *The American Autobiography*, 2.

19 Ibid.

20 Sayre, *The Examined Self*, xix.

21 Linda Wagner-Martin, *Telling Women's Lives* (New Brunswick: Rutgers University Press, 1994), 1.

22 Patricia Meyer Spacks, "Stages of Self: Notes on Autobiography and the Life Cycle," *The American Autobiography*, 49.

23 Sayre, "The Proper Stud: Autobiography in American Studies," *The American Autobiography*, 24.

24 Sayre, *The Examined Self*, xvii.

25 Patricia Meyer Spacks, "Selves in Hiding," *Women's Autobiography, Women's Autobiography*, Estelle C. Jelinek, ed., (Bloomington: Indiana University Press, 1980), 113.

26 Ibid.

27 Ibid., 116.

28 Tillie Olsen, *Silences* (New York: Delacorte Press, 1978).

29 Estelle C. Jelinek, ed., *Women's Autobiography* (Bloomington: Indiana University Press, 1980).

30 Blanche Wiesen Cook, "The Historical Denial of Lesbianism," *Radical History Review* 20 (1979), 60.

31 Blanche Wiesen Cook, *Eleanor Roosevelt, Vol.1* (New York: Penguin Books, 1992), 9.

32 Patricia Meyer Spacks, "Selves in Hiding," 112-132.

33 Adrienne Rich, "It is the Lesbian in Us ..." *On Lies, Secrets, and Silence* (New York: W.W. Norton and Company, 1979), 199.

34 Spacks, "Selves in Hiding," 122.

35 Ibid. 128.

36 Adrienne Rich, 35.

37 Ibid.

38 The Personal Narratives Group, ed., *Interpreting Women's Lives*
    (Bloomington: Indiana University Press, 1989), 8.

39 Ibid., 5.

40 Robyn R. Warhol and Diane Price Herndl, ed., *Feminisms* (New Jersey:
    Rutgers University Press, 1997), 1009.

41 Linda Wagner-Martin, *Telling Women's Lives: The New Biography*
    (New Jersey: Rutgers University Press, 1994), x.

42 Jelinek, Women's Autobiography, 10.

43 Blanche Wiesen Cook, "Female Support Networks and Political
    Activism," *A Heritage of Her Own*, ed. Nancy F. Cott and Elizabeth H.
    Pleck (New York: Simon and Schuster, 1979), 416.

44 Jelinek, *Women's Autobiography*, 13.

45 Frank Harris, letter to Emma Goldman, January 23, 1925.

46 Emma Goldman, letter to Frank Harris, August 7, 1925.

47 Sidone Smith, *A Poetics of Women's Autobiography* (Bloomington:
    Indiana University Press, 1987), 9-10.

48 The Personal Narratives Group, 5.

49 Janet Burstein, *Writing Mothers, Writing Daughters* (Chicago:
    University of Illinois Press, 1996), 1.

50 Cynthia Ozick, "Notes toward Finding the Right Question," *On Being
    a Jewish Feminist: A Reader*, ed. Susannah Herschel (New York:
    Schoken Books, 1983) 125.

51 Burstein, 3.

52 Ibid.

53 Andrew R. Heinze, *Adapting to Abundance: Jewish Immigrants, Mass
    Consumption and the Search for American Identity* (New York:
    Columbia University Press, 1970), 166-182.

54 Goldman, *Living My Life*, 12.

55 Charlotte Baum, Paula Hyman and Sonya Michel, *The Jewish Woman
    in America* (New York: Dial Press, 1976), 5.

56 Anzia Yezierska, *Bread Givers* (New York: Persea Books, 1999), 7.

CHAPTER SEVEN

1 Goldman, *Living My Life*, 153.

2 Albert E. Stone, *Autobiographical Occasions and Original Acts*,
   (Pennsylvania: University of Pennsylvania Press, 1982), 151.

3 Alix Kate Schulman, *Between Women,* Carol Ascher, Sara Ruddick, and Louise DeSalvo eds., (New York: Beacon Press, 1984), 13.

4 Emma Goldman, letter to Alexander Berkman, November 18, 1931.

5 Goldman, *Living My Life,* v.

6 Emma Goldman, letter to Arthur Ross, June 25, 1928.

7 Drinnon, *Rebel in Paradise,* 257.

8 Alexander Berkman, letter to Emma Goldman, 27 December, 1927.

9 Wexler, *Emma Goldman in Exile,* 135.

10 Emma Goldman, letter to Alexander Berkman, December 3, 1927.

11 Emma Goldman, letter to Arthur Ross, 25 June, 1928.

12 Wexler, *Emma Goldman in Exile,* 136.

13 Eleanor Fitzgerald was a companion/lover of Berkman's during World War I; she later became the secretary of the Provincetown Players.

14 Emma Goldman, letter to Alexander Berkman, September 4, 1925.

15 Emma Goldman, letter to Alexander Berkman, June 29, 1928.

16 Wexler, *Emma Goldman in Exile,* 136.

17 Emma Goldman, letter to Ted McLean Switz, March 10, 1930.

18 Emma Goldman, letter to Leonard Ross, January 13, 1929.

19 Wexler, *Emma Goldman in Exile,* 136.

20 Ibid., 138.

21 Alexander Berkman, letter to Emma Goldman, June 25, 1928.

22 Theodore Dreiser, *Sister Carrie* (New York: Penguin Books, 1981), 3.

23 Goldman, *Living My Life,* 3.

24 Dreiser, *Sister Carrie,* 3.

25 Goldman, *Living My Life,* 3.

26 Dreiser, *Sister Carrie,* 3.

27 Goldman, *Living My Life,* 3.

28 Claire Eby, "Cultural and Historical Contexts for *Sister Carrie,*" Dreiser Web Source, http://www.library.upenn.edu/collections/rbm/dreiser/scculhist.html (accessed December 1, 2007).

29 Ibid.

30 Emma Goldman, letter to Evelyn Scott, October 17, 1927.

31 Emma Goldman, letter to Alexander Berkman, June 29, 1928

32 Wexler, *Emma Goldman in Exile,* 134.

33 Ibid., 134.

34 Evelyn Scott (1893–1963) was one of Goldman's close acquaintances she met through her Greenwich Village friends. Goldman and Scott stayed in contact through all of her life.

35 Evelyn Scott, letter to Emma Goldman, July 31, 1928.

36 Alexander Berkman, letter to Emma Goldman, April 11, 1929.

37 Wexler, *Emma Goldman in Exile*, 134.

38 Ibid., 134.

39 Evelyn Scott, letter to Emma Goldman July 31, 1928.

40 Emma Goldman, letter to Alexander Berkman, June 29, 1928.

41 Alexander Berkman, letter to Emma Goldman, November 19, 1928.

42 Alexander Berkman, letter to Emma Goldman, late November 1928.

43 Alexander Berkman, letter to Emma Goldman, late November 1928.

44 Wexler, *Emma Goldman in Exile*, 135.

45 Alexander Berkman, letter to Emma Goldman, May 26, 1929.

46 Alexander Berkman, letter to Emma Goldman, April 11, 1929.

47 Emma Goldman, letter to Alexander Berkman, May 28, 1925.

48 Emma Goldman, letter to Alexander Berkman, September 10, 1925.

49 "As I may, inadvertently and indirectly, bear some responsibility for the extrapolation from authentic text to familiar paraphrase, I would like to confess and set the record straight. Here is what happened. Sometime early in 1973 I received a phone call from one Jack Frager, an old-time anarchist who worked in the anarchist center at 339 Lafayette Street in Lower Manhattan — a building where to this day various radical groups, including anarchists and the War Resisters League, have their offices. Like many dedicated radicals of the era before desktop publishing, he was a printer; now he had the original idea to raise funds for the Cause by printing up a batch of Emma Goldman T-shirts to hawk in Central Park at the huge upcoming festival celebrating the end of the Vietnam War. Having heard me lecture to the anarchists on Emma's feminism (after decades of obscurity during which all of her works were out of print, Emma was suddenly returning to the public eye as a hero of women's liberation), Jack was phoning to solicit my help.

Delighted by the opportunity to publicize Emma's feminist side, particularly among followers sometimes reluctant to share her with any movement not strictly anarchist, I offered him a glossy shot of a stalwart, hatless Emma in a pince-nez and referred him to several prose passages, particularly the dancing episode, which seemed to me to embody her most lively feminist spirit. Did I propose Emma's statement about "freedom, the right to self-expression, everybody's right to beautiful radiant things"? Perhaps. In gratitude, Jack promised me all the T-shirts I wanted, at cost.

Several days later, when I picked up my shirts along with my precious glossy, I was surprised to find a succinct abridgement of Emma's dance story spread boldly across the shirt – the first (and most common) version of the now-famous slogan: "If I can't dance I don't want to be in your revolution."

I searched Emma's texts for the statement; it was nowhere to be found. But Jack was so pleased, the festival was so soon, Emma looked so lively printed in red and black on a variety of rich background colors, that I hadn't the heart to register an objection in the name of scholarship. After all, the apocrypha appeared on a mere gross or two of T-shirts, which surely could not require the same standards of accuracy as, say, book blurbs extracted from book reviews – and the sentiment expressed was pure Emma indeed.

But history (and fashion) exploded so quickly in those hungrily feminist days that the slogan on the original shirt-run was soon dispersed and copied and broadcast nationwide and abroad, underground and above, sometimes, absent a text to be checked against, changing along the way like a child's game of Telephone, until Jack's initial lighthearted liberties had taken wing as quotable lore and soared up into the realms of myth." Alix Kates Shulman, *Women's Review of Books*, 9:3 (1991), 13.

50 Wexler, *Emma Goldman in Exile*, 135.

51 Emma Goldman, letter to Alexander Berkman, February 20, 1929.

52 Emma Goldman, letter to Alexander Berkman, February 20, 1929.

53 Emma Goldman, letter to Alexander Berkman, February 20, 1929.

54 Emma Goldman, letter to Alexander Berkman, February 20, 1929

55 Alexander Berkman, letter to Emma Goldman, May 11, 1929.

56 In a letter to Emma Goldman on May 26, 1929, Berkman told her that he had no intention of taking down any of Goldman's photographs he had around the house as he considered it "educational" for Eckstein.

57 Alexander Berkman, letter to Emma Goldman, May 26, 1929.

58 Drinnon, *Rebel in Paradise*, 268.

59 Arthur Leonard Ross was a lawyer who worked with Goldman and Berkman constantly through their exile in an attempt to raise the possibility they would be allowed return to the States.

60 Her French expulsion order had been squashed and she had a new order from the Minister of the Interior that allowed her to stay.

61 Michael Cohn had been a sometime supporter of anarchist causes. His lack of consistency was annoying to Berkman.

62 Alexander Berkman, letter to Michael Cohn, June 6, 1939.

63 Drinnon, *Rebel in Paradise*, 269.

64 Wexler, *Emma Goldman in Exile*, 153.

65 John Chalberg, *Emma Goldman: American Individualist* (New York: Harper Collins, 1991), 167.

66 Judith Butler, *Gender Trouble: Feminism and the Subversion of Identity* (New York: Routledge, 1999), xi.

67 Ibid., xxv

68 Ibid., xxix.

69 Wexler, *Emma Goldman in Exile*, 152.

70 Ibid., 149.

71 Ben Reitman, letter to Emma Goldman, December 6, 1931.

72 Mecca Reitman Carpenter, *No Regrets: Dr Ben Reitman and the Women Who Loved Him* (Boston: Southside Press, 1999) 1-2.

73 Goldman, *Living My Life*, 435.

74 Ibid., 422.

75 Ibid., 423.

76 Ibid., 694.

77 Ibid., 694.

78 Ibid., 694.

79 Ibid., 435.

80 Ibid., 435.

81 Ibid., 435.

82 Ibid., 436.

83 Emma Goldman, letter to Alexander Berkman, May 14, 1929.

84 Emma Goldman, letter to Alexander Berkman, May 24, 1929.

85 Emma Goldman, letter to Alexander Berkman, May 14, 1929.

86 Emma Goldman, letter to Alexander Berkman, May 14, 1929.

87 Emma Goldman, letter to Ben Reitman, December 30, 1927.

88 Ben Reitman, letter to Emma Goldman, July 20, 1928.

89 Goldman, *Living my Life*, 84.

90 Ibid., 162.

91 Ibid., 32.

92 Ibid., 32.

93 Ibid., 61.

94 Ibid., 56.

95 Ibid., 36.

96 Ibid., 40.

97 Ibid., 29.

98 Ibid., 29.

99 Ibid., 126.

100 Goldman, "Johann Most."

101 Ibid.

102 Emma Goldman, letter to Alexander Berkman, November 23, 1928.

103 Wexler, *Emma Goldman in Exile*, 151.

CHAPTER EIGHT

1 Goldman, *Living My Life*, 23.

2 Burstein, 37.

3 Avrich, *Anarchist Voices*: "several dwell on her physical appearance and her powerful appetite for sex," 35.

4 Wexler, *Emma Goldman: An Intimate Life*, 280.

5 *New York World*, 1893.

6 *New York World*, 1893.

7 Frank Harris, letter to Emma Goldman, January 23, 1925.

8 Emma Goldman, letter to Frank Harris, August 7, 1925.

9 Emma Goldman, letter to Hutchins Hapgood, October 26, 1927.

10 Wexler, *Emma Goldman: An Intimate Life*, xvii.

11 Ibid., xvii.

12 Goldman, *Living My Life*, 21.

13 Ibid., 23.

14 Ibid., 22.

15 Ibid., 23.

16 Ibid., 23.

17 Christine Stansell, *American Moderns: Bohemian New York and the Creation of a New Century* (New York: Metropolitan Books, 2000), 120.

18 Goldman, *Living My Life*, 553.

19 In the research I have done, I have come across over fifty male lovers.

20 Alexander Berkman, letter to Emma Goldman, May 26, 1929.

21 Emma Goldman, letter to Alexander Berkman, February 20, 1929.

22 Goldman, *Living My Life*, 555.

23 Ibid., 555-556.

24 Ibid., 556.

25 Emma Goldman, letter to Evelyn Scott, November 21, 1927.

26 Ibid.,

27 Linda Wagner-Martin, 76.

28 Ibid., 77.

29 Cook, "The Historical Denial of Lesbianism," 60-65.

30 Candace Falk, *Love, Anarchy and Emma Goldman* (New York: Holt, Rineholt and Winston, 1984), 170.

31 Emma Goldman, "White Slave Traffic," *Mother Earth*, 4: 344-351.

32 Falk, 172.

33 Ibid., 171.

34 Ibid., 175.

35 Ibid., 176.

36 Wexler, "Emma Goldman on Mary Wollstonecraft," *Feminist Studies*, 1, 1981, 113-133.

37 Falk, 233.

38 Ibid., 173.

39 Ben Reitman, letter to Emma Goldman, 1934.

40 As have her probable intimate relationships with Margaret Anderson, Louise Michel, and Kate O'Hare.

41 Chalberg,109.

42 Ibid., 110.

43 Falk, 174.

44 Ibid., 169.

45 Ben is Ben Reitman.

46 Falk, 177.

47 Falk, 171.

48 Alice Wexler, *Emma Goldman: An Intimate Life*, 182.

49 Ibid., 182.

50 Ibid., 182.

51 Cook, "The Historical Denial of Lesbianism," 417.

52 Ibid., 418.

53 Cook, *Eleanor Roosevelt* (New York: Penguin Books, 1992), 13.

CHAPTER NINE

1 Wexler, *Emma Goldman in Exile*, 245.

2 John Rodden, *The Politics of Literary Reputation: The Making and Claiming of 'St. George' Orwell* (Oxford: Oxford University Press, 1989), ix.

3 Ibid.,3.

4 Ibid.,142.

5 Ibid.,146.

6 Ibid.,5.

7 Oz Frankel, "Whatever Happened to 'Red Emma'? Emma Goldman from Rebel to American Icon," *The Journal of American History*, 83: 1996, 903.

8 Hippolyte Havel, "Biographic Sketch," Emma Goldman, *Anarchism and Other Essays* (New York: Dover Publications, 1969), 1.

9 Frankel, "Whatever Happened to "Red Emma"? Emma Goldman from Rebel to American Icon," 903.

10 Ibid., 904.

11 Ibid., 940.

12 Ibid., 940.

13 Ibid.,, 940.

14 Ibid., 934.

15 Ibid., 935.

16 Ibid., 935.

17 Ibid., 935.

18 Drinnon, *Rebel in Paradise*, vii- viii.

19 Ibid., vii.

20 Ibid., vii.

21 Ibid., 314.

22 Ibid., 314.

23 Alix Kates Shulman, "Dances with Feminists," *Women's Review of Books*, 9:3, 1991, on *The Emma Goldman Papers*, www.sunsite3.berkeley.edu/Goldman (Accessed: January 12,2007).

24 Ibid.

25 Martha Solomon, *Emma Goldman* (Boston: Twayne Publishers, 1987), 175.

26 Falk, *Love, Anarchy and Emma Goldman*, xiii.

27 Ibid., xiii.

28 Ibid., xiii-xiv.

29 Ibid., xv.

30 Ibid., xv.

31 Alice Wexler, "The Anxiety of Biography," *The Challenge of Feminist Biography*, eds., Sara Alpern, Joyce Antler, Elisabeth Israels Perry, and Ingrid Winther Scobie, (Chicago: University of Illinois Press, 1992), 37-38.

32 Solomon, ii.

33 Marian Morton, *Emma Goldman and the American Left: Nowhere at Home* (New York: Twayne Publishers, 1992), x.

34 Ibid., x.

35 Ibid., x.

36 John Chalberg, 6.

37 Bonnie Haaland, *Emma Goldman: Sexuality and the Impurity of the State* (Montreal: Black Rose Books, 1993), vii.

38 Ibid., vii.

39 Ibid., xvii.

40 Ibid., viii.

41 Leslie A. Howe, *On Goldman* (California: Wadsworth Thompson Learning, 2000), 72.

42 Ibid., 72.

43 Ibid., 72.
44 Wexler, *Emma Goldman in Exile*, 3.
45 Ibid., 3.
46 Ibid., 5.
47 Haaland, vii.
48 Ibid., vii.
49 Ibid., vii.
50 Ibid., 187.
51 Frankel, 906.
52 Drinnon, *Rebel in Paradise*, 268.
53 Chalberg, 165.
54 Morton, 133.

CONCLUSION

1 Goldman, *Living My Life*, 529.
2 Goldman, "A New Declaration of Independence," *Mother Earth*, July 5, 1909.
3 Goldman, "What I Believe," Red Emma Speaks, 48-60.
4 New York Times, 15 May 1940.
5 Linda Kerber, *Toward an Intellectual History of Women* (Chapel Hill: The University of North Carolina Press, 1997).
6 McFadden, 1-13.
7 Goldman, *Living My Life*, 10.
8 International Anarchist Congress, Amsterdam, August 26-31, 1907, 5.
9 Ibid., 10.
10 Charles Pierce Lewarne, *Utopias on Puget Sound, 1885–1915* (Seattle: University of Washington Press, 1978), 175.
11 Francis Robert Shor, *Utopianism and Radicalism in a Reforming America: 1888-1918.* (New York: Greenwood Press, 1977), 129, and Carlos A. Schnantes, "Free Love on the Pacific Northwest Frontier," *Oregon Historical Quarterly*, 82 (1982), 271-293.
12 Lewarne, 176.
13 Emma Goldman, "Educational Experiment in Germany," Unpublished Paper.
14 Ibid.
15 Avrich, *The Modern School Movement*, 39.
16 Ibid., 43.
17 Ibid., 34-69.
18 Emma Goldman, Letter to Comrades, July 12, 1936.

19 Ibid.

20 Ibid.

21 Ibid.

22 Ibid.

23 Ibid.

24 Wexler, *Emma Goldman in Exile*, 235.

25 Ibid., 235.

26 Harry Weinberger, *Speech at Funeral of Emma Goldman* (Berkeley Heights, New Jersey: Oriole Press, 1940).

27 Ibid.

28 Ibid.

29 Emma Goldman, "Was My Life Worth Living?" in *Red Emma Speaks*, Alix Kate Shulman, (New York: Random House, 1975), 397-398.

30 Wexler, *Emma Goldman in Exile*, 241.

31 Charles Burress, "UC finds anarchist's words too red hot," *Sfgate.com* (accessed January 1, 2007).

32 Dean E. Murphy," Old Words on War Stirring A New Dispute at Berkley," *New York Times*, January 14, 2003, Section A, 1.

33 Charles Burress, "UC finds anarchist's words too red hot," *Sfgate.com* (accessed January 1, 2007).

Index

Adamic, Louis: *Dynamite*, 67
Addams, Jane, 133
African Americans, 28-29, 116
Alexander III, 41, 52-53
Alfonso XIII, 109
Alien Property Custodian, 32-33
Alsberg, Henry, 149
Altgeld, John Peter, 45
Amalgamated Association of Iron
  and Steel Workers, 70
American Civil Liberties Union, 1
American Journal of Insanity, 93
American Mercury, 160-161
Americanism, 30
Amsterdam, Netherlands, 109,
  192
Anarchism, xii, 1, 3, 25, 47, 67,
  80, 101, 111-112, 114, 122,
  160, 163, 165, 171, 175, 182,
  184, 192-193, 195-197, 200;
  Berkman's questions about, 115-
  116; definitions, 4-5; and
  Goldman's autobiography, 162;
  Goldman's concerns about, 21,
  77, 103-104, 109-110, 125, 148,
  152, 194; Goldman's introduction to, 48-49, 96-97, 99, 145,
  191; and Haymarket Riot, 47,
  55-56, 66; historical background, 5-19; and Homestead
  Strike, 72, 74-76; Justice
  Department response to, 34-38;
  lure in America, 54-61, 65-66;

and McKinley assassination, 85-
  95; Most's views of, 50-52
Anarchist, 78
Anarchist communism, 17
Anderson, Margaret, 176; *My
  Thirty Years War*, 119-120
Andrews, Stephen Pearl, 59
Angiolillo, Michele, 94
Assassinations, 18, 31-34, 36, 41,
  50-53, 72-76, 78, 81-87, 89-91,
  93-95, 161, 164
Atheism, 114
Atlanta, Ga., 123-124
Augsburg, Germany, 50
Austria, 51-52, 101
Avrich, Paul, 163; *Anarchist
  Voices*, 3, 47, 50, 55, 79; *The
  Modern School Movement*, 105,
  110-111, 121-122, 194

Bakunin, Michael, 8, 10-14, 17-
  18, 59-60, 111; *Reaction in
  Deutschland*, 10; *Revolutionary
  Catechism*, 12
Baldwin, Roger, 1, 130
Ballantine, Stella, 123
Banking, 59-60
Baseball, 30-31
Basel, Switzerland, 13
Bauer, Henry, 74
Belgium, 155
Berkman, Alexander, 4, 40, 77,
  80, 96-97, 99, 110-111, 118,

120-122, 129-130, 140, 169,
175, 184, 190; background of,
53-54; death of, 194-197; deportation of, xii, 23, 37-39, 123-
125, 127-128; failed assassination of Frick, 50, 69-76, 78-79,
81-82; and Goldman's autobiog-
raphy, 131, 137, 141-145, 148-
161, 170; and McKinley assassi-
nation, 83, 87, 94-95; meets
Goldman, 49; photographs of,
ix-x; questions about anarchist
revolution, 115-116; relationship
with Goldman, 67-69, 164, 166
WORKS: *Prison Memoirs of an
Anarchist*, 53, 81, 154; *What Is
Communist Anarchism?* 150
Berkman, Maxim, 53
Bill of Rights, 89, 114
Birth control, 169-170
Bismarck, Otto von, 61, 64, 83-84
"Black International," 65
Blackwell's Island, 87, 96-97, 191
Bly, Nellie, 164
Boer War, 101
Bologna, Italy, 14
Bolshevism, 30, 38, 127-129
Bonfield, Inspector, John, 47
Boston, Mass., 26-27, 30, 32, 35
Boston Globe, 49, 59, 98
Botesen, Bayard, 111
Brady, Edward, 97, 101, 118, 166,
170
Bresci, Gaetano, 94
Briggs, Vernon, Lloyd, 92-93
Brussels, Belgium, 8-9
Buffalo, N. Y., 34, 68, 83, 85-87,
91-92
Buford, S. S., 23-24, 126-127
Bull, William S., 86

Burstein, Janet Handler: *Writing
Mothers, Writing Daughters*,
127, 138, 163

Caffey, Francis, 200
Caminetti, Anthony, 125
Camus, Albert, 180
Canada, 197
Capitalism, 8, 17, 51-52, 55, 57,
59, 65, 127
Carnegie, Andrew, 70-71, 180,
183
Carnegie Steel Company, 74
Carpenter, Edward, 165, 171
Carpenter, Mecca Reitman: *No
Regrets*, 157
Catholicism, 108-109, 112
Cavendish, Frederick, 18
Chalberg, John, 176-177; *Emma
Goldman*, 182-183, 187
Chamber of Commerce, 43
Channing, Walter, 92-93
Charleston, S. C., 28
Chernyshevsky, Nikolai: *What Is
to Be Done?* 19, 40, 73
Chevigny, Bell Gale, 179
Chicago, Ill., 25, 28-29, 44-48,
56, 63, 65-66, 78, 85-87, 119-
120, 122-123, 145-147, 176,
198
Chicago Labor Movement, 63
Chicago Social Revolutionary
Congress, 65-66
Chicago Tribune, xii, 47, 85
Christianity, 5, 114
Civil War, 61-62
Clark University, 168
Clayton Antitrust Act, 32
Cleveland, Ohio, 29, 32, 35, 68,
86-87, 90-91

Cohn, Michael, 155, 194-195
Coleman, Emily Holmes, 137, 148-149, 156, 194
Coleman, Lloyd Ring, 148-149
Collectivism, 10-12, 17
Colorado Fuel and Iron Company, 120
Colton, James, 142
Commins, Saxe, 148
Communalism, 56-57
Communism, 8, 11, 14, 17, 29, 34, 52, 129
Comstock, Anthony, 114, 168-169
Comstock Laws, 168-169
Congress, U.S., 32, 36, 38-39, 58, 64, 71, 88-89, 124
Cook, Blanche Wiesen, 133, 135, 172, 179
Coolidge, Calvin, 30
Corner, George E., 86
Crego, Floyd D., 92
Creighton, John, 35, 37
Crime, 114-117
Curti, Merrill, 191
Czolgosz, Leon, xii, 25, 83-87, 90-95, 124, 161

Dana, Charles A., 9
Darwin, Charles, 15-16, 60, 148; *The Descent of Man*, 16
Darrow, Clarence, 89
Davis, Harry, 32
Dearborn Independent, 31
DeCleyre, Voltairine, 109, 170
Degan, Mathias J., 45
Democracy, 113, 186
Detroit, Mich., 29, 46, 118
Dewey, John, 112
Diamond, Freda, 3
Diggers, 5

Doherty, Thomas P., 131
Dostoyevsky, Fyodor: *Crime and Punishment*, 73
Draft Act, 123
Dreiser, Emma, 145-148
Dreiser, Theodore, 20, 82, 142; *Sister Carrie*, 145-148
Drinnon, Richard, 176-177; *Rebel in Paradise*, 180, 185-187
Drysdale, George, 102
Dublin, Ireland, 18
Duffus, R. L., 156

Eastman, Crystal, 28
Eastman, Max, 28
Eby, Claire, 148
Eckstein, Emmy, 143, 153-154, 194-197
Edison, Thomas, 84
Education, 105-112, 193-194
Education and Defense Society, 63-64
Einstein, Albert, 155
Eliezer, Rabbi, 139
Ellis, Havelock, 165, 171
Emerson, Ralph Waldo, 97, 104, 112
Emma Goldman Papers, 181, 199-200
Emma Goldman Spanish Refugee Rescue Fund, 197
Engel, George, 45
Engels, Friedrich, 10, 13, 51
England, 5-6, 15, 18, 51-52, 99, 101, 164-165
Enlightenment, 5
Esperanto, 111
Espionage Act, 123

Fabian Society, 100, 165

Falk, Candace, 176-177, 199-200; *Love, Anarchy, and Emma Goldman*, 181-182, 185, 187
Faure, Sebastian, 106-107
Federal Bureau of Investigation, xii, 31, 36-37
Federal Farm Loan Act, 32
Federal Reserve System, 32
Federal Trade Commission, 32
Federation of Organized Trades and Labor Unions, 46
Federation of the Union of Russian Workers, 23
Fellowship of the New Life, 165
Ferrer, Francisco, 106, 108-112, 193
Feuerbach, Ludwig, 10; *Essence of Christianity*, 7
Fichte, Johann Gottlieb, 10
Fielden, Samuel, 45-46
First Amendment, 169
First Anarchist Congress, 102
Fischer, Adolph, 45, 47
Fitzgerald, Eleanor, 143-144
Fitzgerald, F. Scott: *The Great Gatsby*, 31
Flynn, William F., 35-36, 125
Ford, Henry, 31
Fourier, Charles, 8.
Fowler, Joseph, 92-93
France, 5, 7-8, 15, 102, 105-106, 108, 129-130, 142, 149-151, 154-155, 178, 194-197
Francisco Ferrer Association, 110—112, 194
Franco-Prussian War, 10
Frankel, Oz, 179-180, 187-188
Franklin Liberal Club, 86, 90
Free Society, 89-91, 94
Freiheit, 49-52, 78, 87

Freud, Sigmund, 101, 168, 182
Frick, Henry Clay, 50, 70-74, 78, 80-82, 121, 164
Fuller, Melville, 89

Galleani, Luigi, 34
Gandhi, Mohandas K., 75
Gandil, Arnold "Chick," 30
Ganguli, B. N.: *Emma Goldman*, 181
Garfield, James, 84
Garson, Leopold, 43
Garvan, Francis P., 35
Gary, Joseph, 45, 48
Gay, Martin and Kathleen: *The Importance of Emma Goldman*, 184
Geilert, S. S., 41
Gentry, Curt, 38
Georgetown University, 36
Georgia, 31
Gerin, Dr. John, 92
German immigrants, 43, 61-64, 139-140, 161
Germany, 6-7, 11, 14, 33, 37, 50-52, 54, 61, 64, 83-84, 123, 193
Gershoy, Ida, 4
Gigerich, A., 88-89
Gladstone, William, 18

Godwin, William, 111, 165; *Enquiry Concerning Political Justice*, 5-6
Gold, Max, 32
Goldman, Abraham (father), 39-41, 44, 48, 139
Goldman Emma, 3-4, 19-20, 22, 50, 66; background of, 39-41; concerns about anarchism, 21, 77, 103-104, 109-110, 125, 148,

152, 194; on crime, 114-117; and death of Berkman, 194-197; deportation of, xii, 23-25, 37-39, 123-127; early years in America, 41-44; on education, 104-112; European travels of, 99-102, 105-107; in France, 129, 142, 155; and Haymarket Riot, 44, 56; and Homestead Strike, 72, 74-76, 81-82, 160; introduction to anarchism, 48-49, 96-97, 99, 145, 191; involvement with Most, 48-49, 67-68, 78-80, 140, 157, 160-161; jailed on Blackwell's Island, 96-97, 191; last years of, 197-198; and McKinley assassination, 82-83, 85-87, 89-91, 93-95; as nurse, 98-99, 101, 117; opposition to World War I, 122-123; photographs of, ii, ix-xii; relationship with Berkman, 49, 67-69, 78, 80, 140, 157-160, 164, 166; relationship with Reitman, 118-120, 122, 157-160; on religion, 113-114; reputation of, 77, 178-188, 199-200; on sex/sexuality, 136, 163-177; in Soviet Russia, 127-129; on violence, 74-76, 81, 91, 94, 103-104

WORKS: "Declaration of Independence," 96, 98-99; *Living My Life*, 19, 21, 23-24, 41-45, 56, 67-70, 72, 75-76, 79-81, 87, 96-97, 127, 129-132, 136-137, 140-162, 166-171, 175-176, 178, 181, 187-189, 191, 196; *My Disillusionment with Russia*, 128, 154; "What I Believe," 189-190

Goldman, Helena (sister), 41-42, 48, 123

Goldman, Morris (brother), 95

Goldman, Tuabe Bienowitch (mother), 39, 41, 44, 48, 123

Greece, ancient, 5-6

Greeley, Horace, 59

Greenback Party, 64

Greene, William B.: *Mutual Banking*, 59

Gregory, Francis W., 33

Grinnell, Julius, 47

Grun, Karl, 8

Guggenheim, Peggy, 142

Guillaume, James, 14-15

Haaland, Bonnie, 20, 179; *Emma Goldman*, 163, 183-184, 186

Hague, Netherlands, 14

Hanson, Ole, 29-31, 34

Hapgood, Hutchins, 111, 165, 175

Harding, Warren, 33

Hardwick, Thomas, 31

Harper's Weekly, xiii, 49, 84, 198

Harris, Frank, 81, 165; *My Life and Loves*, 136, 165

Harrison, Carter, 46

Havel, Hippolyte, 81, 85, 90, 101, 179

Hawthorne, Nathaniel, 97

Hayden, Robert, 32

Haymarket Riot, 44-48, 55-56, 66, 89, 146, 191, 198

Hegel, Georg Wilhelm Friedrich, 6-8, 10

Heiner, Frank, 170

Heinze, Andrew R., 138-139

Henri, Robert, 19, 189

Herbert, Auberon, 59
Heywood, Ezra, 59
History, 607, 11, 16, 100
Homestead Strike, 69-71, 74, 121, 160
Homosexuality, 171-177
Hoover, J. Edgar, xii, 31, 36-39, 44, 124-126, 130, 185
Hopkins, L. A., 145-146
Howe, Leslie A,: *On Goldman*, 184
Huxley, T. H., 15-16

Ibsen, Henrik, 1
Illinois, 45-47, 64, 87, 105
Imlay, William, 165
Immigrants, 42-44, 61-63, 65, 89, 91, 124, 132, 139-140, 161, 182
Immigration Act, 35-36, 89, 124
Indiana, 56-57
Individualism, 5, 7, 11, 17, 57, 59-60, 102, 129, 193, 198
Individualistic anarchy, 7
Industrial Workers of the World, 30
Industrialization, 7, 9, 61-62, 101
Influenza epidemic, 27-28, 30
Ingalls, Joshua K., 59
International Alliance for Social Democracy, 13-14
International Movement, 55
International Revolutionary Movement, 10
International Working Men's Association, 12-13, 51
Ireland, 6, 18
Issak, Abe and Mary, 90
Italian immigrants, 105
Italy, 34

Jefferson, Thomas, 56
Jefferson City, Mo., 123
Jelinek, Estelle: *Women and Autobiography*, 135-136
Jews, 31, 39, 41-43, 48, 53-54, 68, 76-77, 97, 127, 138-140, 160, 182, 191
Justice Department, U.S., 33-35, 37, 124-125, 129

Kelly, Henry, 110, 155
Kerber, Linda, 190
Kersner, Jacob, 43-44, 48, 124-125
Kloppenberg, James T.: *Uncertain Victory*, 100
Knights of Labor, 43
Knopf, Alfred A., 155-156
Kovo (Kaunas), Lithuania, 39
Kronstadt Mutiny, 128
Kropotkin, Peter, 10, 14-17, 101, 113, 115, 148; *The Conquest of Bread*, 16; *Mutual Aid*, 16

Labor Standard, 63
Landis, Kennesaw, 31
Latvia, 128
Lehr-und-Wehr Verein, 63-64
Leishman, John G. A., 73
Lender, Mark: *Drinking in America*, 26
Lenin, V. I., 15
Lerner, Miriam, 137
Lever Food and Fuel Control Act, 26
Liberator, 28
Libertarianism, 17
Liberty, 59
Library of Congress, 36-37
Lincoln, Abraham, 84

Lingg, Louis, 45
Lithuania, 39, 200
Lodge, Henry Cabot, 87
London, England, 10, 13, 15, 51,
  101, 106, 129, 142
London Social Revolutionary
  Congress, 65-66
Ludlow Massacre, 120-121
Lusk, Clayton R., 34

MacDonald, Carlos F., 92
Mackay, John Henry, 59
Malatesta, Errico, 101
Malcolm X, 180
Mann, Mathew, 84
Mann, Thomas, 155
Martin, James J.: Men Against the
  State, 49
Martindale, Anna, 122
Martins, Ludwig, 38
Marx, Karl, 8-10, 13-14
Marxism, 6, 11, 13, 17
Massachusetts, 32
Masses, 28
Masters, Edgar Lee, 89
McCormick Harvesting Machine
  Company, 46
McFadden, Margaret H.: Golden
  Cables of Sympathy, 99-100,
  191-192, 194
McKay, Claude: "If We Must
  Die," 28
McKellar, Senator, Kenneth, 38
McKinley, William, 25, 34, 82-85,
  88-91, 93-95, 161
Mellon, Andrew, 71
Michel, Louise, 101, 105-106, 170
Mill, John Stuart, 56
Milwaukee, Wis., 46
Minkin, Helen, 69

Missouri, 123
Modern School Movement, 105-
  112, 193-194
Montana, 64
Morality, 10, 17, 26, 72, 168
Moritzs, Theresa: The World's
  Most Dangerous Woman, 184
Morral, Mateo, 109
Morton, Marian: Emma Goldman
  and the American Left, 182-183,
  187
Moscow, Russia, 10, 15, 128
Most, Johann, 47-52, 54, 60, 65,
  67-68, 78-81, 87, 96-97, 140,
  152, 157, 160-161, 170, 191;
  Revolutionary War Science, 52,
  73
Most, John J., 50, 79
Mother Earth, 96, 107, 115, 117-
  119, 121-122, 129, 173, 175
Mutual aid, 15-16, 113
Mutual banking, 60
Mutualism, 9, 17

Napoleon III, 8, 106
Narodnaya Volya, 41
National Hockey League, 30
National Socialist, 63
Nazimova, Alla, 117
Nechaev, Sergei, 12; Revolutionary
  Catechism, 12
Neebe, Oscar, 45
Neo-Malthusian Congress, 102
Nettlau, Max, 75, 79
New England Labor Reform
  League, 59
New Harmony, Ind., 56-57
New Haven, Conn., 49
New Jersey, 32, 35
New Mexico, 87

New Orleans, La., 55
New York (state), 34, 87
New York City, 24, 32, 35, 42,
  44, 46, 48-49, 51-52, 68-69, 72-
  73, 87, 95-99, 101-102, 111,
  117, 121, 123-125, 130, 140,
  145-147, 152, 168-169, 175
New York Society for the
  Suppression of Vice, 168
New York Sun, 91, 97
New York Times, 23-26, 47, 49,
  77, 80, 89, 91, 129, 157, 190,
  200
New York Tribune, 9
New York World, 76, 96, 164,
  189
Nice, France, x, 195
Nietzsche, Friedrich, 59
Nihilism, 40-41, 44, 54, 72
Nold, Carl, 74
Norris, J., 85
North American Review, 92
Nott, Charles, Jr., 32
Nurses' Settlement, 99

O'Brien, Jack Lord, 37
Oerter, Frank, 170
Oglesby, Richard J., 45
O'Hare, Bonnie, 22
Ohio, 61
O'Loughlin, Mathew J., 86
Olsen, Tillie, 133
O'Neill, Chief, Francis, 87
O'Neill, Eugene, 111
Orwell, George, 191
Oswald, F. L., 92
Overholt, Abraham, 71
Owen, Robert, 56-57
Ozick, Cynthia, 138

Paine, Thomas: The Rights of
  Man, 6
Palmer, Mitchell, 32-37
Pan-American Exposition, 83-84
Pankhurst, Emmeline, 134
Paris, France, 8-10, 102, 105-106,
  108, 115
Paris Commune, 10, 16, 18, 63
Parsons, Albert, 45, 55, 62-63
Paterson, N. J., 87
Payne, Henry C., 88
Peaceful Revolutionist, 57, 61
Penney, Thomas, 83, 87, 91
Pennsylvania, 32
People's Bank, 9-10
People's Will, 41
Peritas, José: Emma Goldman
  Anarquista de Ambos Mundos,
  181
Pesotta, Rose, 191
Petrushka, 166-167
Philadelphia, Pa., 32, 35
Piez, Charles, 29
Pinkerton guards, 70-72, 121
Pioneers of Liberty, 54
Piscan, Carlo, 18
Pittsburgh, Pa., 35, 69, 72-74, 82,
  160, 172-173, 177
Poland, 10
Powers, Leland W., 32
Prohibition, 26
Proletariat, 13-15, 34, 55, 65
Propaganda by deed, 18, 91
Property, 10-13, 17, 57-58, 60-61,
  65, 103, 113
Protestantism, 7, 26
Proudhon, Pierre-Joseph, 7-11, 14-
  15, 17, 59-60; On Justice, 8;
  System of Economic
  Contradictions, 8; Warning to

Proprietors, 8; *What Is Property?* 8-9
Putman, James W., 92

Quackenbush, James, 91
Quakers, 32-33

Race riots, 28-29
Radical Review, 59
Reds (film), 20
Reformation, 7
Reinhart, Robert, 130
Reitman, Ben, 118-120, 122, 157-159, 161, 166, 170, 174-176, 181, 185, 187
Religion, 114
Republican Party, 88
Revolution, 10-19, 24, 52, 61, 63-65, 72-76, 98, 102-106, 113, 116, 148, 153, 184, 193-194
Revolutionary Socialist Party, 65
Rich, Adrienne, 134-136
Robin, Paul, 102, 105-106
Rochester, N. Y., 42-44, 48, 68, 90, 145, 152
Rockefeller, John D., 32, 120-122
Rocker, Rudolf, 144, 149
Rodden, John: *The Politics of Literary Reputation*, 178, 185
Rogers, Daniel: *Atlantic Crossings*, 100
Romanticism, 61
Rome, ancient, 6
Roosevelt, Eleanor, 33, 133-134
Roosevelt, Franklin, 33, 134
Roosevelt, Theodore, 32, 83, 87-88, 104
Rosenberg, Karen, 179
Ross, Arthur, 137, 143-144, 155-156

Rothstein, Arnold, 31
Rubenstein, Mr., 43
Rudahl, Sharon: *Dangerous Woman*, 184
Runyon, Damon: *The Idyll of Miss Sarah Brown*, 31
Russell, Bertrand, 155
Russia, 1, 10, 12, 14-15, 24, 40-44, 51, 53-54, 69-70, 72-73, 97, 114, 116, 125-129, 139, 148, 166-167, 200
Russian immigrants, 42-44, 62, 139-140, 182
Russian Revolution, 15, 25, 29

St. Louis, Mo., 1, 85, 124
St. Petersburg, Russia, 10, 14, 40-41, 53, 167
St. Tropez, France, ix, 129, 150-151, 178
Saint-Simon, comte de (Claude de Rouvroy), 8
Sanger, Margaret, 169
Sayre, Robert F.: *The Examined Self*, 131-132
Schaack, Captain, Michael, 46
Schelling, Friedrich von, 10
Schopenhauer, Arthur, 1
Schreiner, Olive, 165
Schwab, Michael, 45, 97
Scotland, 6, 101
Scott, Evelyn, 141, 148-150, 171-172
Seattle, Wash., 29-30, 34, 193
Second Anarchist Conference, 109, 192
Secret Service, 83
Segregation, 29
Sex/sexuality, 21, 68-69, 95, 114, 136, 147, 162-177, 182, 184, 186

Shaw, George Bernard, 59; *Mrs. Warren's Profession*, 168
Shulman, Alix Kate, 176; *Between Women*, 141; *To the Barricades*, 180-181, 185-187
Siberia, 10, 14, 24, 53
Sinclair, Upton, 191
Slavery, 62
Smith, Mary Rozet, 133
Smith, Sidone: *A Poetics of Women's Autobiography*, 137
Social Democratic Movement, 62
Social revolution, 14-15
Socialism, 8, 13, 49, 51-52, 55, 61, 63-66, 97, 99-100, 186
Socialist, 63
Socialist Labor Party, 63-64
Solomon, Martha, 176; *Emma Goldman*, 182-183
Solotaroff, A., 49
Soviet Union, 126-129, 148, 184, 200
Spacks, Patricia Meyers, 132-134
Spain, 108-110, 112, 181, 195-197
Spencer, Herbert, 59, 189
Sperry, Almeda, 172-177
Spies, August, 45-47
Spirit of the Age, 9
Spitzka, Edward A., 92
Spooner, Lysander, 59
Springfield, Mass., 69
Stanley Cup Finals, 30
Stapleton, Maureen, 20
Statue of Liberty, 24, 41
Stein, Modest, 68-70, 72, 79, 82
Stirner, Max, 7, 17, 59
Stone, Albert E., 132; *Autobiographical Occasions and Original Acts*, 141

Strikes, 22, 29-30, 46, 61-63, 69-71, 120-121
Sunday, Billy, 26
Supreme Court, U.S., 29, 45, 123, 125
Swain, Joseph H., 65-66
Swenson, Arthur, 170
Swinton, John, 97, 99
Swtiz, Ted McLean, 144
Switzerland, 10, 12, 15, 51

Taft, William Howard, 25-26, 32-33
Thompson, William, 32
Thoreau, Henry David, 97, 102, 112
Tolstoy, Leo, 88
Tompkins, Jane, 159-160
Traubel, Horace, 172
Treaty of Brest-Litovsk, 25
Tucker, Benjamin, 56, 58-61, 65-66; *Proudhon and His "Bank of the People"*, 10
Turner, John, 89

Underwood Tariff, 32
Unions, 22, 29-30, 46, 48, 52, 70-71
United Jewish Charities, 43
University of California, 199-200
Utopian communities, 193

Valdinoci, Carlo, 34
Vallely, James, 83
Van Patten, Philip, 64-66
Van Valkenburgh, W. S., 142
Verne, Madeline, 102
Veysey, Laurence: *The Communal Experience*, 112
Vienna, Austria, 51, 99, 101, 168, 182

Violence, 10, 12, 17-19, 21, 34,
  52, 60-66, 72, 74-79, 81, 91,
  94, 101, 103-104, 116-117, 161

Wage slavery, 62, 65, 168
Wagner-Martins, Linda, 132, 172
Wales, 6, 142
Warren, Josiah, 56-61; *True
  Civilization*, 59
Washington, D. C., 28, 33, 36
Washington Post, 35
Weinberger, Henry, 23, 198
Wenzer, Kenneth C.: *Anarchists
  Adrift*, 183-184
Wexler, Alice, 20, 163, 165-166,
  175, 177, 188; *Emma Goldman*,
  81, 105, 112-114, 121, 131,
  182, 187; *Emma Goldman in
  Exile*, 157, 182, 186
Whitehead, Don: *The FBI Story*,
  39

Whitman, Walt, 97, 171-172
Wilson, Woodrow, 30-33, 183
Winstanley, Gerrard, 5
Wisconsin, 64
Wollstonecraft, Mary, 165, 174-
  175
Women, 98-101, 114, 127, 132-
  140, 148, 152, 169, 190-193
Word, 59
World Series, 30-31
World War I, 15, 25-27, 31-33,
  35, 37, 122-123, 175, 200
World War II, 197

Yezierska, Anzia: *Bread Givers*,
  139
Yiddischer Arbeiter Verein, 54

Zeno, 5
Zurich, Switzerland, 51, 101

PARTICIPATORY DEMOCRACY

Prospects for Democratizing Democracy

Dimitrios Roussopoulos, C.George Benello, editors

A completely revised edition of the classic and widely consulted 1970 version

First published as a testament to the legacy of the concept made popular by the New Left of the 1960s, and with the perspective of the intervening decades, this book opens up the way for re-examining just what is involved in democratizing democracy.

With its emphasis on citizen participation, here, presented in one volume, are the best arguments for participatory democracy written by some of the most relevant contributors to the debate, both in an historic, and in a contemporary, sense.

> The book is, by all odds, the most encompassing one so far in revealing the practical actual subversions that the New Left wishes to visit upon us. —*Washington Post*

Apart from the editors, contributors include: George Woodcock, Murray Bookchin, Don Calhoun, Stewart Perry, Rosabeth Moss Kanter, James Gillespie, Gerry Hunnius, John McEwan, Arthur Chickering, Christian Bay, Martin Oppenheimer, Colin Ward, Sergio Baierle, Anne Latendresse, Bartha Rodin, and C.L.R. James.

DIMITRIOS ROUSSOPOULOS was a prominent New Left activist in the 1960s, locally and internationally, and is the author and/or editor of some eighteen books, most recently *Faith in Faithlessness: An Anthology of Atheism*.

C.GEORGE BENELLO (1927-1987) taught sociology at Goddard College in Vermont until his untimely death. He was author of *From the Ground Up: Essays on Grassroots and Workplace Democracy*.

2004: 380 pages
Paperback ISBN: 1-55164-224-7 $24.99
Hardcover ISBN: 1-55164-225-5 $53.99

THE NEW LEFT
Legacy and Continuity
Dimitrios Roussopoulos

As the contributors to this anthology revisit the sixties to identify its ongoing impact on North American politics and culture, it becomes evident how this legacy has blended with, and influenced today's world-wide social movements, in particular, the anti-globalization movement, and the 'Right to the City' movement: the successes and failures of civil society orgnisations as they struggle for a voice at all levels of decision-making are examined, as are the new movements of the urban disenfranchised—the homeless, the alienation of youth, the elderly poor.

Apart from evoking memories of past peace and freedom struggles from those who worked on the social movements of the 1960s, this work also includes a number of essays from a rising generation of intellectual and activists, too young to have experienced the 1960s firsthand, whose perspective enables them to offer fresh insights and analyses.

> An eclectic mix of memoir and commentary that accents the legacies of the 60s rebellious youth, and the continuities of the political dissent and oppositional challenges of that decade. —*Canadian Dimension*

Contributors include: Dimitrios Roussopoulos, Andrea Levy, Anthony Hyde, Jacques Martin, Mark Rudd, Katherina Haris, Gregory Nevala Calvert, Natasha Kapoor, and Tom Hayden.

DIMITRIOS ROUSSOPOULOS was a prominent New Left activist in the 1960s, locally and internationally. He continues to write and edit on major issues while being a committed activist testing theory with practice.

2007: 224 pages
Paperback ISBN: 978-1-155164-298-7 $19.99
Hardcover ISBN: 978-1-155164-299-4 $48.99

Printed by the workers
of Imprimerie Gauvin
for Black Rose Books